MUSIC OF THE TWENTIETH CENTURY

Picasso—*Man with Violin*

Philadelphia Museum of Art: The
Louise and Walter Arensberg Collection.

MUSIC OF THE TWENTIETH CENTURY

WILLIAM R. MARTIN
and
JULIUS DROSSIN

Cleveland State University

PRENTICE-HALL, INC., Englewood Cliffs, N.J. 07632

Library of Congress Cataloging in Publication Data

MARTIN, WILLIAM R. (date)
   Music of the twentieth century.

   Bibliography: p.
   Includes index.
   1. Music—History and criticism—20th century.
I. Drossin, Julius, joint author. II. Title.
ML197.M1745   780'.904   79-19740
ISBN 0-13-608927-5

To Norene and Barbara

Editorial/production supervision by Frank J. Hubert
Page layout by Mary Greey
Cover design by R L Communications
Manufacturing Buyer: Harry P. Baisley

PRINTED IN THE UNITED STATES OF AMERICA

10 9 8 7 6 5 4 3 2 1

PRENTICE-HALL INTERNATIONAL, INC., *London*
PRENTICE-HALL OF AUSTRALIA PTY. LIMITED, *Sydney*
PRENTICE-HALL OF CANADA, LTD., *Toronto*
PRENTICE-HALL OF INDIA PRIVATE LIMITED, *New Delhi*
PRENTICE-HALL OF JAPAN, INC., *Tokyo*
PRENTICE-HALL OF SOUTHEAST ASIA PTE. LTD., *Singapore*
WHITEHALL BOOKS LIMITED, *Wellington, New Zealand*

Contents

chapter 1

Introduction

"In art there are only fast or slow developments. Essentially it is a matter of evolution, not revolution" (Bartók); "I hold that it was error to regard me as a revolutionary . . . [for stepping] outside the bounds of established convention" (Stravinsky); "I personally hate to be called a revolutionary, which I am not" (Schoenberg). These three composers were among the most influential in bringing about the innovations that characterize much of the music of the twentieth century. Their view of themselves as nonrevolutionaries, however, has not been shared universally by audiences throughout this century. Particularly during the first decades of the twentieth century, audiences felt that the "new music" had assaulted their ears and compromised their sensibilities. What, they wondered, had happened to the sanity of the new generations of composers? Beethoven, Wagner, Brahms, and Tchaikovsky were staples in their musical diet—the norm by which they measured the music of the new age. For many who have been almost completely nurtured on music predating the twentieth century, this value judgment persists even to the present; for others, time and understanding have brought about enthusiastic acceptance of that which was once thought revolutionary. Many of the same works that aroused adverse criticism when first presented are, in fact, now considered twentieth-century classics.

One must come to realize that change has been an inevitable part of the human condition throughout history, and that the closer one is in time and experience to these elements of change, the more likely one is to resist them. Furthermore, the more rapidly these changes take place, the less likely they are to gain ready acceptance. The early part of the twentieth century was a period of particularly rapid musical change—so much so, in fact, that the music of these years is referred to as the New Music. Just twice before in the history of music (interestingly enough at intervals of three hundred years) has the process of change reached a degree of intensity sufficiently strong for contemporaries to appropriate the word *new* to describe it, once about the year 1300 (*ars nova*) to describe innovations in rhythm and meter, and the other in 1600 (*nuove musiche*) to describe the new style of accompanied monodic recitative.

Marked as some changes may seem to have been at the beginning of this century, the musical inheritance from the previous century was very strong, both through its evolutionary role, and as old practices that persisted for a long time beside the new. The present may not, then, be understood completely in terms of itself. Only as we view the past and present as a continuum can we truly comprehend what has occurred in the twentieth century.

ANTECEDENTS—A BRIEF SUMMARY

By 1825, the era of classicism had given way to a new kind of creative expression in which the tenets of formalism appropriated from Greek and Roman civilizations were no longer compatible with the creative artist's passion for self-expression. The romantic movement in literature served as a point of departure for the musical revolutionary who, wishing to discard the restricting effects of classical form, explored the works of Goethe, Heine, and Schiller, medieval folklore, and Shakespeare (by then available in translation), as sources for his inspiration. The program music produced through this process thus became one answer in the romanticist's search for a new aesthetic unity. Large works could now be unified through the use of a program expressing pictorial, narrative, and emotional ideas that were essentially nonmusical in origin. Romantic emotionalism, typified by a dominance of lyric expression and programmatic tendencies, permeated even the symphony, classicism's ideal absolute music expression.

The classicist's techniques of contrapuntal development were now largely replaced by the use of harmonic change as a means for giving variety to the repetition of melodic and motivic content. Choices of thematic content and key relationships were frequently made more on the basis of dramatic potential than on formal considerations. Inevitably these procedures resulted in a broadened approach to the classical concepts of balance in the sonata cycle.

Two nineteenth-century revolutionaries, Franz Liszt (1811–86) and Richard Wagner (1813–83), supported the view that music's only salvation was in conjunction with poetry: "the music of the future." While Liszt's tone poems provided an "inner connection" between poetry and music, Wagner, in his music-dramas, advanced a more complete interpretation regarding the total affinity between the two. Wagner enhanced the continuity of his music-dramas, and incidentally, the significance of the orchestra, through a highly refined system of associative musical themes called *Leitmotive* (singular, *Leitmotiv*). These "leading motifs" were used within the musical continuity of the music drama to represent or associate with a specific character, thing, emotion, or idea. The centrality of Wagner's orchestra was further effected through his highly developed skill in the use of chromatic harmony. By making half-step chromatic alterations in the diatonic scale tones normally used as the basis of harmonic structures, and by using modulating sequences and unconventional dissonance practices, he was able to blur the traditional dominant-to-tonic harmonic relationships generally associated with pre-Wagnerian music. As a consequence, phrases could be extended to almost limitless proportions. *Tristan und Isolde* (1857–59) particularly exemplifies Wagner's capacity to produce an almost constant feeling of gradual motion, enhancing the opera's mood of longing, passion, and tragedy, through the consistent use of chromatic suspensions, delayed cadences, and non-harmonic tones. The resulting ambiguity of tonality, and its subsequent influence on future composers, gives *Tristan* a position of unusual importance in the history of music.

Although Franz Liszt had experimented extensively with the implications of chromatic harmony, it was Wagner who firmly established the harmonic practices that eventually led to a complete disintegration of tonality. This man, so controversial personally and professionally during his lifetime, left a legacy of theory and practice so significant that nineteenth-century music must be divided in terms of pre-Wagnerian and post-Wagnerian practices.

It was not until the last four decades of the century that a substantial interest in absolute music and its most important form, the symphony, was rekindled. Just as writers of descriptive music had borrowed freely from the formal schemes of absolute music to accommodate their purposes, now symphonists found themselves benefited by an enriched harmonic and melodic vocabulary, and by greatly expanded orchestral resources, through the innovative techniques developed successively by Hector Berlioz (1803–69), Liszt, and Wagner. Anton Bruckner (1824–96) and César Franck (1822–90) reflect these influences positively through their expansive orchestral sound and their use of chromatic harmony. Johannes Brahms (1833–97) and Peter Ilyich Tchaikovsky (1840–93) both reflect a reaction against many of these influences, particularly Wagnerianism—Brahms by his almost complete avoidance of programmatic elements and by his reworking and giving new life to the classical forms, and Tchaikovsky principally by his rejection of excessive chromatic harmony. Antonin Dvořák (1841–1904), influenced by the Wagnerian sound, particularly in his early works, later became the leading exponent of absolute forms in the Brahms manner.

By the end of the nineteenth century, the luster of romanticism had worn thin, and what had been an exciting communication of direct musical emotionalism now grew overblown and self-conscious in its expression. Many of the art products of this declining era had become preoccupied with suffering and death through an intensification of Wagner's philosophy that ultimate fulfillment is possible only through dying. Wagner's influence was further reflected in a developing orchestral gigantism, which required scores of thirty to forty staves, increased orchestral sonorities, and expanded technical virtuosity. The sensuous, chromatic harmony of *Tristan* was also developed and exploited to a point where, by the end of the century, traditional concepts of harmony and tonality were seriously challenged.

Although romanticism's end was imminent, its final statement was not sharply defined; in fact, the years immediately preceding and following the beginning of the twentieth century comprised a transition period of great musical activity during which composers sought identity within the changing scene. Three divergent paths of general activity soon became identifiable: *conservatism,* characterized by an extension of romantic traditionalism: *intensification* marked by the expansion of the technical and harmonic resources of the romantic era; and *radicalism,* the rejection of traditional romanticism by composers who searched for new paths of musical expression without the restraints of the past. Those composers identified with the first two paths—the postromantics—marked the end of an era, although many lived well beyond it; the third path marked the beginning of a new era.

part I

FORERUNNERS

chapter 2

Postromanticism

Richard Strauss (1864–1949)

The role of harmony as a principal determining factor in musical form had been significantly challenged by the end of the nineteenth century. Traditionally, harmonic progressions defined phrase lengths, sectional limits, and formal outlines, but now the gradual disintegration of the harmonic "system," through an ever-increasing use of chromaticism and free modulation, deprived music of this important organizational format. Composers in Germany reacted in several ways: some simply turned the clock back and wrote in a traditional romantic style; some attempted a synthesis of romantic and baroque practices by grafting a severe contrapuntal idiom onto extant harmonic procedures; others, notably Richard Strauss, sought structural unity within the expanding implications of chromaticism by writing descriptive music.

Strauss produced some exceedingly beautiful original music before he was twenty, including his first two symphonies, a sonata for cello and piano, the *Burlesk* for piano and orchestra, a set of eight songs that includes the beautiful "Allerseelen" ("All Souls' Day") and "Zueignung" ("Dedication"), and a delightful Serenade for Thirteen Wind Instruments. The formal structures of these works reflect the thoroughness of his early training in the compositions of Bach, Haydn, Mozart, and Beethoven. These years of young Strauss's development were supervised

Richard Strauss

by his father, a leading French horn player of his time, in an attempt to shield him from any Wagnerian "contamination."

When Strauss was twenty, two important events precipitated a significant change in his work: he became assistant to the famed conductor Hans von Bülow, marking the beginning of his career as an internationally acclaimed conductor; and he met Alexander Ritter, an ardent Wagnerian who urged Strauss, in his search for musical identity, to explore the expressive means utilized by Berlioz, Liszt, and Wagner. Each of these composers contributed significantly to Strauss's new compositional profile: Berlioz through his programmatic realism; Liszt through the symphonic-poem format; Wagner through a distinctive harmonic vocabulary and the *Leitmotiv;* and both Berlioz and Wagner by becoming models for Strauss in the development of the orchestra as a gigantic virtuoso ensemble.

During the next decade, following his transitional work *Aus Italien* (1886) and the relatively unsuccessful *Macbeth* (1886), he wrote the sym-

8

phonic poems that catapulted him to worldwide fame: *Don Juan* (1888), *Tod und Verklärung (Death and Transfiguration;* 1889), *Till Eulen-spiegels lustige Streiche (Till Eulenspiegel's Merry Pranks;* 1895), *Also sprach Zarathustra (Thus Spake Zarathustra;* 1896), *Don Quixote* (1897), and *Ein Heldenleben (A Hero's Life;* 1898).

Recognizing the organizational dangers in completely adopting the diffuse formal structure of the Liszt symphonic poem, Strauss continued using classical forms in these descriptive works while stressing Liszt's concept of theme transformation. *Don Juan* and *Tod und Verklärung* are both in sonata-form; *Till Eulenspiegel,* although called a rondo form by Strauss, is essentially a variation form with two themes; *Don Quixote* is in classical variation form; and *Ein Heldenleben,* though structurally diffuse, does in many respects resemble a large sonata-form movement.

With Strauss, musical realism became an end in itself, accomplished through both his superb orchestral virtuosity and his use of the motive as a musical counterpart of the gesture or idea. For example, in *Don Quixote* he imitates the bleating of a flock of sheep, and in *Tod und Verklärung,* the labored breathing of a dying man. One can easily "see" Till thumbing his nose as he mocks the Establishment:

Example 1.

Don Juan is depicted tossing his cloak over his shoulder as he strides off on his search for the perfect woman:

Example 2.

Going beyond these more obvious pictorializations into the realm of ideas, Strauss depicts *Wissenschaft* (science, knowledge) in *Also sprach Zarathustra* with a motive that includes all twelve notes of the chromatic scale as the basis of a gigantic fugue:

Example 3.

Shortly after the beginning of the twentieth century, Strauss established an entirely new international reputation, this time as an opera composer, with *Salome* (1905), *Elektra* (1908), and *Der Rosenkavalier* (*The Knight of the Rose;* 1911). Both *Salome* and *Elektra* are one-act lyric tragedies that initially shocked an unsuspecting public with their insane heroines, harsh dissonances, and an enormous orchestra that shrieked and groaned in a paroxysm of realistic expressionism. It is in these two operas that Strauss made his most important contributions to twentieth-century music. The resolution of harmonic and melodic dissonance is frequently delayed or even omitted completely, and in a reflection of the dramatic content of the operas, Strauss creates unorthodox intrusions of musical ideas. *Der Rosenkavalier,* by contrast, is a comedy, whose score is filled with anachronistic waltzes delightfully contemporized through his imaginative harmonizations. With *Elektra* and *Der Rosenkavalier,* Strauss established an enduring collaboration with the librettist Hugo von Hofmannsthal.

Although a number of works Strauss produced during the next thirty-five years contain many inspired moments, these works contributed little that was new to the art of music. The changing currents of twentieth-century music had passed over the one-time *enfant terrible.* Among the more notable of these later works are the operas *Ariadne auf Naxos* (1912), *Arabella* (1932), and *Capriccio* (1941); his *Metamorphosen* (1944) for twenty-three strings; and the *Vier letzte Lieder* (*Four Last Songs;* 1948).

Gustav Mahler (1860–1911)

By the end of the nineteenth century, the symphony had generally evolved into a large, diffuse orchestral work which, while continuing to use the name *symphony,* retained very little of its classical structure.

Gustav Mahler

There were of course a number of notable exceptions, including those by Brahms. Wagnerian chromaticism, "endless melody," increased technical virtuosity, and greatly expanded orchestral resources all contributed significantly to the transformation, which was brought to an effective climax in the symphonies of the postromantic Gustav Mahler.

Mahler was essentially a lyric composer whose interest in song and the voice as an important expressive medium was established early in his career with the song cycle *Lieder eines fahrenden Gesellen* (*Songs of a Wayfarer;* 1883). Later, he wrote a cycle of twelve songs, *Des Knaben Wunderhorn* (*The Boy's Magic Horn;* 1888–99), and the touching *Kindertotenlieder* (*Songs on the Death of Children;* 1901–4).

The degree of importance that he attached to these works for voice is best pointed up by the significant number of themes he borrowed from them for use in his symphonies. The First Symphony uses material from *Lieder eines fahrenden Gesellen* and the next three symphonies all include themes from the cycle *Des Knaben Wunderhorn.* He further demonstrated his affinity for song within the concept of the symphony by including voices as an integral part of his Second, Third, Fourth, and Eighth symphonies.

Mahler's final vocal work, *Das Lied von der Erde* (*The Song of the Earth;* 1908), is justifiably his best-known composition. It is based on a cycle of six poems translated from the original Chinese by Hans Bethge. Three are scored for solo tenor, the other three for contralto. Although the work was called a symphony by Mahler, the soloists play the dominant role; the orchestra is exploited fully only in the interludes. This work, perhaps more than any other, epitomizes that philosophical dualism expressed by Mahler in so many of his compositions: the intoxication with earthly joys against the background of awaiting death. Even the title of the first song is revealing: "Trinklied vom Jammer der Erde" ("The Drinking Song of Earth's Sorrow").

A large measure of Mahler's extraordinary sensitivity for orchestral color and balance may be attributed to his remarkable gifts as an orchestral and operatic conductor. It was during his tenure as conductor of the Vienna Imperial Opera (1897–1907) and subsequently of the New York Philharmonic that he produced the greater part of his compositions, writing during the summers and then orchestrating these works during his regular conducting season. The heritage of Wagner's orchestra was of course at his command, but he found that these resources simply did not meet his needs. He therefore considerably enlarged each division of the orchestra to give himself both the size and the flexibility he required. His Eighth Symphony, sometimes called the *Symphony of a Thousand*, requires, in addition to an enormously expanded orchestra, the services of two mixed choruses, a boys' chorus, and seven soloists. Actually Mahler employed the orchestral *tutti* sparingly, juxtaposing it with his use of varied and expanded color possibilities within each section.

In addition to his experimentation with orchestration, Mahler's forward-looking contrapuntal and harmonic procedures distinguish him within the postromantic period as a transitional composer of considerable importance. With Bach as his model, Mahler learned canonic imitation, use of the ostinato, and the ability to expand two or more musical ideas simultaneously, enhancing each through the interrelationship. By long delaying of cadence points, Mahler expanded phrase structures to remarkable lengths, creating seemingly endless melodic lines. Although his music never denies the cohesive principle of tonality, particularly with regard to tonal functions, he does significantly weaken its formal role through far-ranging modulations, abrupt modulations between phrases, and the avoidance of the traditional formal necessity for a return to an original tonal center. Although during his lifetime Mahler's critics far outnumbered his champions, succeeding generations of twentieth-century composers—particularly Schoenberg, Berg, and Webern—owed much to his innovative practices.

Mahler: SYMPHONY NO. 4 IN G MAJOR

Mahler wrote the first three movements of this symphony during the summers of 1899 and 1900 while on holiday from his position as director of the Vienna Imperial Opera. The fourth movement, composed before the others, was originally intended as a final movement (number seven) for his Third Symphony. It was to be titled "What the Child Told Me," as a sequel to the symphony's sixth movement, "What Love Tells Me." Eventually, however, he gave up his intention to extend the Third Symphony and made this movement the musical and programmatic aim of a new symphony. The result is a completely joyous work, diminutive in size, relatively conventional in form, and readily accessible to the inexperienced Mahler listener.

First Movement. An unpretentious three-measure introduction by the flutes and sleigh bells joined by the clarinet sets the mood of this delightful lyric movement and serves as both a unifying motive throughout the movement and a remembrance motive in the finale. The first subject is strongly reminiscent of Austrian folk song. It consists of three phrases (identified as *a, b, c* in example), each of which contains distinctive motives that achieve subsequent prominence in the development of the movement:

Example 4.

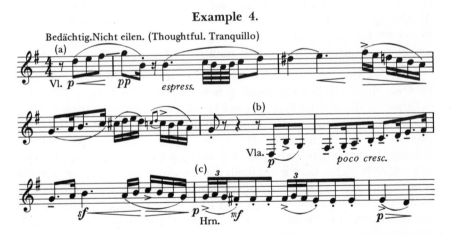

All three phrases are repeated and extended, reaching a *fortissimo* climax before being cut off abruptly to end this statement of the first subject. The second subject is a broad lyric melody built on the two phrases stated below, in the form *aaba.* It is sung by the cellos in the dominant key (D major):

13

Example 5.

a. **Breit gesungen (broadly singing)**

b.

A solemn rhythmic figure, played at a slightly slower tempo, is repeated by various instruments before dying away. The flutes and sleigh bells then return with their opening idea. The exposition closes with the cellos playing a slow, yearning new theme.

The sleigh bells open the development, and the various themes, as if participating in a conversation, are reintroduced, extended, and imaginatively developed within a continually shifting tonal affinity. Additional material finds its way into this section, previewing its appearance in the last movement. A marchlike fanfare in the brass and woodwinds brings the development to a climax, and then as it subsides, the oboes and clarinets begin the recapitulation with the opening subject while the remainder of the orchestra brings the development section to a close. Mahler further explores the latent power and passion implicit within the movement's subject matter in the recapitulation and coda, giving this section a character quite different from that of the exposition.

Second Movement. This movement is a scherzo, half humorous, half sardonic, in the following form: Scherzo—Trio I—Scherzo—Trio II—Scherzo—Coda. Mahler here pictures Death as a fiddler playing a tune to which reluctant souls of the world ultimately dance their way into the Beyond. To heighten the bizarre nature of this once-popular medieval notion, Mahler instructs the concertmaster-soloist to tune his instrument a whole step higher than normal, giving the violin a shrill, more piercing tone than usual. This deliberate abnormal tuning of a stringed instrument is known as *scordatura.* He also instructs the concertmaster to play his instrument in the manner of a street fiddler. His raucous tune is accompanied by muted strings:

Example 6.

In gemächlicher Bewegung. (Andante con moto)

14

Following a brief interlude, the solo violinist returns with his insistent tune. A descent by the bass instruments using the rhythmic motive of the introduction leads to the first trio.

It is slower than the scherzo, and begins with the clarinet playing a dance tune in $\frac{3}{8}$. The tune is answered by a lovely phrase played by the violins accompanied by a contrapuntal figure in the horn:

Example 7.

The second appearance of the scherzo is longer and more fully orchestrated than at the opening. The second trio, like the first, is slower than the scherzo, and though distinctly rhythmic in orientation, it still retains a lyric folklike character. The violins' phrase from the first trio reappears, leading to the return of the scherzo, played as at the beginning. The coda gradually diminishes in volume until the movement ends abruptly.

Third Movement. The lyric slow movement (*Poco adagio*) opens with a broad melody played by one division of the cello section accompanied by the violas and the remainder of the cellos. The basses pluck a rhythmic figure that continues throughout the movement:

Example 8.

The violins then repeat the theme. Next, a new theme is introduced by the oboe and is then immediately extended by the violins. The emotional impact of this passage is intensified through Mahler's characteristic use of a series of appoggiaturas:

Example 9.

16

The dramatic quality of both themes suggests a programmatic content; in fact, Mahler did write a detailed program for each of his first four symphonies but later suppressed them. Only after the close of this section, when Mahler effectively juxtaposes variations on his two principal ideas, does it become evident that the movement is in theme-and-variation form. Mahler lightens the mood in the first variation by means of a somewhat faster tempo and a beautiful countermelody played by the clarinet. Soon, however, the emotional level is again intensified by a variation of the section previously described, and a connecting passage by the cello leads to the next variation.

It begins as a lighthearted *Allegretto*, moves gracefully through the two themes with two increases of tempo, and then abruptly returns to the original tempo of the movement. As the sound gradually disappears, an outcry from the entire orchestra suddenly intrudes—the underlying rhythm figure is pounded out *fortissimo*, and the horns blare a hint of the theme of the fourth movement. Just as suddenly, quiet is restored and the movement closes on the sighing appoggiatura phrase of the second theme.

Fourth Movement. The finale, scored for soprano and small orchestra, is a child's artless expression of unrestrained delight in his view of heaven. The parable text is from the folk poetry of *Des Knaben Wunderhorn,* some of whose verses Mahler had already used in his songs. The opening depicts the joys of an angel's peaceful life filled with singing and dancing watched over by Saint Peter. The clarinet begins the movement playing the main theme; the voice soon enters singing "with childishly joyous expression, but without any parody":

Example 10.

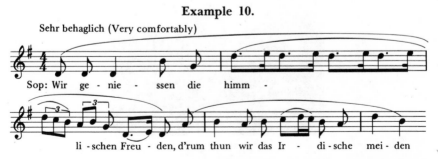

Translation: We delight in heaven's pleasures, where
we avoid all that which is earthbound.

The jingling interlude separating the first two strophes is taken from the opening of the first movement. The poetry next relates that while Herod the butcher watches, Saint John releases his small lamb, and that we are leading a blameless little lamb to its death. In heaven, Saint Luke slays the ox, wine never costs a penny, and the angels bake bread. Although the tune of the second strophe is different from the others, its close is similar. There is another twittering, jingling interlude, and then the soloist describes the vegetables and fruits of the heavenly garden. Saint Peter is seen catching fish with his net in the heavenly pond. Saint Martha does the cooking. The customary interlude begins but is considerably extended through the use of additional material. The soprano then continues, "There is no music on earth which can be compared to our own; eleven thousand maidens dance, and even Saint Ursula laughs. Saint Cecilia and her relatives are marvelous court musicians; our senses are so refreshed by their angelic voices that everything joyously awakens." A beautiful countertheme played by the violins accompanies the voice throughout this final strophe, which is marked "very tender and mysterious to the end."

Hugo Wolf (1860–1903)

Hugo Wolf belongs to the line of distinguished nineteenth-century *Lieder* writers begun by Schubert and continued by Schumann and Brahms. Although Wolf wrote an opera (*Der Corregidor;* 1896), a symphonic poem, and some chamber music, these compositions are relatively

Hugo Wolf
Doubleday & Company, Inc., New York.

unimportant when compared with his significant output of nearly three hundred songs. He applied many of the artistic principles and harmonic techniques used by Wagner to his song writing and, like Wagner, sought to amplify the meaning of poetry through a completely intimate relationship between poetry and music.

His taste in poetry was superb. Having immersed himself in a select volume of poetry, often by a single writer, Wolf composed in a brief but frenzied period of inspiration. When ideas no longer flowed readily from his pen, he would then fall into a state of depression until the next period of activity. During these creative periods between 1887 and 1897, he produced six volumes of songs which included fifty-three settings of poems by Mörike (1889), twenty by Eichendorff (1889), and fifty-one by Goethe, and from poetry of other countries in German translation, forty-four songs of the *Spanisches Liederbuch,* and forty-six settings in two parts (1892, 1896) of the *Italienisches Liederbuch.*

Jean Sibelius (1865–1957)

During the last decade of the nineteenth century, Jean Sibelius produced the first musical literature of genuine significance to come from the pen of a Finnish national. His interest in Finland's folklore, including

Jean Sibelius

Music Division, The New York Public Library at Lincoln Center. Astor, Lenox and Tilden Foundations.

the national epic *Kalevala,* provided general programmatic material for a number of his well-known early works, particularly *En Saga* (1892), *The Swan of Tuonela* (1893), *Leminkäinen's Homecoming* (1895), and *Finlandia* (1899). It is interesting to note, however, that Sibelius's musical nationalism does not reflect the folk-song tradition of his country; instead, he developed a capacity for depicting the character of the Finnish people and the somber, natural beauty of their country in his imaginative scores.

Sibelius's international reputation is based largely upon his seven symphonies. Motivic ideas in these works frequently do not coalesce into themes until a movement is well advanced, making it impossible to analyze his music in terms of traditional concepts of thematic presentation. His music has a definite tonal orientation, occasionally modal but seldom chromatic. The dark colors of the woodwinds in their low register, the explosive capacity of the brass section when used alone, and the effect of the string section playing *pizzicato* are all features of his distinctive orchestral technique.

Sibelius wrote no important works after 1925. Evidently he preferred a quiet retirement in his country home to the rigors of adjusting to the new musical currents of the time.

Only one other Scandinavian composer active during the first quarter of the twentieth century rose to international prominence—Denmark's Carl Nielson (1865–1931). While long recognized in his own country, Nielson remained little known outside Denmark until, about twenty years after his death, his six symphonies and three concertos began to receive critical acclaim throughout the world. Like Sibelius, Nielson did not reflect the more revolutionary aspects of musical change of his time; he did, however, take a rather unconventional approach to tonality and form, particularly in his symphonies No. 1 and No. 5. The brooding subjectivism normally associated with Sibelius finds no role in his more objective, sometimes humorous style.

Alexander Scriabin (1872–1915)

In Russia, the tenets of romanticism under the long-lasting influence of Rimsky-Korsakov and Tchaikovsky persisted well into the twentieth century. The most prominent among the many postromantic Russian composers, Sergei Rachmaninoff (1873–1943), Alexander Scriabin, and Alexander Glazunov (1865–1936), were largely unaffected by the revolutionary musical ideas of the period. Glazunov, a student of Rimsky-Korsakov and a dedicated nationalist, achieved a synthesis of the German and Russian styles in his numerous symphonies, concertos, and ballets. Melodically his music derives from Rimsky-Korsakov and formally from Brahms, although his orchestral writing is lighter and more transparent than that of either of his models. Rachmaninoff, an avowed romantic traditionalist, evinced no desire to reform or transform. He was a distinguished pianist who, in addition to concertizing throughout the world, wrote three symphonies, four piano concertos, two operas, and numerous songs and piano pieces. He derived his general style from the Chopin-Liszt and Tchaikovsky traditions and throughout his long career remained completely oblivious to contemporary trends in twentieth-century music.

Scriabin's early works were piano compositions patterned after Chopin. Later, as he assimilated the techniques used by Liszt and Wagner, his music became increasingly chromatic and took on the lush, expressive Wagnerian sound. In his later years he became a mystic whose beliefs in theosophy and occult philosophy ultimately permeated his thinking to the extent that he dreamed of an ultimate *mysterium*, "in which all arts, all sciences and all religions would be brought together in a hyper-Hegelian synthesis" and of which he himself would be the deviser. His last three symphonic works, all part of a cycle, demonstrate his sincerity in attempting to achieve this ultimate synthesis. In them he departs from classical sonata-form, finding the Lisztian symphonic-poem concept more congenial to his ecstatic, passionate, metaphysical allusions. The titles,

Alexander Scriabin

Cleveland Public Library.

Divine Poem (1903), *Poem of Ecstasy* (1908), and *Prometheus: Poem of Fire* (1910), suggest his programmatic intentions. The *Poem of Ecstasy* is based on a "mystic chord" which Scriabin created, structured in fourths: C, F♯, B♭, E, A, D. *Prometheus* is scored for large orchestra and color organ, making possible the coordination of the mystical qualities of Scriabin's orchestral score with the projection of colors upon a screen.

Many feel that his greatest contributions to music literature are to be found among his piano miniatures and sonatas, particularly the last six of his ten piano sonatas written near the end of his unfortunately brief life. In them, Scriabin seems to be abandoning traditional concepts of tonality altogether by extending his use of chords built on fourths and by utilizing long strings of unresolved dissonances.

OTHER POSTROMANTICS

Gabriel Fauré (1845–1924)

Fauré represents the very essence of French *sensibilité*. The highly civilized, ultra-refined quality of his style is reminiscent of that found in the music of the eighteenth-century French composer Rameau. His music is intimate, with none of the bombast or emotionalism of the German or Russian romanticists; in fact, his finest inspirations are to be

Gabriel Fauré
Cleveland Public Library.

found in his chamber music and songs. Fauré's rich, innovative harmonic idiom reflects a subtle blending of modality and functional tonality within its chromatic framework. He wrote one string quartet, two piano quartets, two piano quintets, and a piano trio which must be numbered among the finest chamber music expressions of the postromantic period. His songs and those of his contemporary, Henri Duparc (1848–1933) provided a substantial foundation for the development of a genuine modern French art song *(chanson)* tradition. His favorite poet was Paul Verlaine, whose refined, evocative poetry was close to his own restrained musical language. His exceptional melodic gifts and masterful capacity for combining words and music are known to audiences through such recital favorites as "Après un rêve" ("After a Dream"), written when he was twenty; "Clair de lune" ("Moonlight"), the first of his Verlaine songs; "Mandoline"; "Nell"; and the song cycle *La Bonne Chanson (A Good Song)*, a setting of nine Verlaine love lyrics. Of his large works only the Requiem and the incidental music he wrote for *Pelléas and Mélisande* have achieved popularity outside France. Maurice Ravel, Georges Enesco, and Nadia Boulanger were among his more significant students.

Ernest Chausson (1855–99)

Chausson reflects the influences of his teacher, César Franck, and of Wagner in a compositional style characterized by sensitivity, excellent construction, and fine command of contrapuntal and melodic skills. His developing individuality as a composer was unfortunately cut short when he was killed in a bicycle accident at the age of forty-four. His only symphony, in B flat major (1898), uses the cyclic form in a manner very close to that used by Franck in his D minor symphony. His rhapsodic *Poème* for violin and orchestra (1897) is perhaps his finest work.

Vincent d'Indy (1851–1931)

D'Indy was a student of César Franck and became his teacher's most ardent champion. Together with other followers of Franck, he continued the work of the master by creating one of France's great musical institutions, the Schola Cantorum, in 1894. As a professor and director of the Schola and as a teacher at the Paris Conservatoire, he influenced an entirely new generation of composers, including Satie, Roussel, and Honegger, whose works have figured so importantly in twentieth-century music. D'Indy's compositional style is a synthesis of both French and German romanticism, and of the forms and techniques of the past as a framework for his very personal expression. Although he wrote a considerable amount of music, only three of his symphonic works are still heard occasionally outside of France: the First Symphony *On a French*

Mountain Air (1887) for orchestra and piano obbligato, the Second Symphony in B flat major (1903)—both based on the cyclic principle of thematic transformation—and the symphonic variations *Istar* (1896).

Edward Elgar (1857–1934)

Sir Edward Elgar was the first English composer to win international fame in over two hundred years. England's lack of an established tradition in composition undoubtedly contributed to the fact that Elgar was a late developer whose first important work, the *Enigma Variations,* did not appear until he was over forty. Once begun, his direction was positive, and he produced his finest works within the space of less than fifteen years. Elgar's music reflects taste and breeding, dignity and nobility; overt passion finds no place in his controlled expression of emotion.

Frederick Delius (1862–1934)

Elgar's English contemporary, Frederick Delius, was also important in the reestablishment of England's prominence in musical composition. By contrast with the music of Elgar, Delius's expression is gentle and inwardly reflective, pictorially oriented to his varied environment. He belongs to no given school, and although there is evidence of eclecticism in his works through his varied exposure to Grieg, Wagner, and the late-nineteenth-century development in France known as impressionism, these influences are vague rather than specific. Viewing nature in a subjective reflection of his own temperament, he produced his most characteristic works, among which the best known are *Appalachia* (1902), *Brigg Fair* (1907), *On Hearing the First Cuckoo in Spring* (1912), and *Sea Drift* (1903), a setting of Walt Whitman's poem, for baritone, chorus, and orchestra.

Leõs Janáček (1854–1928)

Janáček successfully expressed his Moravian heritage throughout the period of postromanticism in a musical style that at first reflected the nineteenth-century influence of Smetana and Dvořák, followed later by a period of significant folk-song interest and the gradual emergence of his own highly personal twentieth-century expression. Ironically, he did not achieve international fame until he was in his sixties, with the Prague performance of his greatest opera *Jenufa* (1894–1903) in its 1916 version. Like Mussorgsky, Janáček identified with the peasantry of his country, used their music and tales, and successfully reflected the rhythmic speech inflections of their language in his vocal works. His mature harmonic expression is characterized by great freedom in his use of chromaticism, the whole-tone scale, and unconventional chord progressions; in fact, key affinities became so nebulous in his late works that he dispensed with key signatures altogether. Some of his greatest works were written during the last ten years of his life: the Slavonic rhapsody *Taras Bulba* (1918); Wind Sextet (1924); Concertino for Piano and Chamber Orchestra (1925); *The Slavonic Mass* (1926); Sinfonietta (1926); and Two String Quartets (1923, 1928).

Giacomo Puccini (1858–1924)

Giacomo Puccini was the most important Italian opera composer of the postromantic period. Although his operas are based upon a combination of the romantic traditions of Verdi and Wagner, he borrowed rather extensively from the harmonic vocabulary and orchestration techniques of a number of his twentieth-century-oriented contemporaries—particularly Debussy—to create the distinctive character of his music. His third opera, *Manon Lescaut* (1893), established the essentials of this highly successful style and brought him considerable recognition. His next two operas, *La Bohème* (1896), and *Tosca* (1900), secured his fame internationally and earned him a substantial fortune. Although *La Bohème* is influenced to some extent by the *verismo* (realism) concept, already ex-

Giacomo Puccini

Music Division, The New York Public Library at Lincoln Center. Astor, Lenox and Tilden Foundations.

plored by Ruggiero Leoncavallo (*I Pagliacci*, 1892) and by Pietro Mascagni (*Cavalleria rusticana*, 1890), its realism is not violent; *Tosca*, on the other hand, is a pure *verismo* "shocker." By contrast, both his next opera, *Madama Butterfly* (1904), and his last, the masterpiece *Turandot* (1924, finished by Alfano in 1926), display Eastern exoticism through their melody, harmony, and orchestral color. Following *Madama Butterfly*, two less successful operas, *La Fanciulla del West* (*The Girl of the Golden West;* 1910) and *La Rondine* (*The Swallow;* 1917) were written before he produced his much praised *Il Trittico* (*Triptych*) of three one-act operas in 1918. The first, *Il Tabarro* (*The Cloak*) is a veristic opera; the second *Suor Angelica* (*Sister Angelica*) is a lyric religious outpouring of great intensity; and the third, *Gianni Schicchi*, the most popular of the three, is a comedy in eighteenth-century opera buffa style.

Puccini's passionate lyric style and such instinct for the theatre, in a viable combination of sentimentality and realism, have earned him the gratitude of generations of singers and opera-goers. Fortunately, Puccini never attempted to exceed his limitations. As the author Donald Grout remarks, Puccini's music "often sounds better than it is, owing to the perfect adjustment of means to ends."

chapter 3

Impressionism and Postimpressionism

IMPRESSIONISM

The term *impressionism* was appropriated by the French art critic Louis Leroy from a painting by Claude Monet (1840–1926) titled *Impression: Soliel Levant (Rising Sun)*, to describe in derisive terms both Monet's painting and a number of others exhibited in a Paris salon in 1874. Soon the term was applied to an entire school of artists that included Monet, Édouard Manet (1832–83), Edgar Degas (1834–1917), and Auguste Renoir (1841–1919). These men ignored conventional formulas of the "true to nature" concept in their paintings, deliberately blurring details in an attempt to capture an impression, together with its emotional overtones, of a fleeting moment in time. Heroic and sentimental subject matter of the romantic tradition was discarded in favor of the commonplace, and traditional form was replaced by the iridescent color and atmospheric moods of the outdoor world, whose constantly changing interplay of light and shade was preferred to the sterile, controlled, environment of the studio.

Concurrent with this development, a movement in poetry known as *symbolism*, first explored by Edgar Allen Poe (1808–49), was introduced in France by Charles Baudelaire (1821–67) and later developed by his countrymen Stéphane Mallarmé (1842–98), Paul Verlaine (1844–96), and Arthur Rimbaud (1854–91). It was an art of suggestion, of subtle imagery,

Monet—*Impression: Soliel Levant* (1872)

Musée Marmottan, Paris.

Degas—*On the Stage* (1880)

The Art Institute of Chicago.

a searching for that abstract quality that traditionally had been the sole property of music. Words were used as much for their sound as for their meaning, and rhyme, rhythm, and form became secondary to the mood or idea the poet was attempting to convey.

Musical impressionism directly reflected the works of these painters and poets. Building an atmosphere, suggesting images, and developing subtle moods all took precedence over the influences of the formalistic logic and excessive extroverted emotional qualities of German late romanticism. While the musical vocabulary required to express this new aesthetic was sufficiently innovative to anticipate a new era, substantial ties with French postromanticism are also readily identifiable in its scores. This dichotomy places impressionism in a bridgelike position between the romantic past and twentieth-century modernism.

Claude Debussy (1862–1918)

This period is exemplified principally in the works of one man, Claude Debussy. As a student at the Paris Conservatoire, he was in constant rebellion against the rules of the theorists and academicians—the only rules he chose to follow were his own. He constantly sought new sounds, new cadences, innovative progressions, and novel tone colors. In 1884 he won the Conservatoire's highest award, the *Prix de Rome,* with his cantata *L'Enfant prodigue* (*The Prodigal Son*). He shortened his required residence in the Italian capital to return to Paris, where he joined the circle of avant-garde symbolists and impressionists who gathered weekly at the home of Mallarmé. He quickly perceived that these artists were expressing themselves in poetry and painting in a manner that he had been striving for in music. The following year, at the Paris Exposition of 1889, the exotic Far Eastern sounds of Javanese and Indonesian *gamelan* orchestras further stimulated his imagination. During this same period in his development he heard Rimsky-Korsakov conduct works by Borodin and Mussorgsky. Mussorgsky's *Boris Godunov* in particular made a lasting impression on him and significantly influenced his only opera. His friendship with Erik Satie a few years later further helped crystallize his ideas about music. This period of transition is beautifully summed up in his String Quartet (1893), which combines his impressionistic harmonic and rhythmic characteristics with classical form and the cyclic concepts of Franck and d'Indy. Debussy's first major impressionistic work, the *Prélude à l'après-midi d'un faune* (*Prelude to the Afternoon of a Faun*), completed in 1894, successfully synthesized the innovative procedures he had been developing over a number of years. This orchestral work is based on Mallarmé's symbolic poem *L'Après-midi d'un faune,* whose sensual, evocative meaning was captured perfectly within the atmosphere of dreamy illusion contained in Debussy's score.

Claude Debussy

Debussy's innovative use of harmony for coloristic effect constitutes one of the most striking aspects of musical impressionism. To him, dissonance was an end in itself requiring no resolution, and the chord was no longer part of a harmonic progression but a unity that existed for its sonorous quality, much as the word in symbolist poetry was used for its sound as well as its meaning. The implications of this concept freed him to disregard traditional cadential formulas in favor of more subtle relationships to a key center, and by recognizing varying degrees of dissonance, he explored the effect of using "mild" dissonance as a kind of relaxation following the tension created by "harsh" dissonance. This revolutionary theory opened an entirely new world of harmonic possibilities for himself and his contemporaries. It should be mentioned parenthetically, however, that Aristoxenus, the Greek philosopher, had already stated during the fourth century B.C. that "the distinction between consonance and dissonance is merely a relative matter."

By sounding chords with a fixed structure, either consonant or dissonant, on successive tones, Debussy created another typically impressionistic effect. These *parallel,* or "gliding," chords deny the basic functional character of traditional harmony; Debussy uses them instead for their sonority and expressive qualities:

Example 11. *Pelléas et Mélisande*

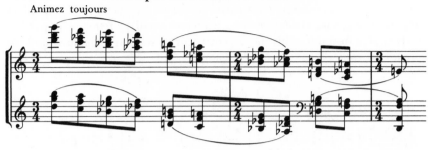

This parallel effect achieves a characteristically archaic sound, in imitation of a type of ninth-century polyphonic church music known as *parallel organum,* when the parallelism involves a series of chords in which the third has been omitted:

Example 12. "Cathédrale engloutie" ("The Sunken Cathedral")

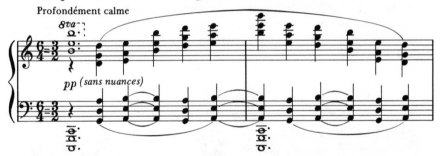

Debussy found the implications of the *whole-tone* scale useful in his composition. This scale is constructed completely of whole steps, for example, E-F♯-G♯-A♯-C-D-E. Because of its lack of half steps, the whole-tone scale avoids the sense of direction to the tonic that we feel in traditional major and minor scales. As a consequence, it avoids normal tonal and harmonic implications and adds to the vague, subtle, suggestive quality so much sought after by the impressionists:

Example 13. "Voiles" ("Sails") from First Book of Preludes

Debussy also used the *pentatonic* scale occasionally. This scale contains just five tones and can be most easily produced by playing only the black keys on the piano. He found the distinctive quality of this scale particularly useful in some of his more exotic works, such as "Pagodas" and the orchestral tone poem "Nuages" ("Clouds"):

Example 14.

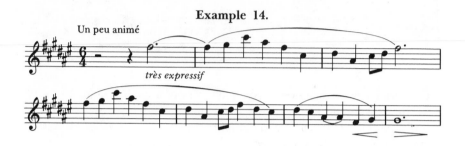

The rhythmic pulse itself is often disguised in impressionistic music through syncopation, frequent meter and tempo changes, and irregular subdivisions of the beat. The opening of *Prélude à l'après-midi d'un faune* illustrates the nearly arhythmic structures found in Debussy's music:

Example 15.

The French had never been particularly enthusiastic about using the large forms of the sonata cycle, and now the sensual quality of impressionism was found to be particularly opposed to the intellectual restraints of the developmental forms. Even in the miniature forms, formal outlines were deliberately blurred and phrase outlines distorted. The names for many of these miniatures Debussy borrowed from the painter: *images, estampes,* and *esquisses* (images, engravings, and sketches); others are poetic in their inspiration: "Jardins sous la pluie" ("Gardens in the Rain"), "Reflets dans l'eau" ("Reflections in the Water"), "Les Sons et les Parfums Tournent dans l'air du soir" ("Sounds and Perfumes Turning in the Evening Air"), and "Feuilles mortes" ("Dead Leaves").

Renoir—*San Marco* (1881)

The Minneapolis Institute of Arts, Minneapolis.

In addition to the well-known *Prélude à l'après-midi d'un faune,* several other works among Debussy's small output for orchestra have achieved an importance in twentieth-century music completely disproportionate to their number. In 1899, he completed a set of three Nocturnes for Orchestra; "Nuages" ("Clouds"), "Fêtes" ("Festivals"), and "Sirènes" ("Sirens"). This descriptive music captures the pictorial and emotional essence of each subject with remarkable musical insight, from the constantly drifting motion of clouds depicted in the first to the textless chorus of the Sirens in the last. *La Mer (The Sea;* 1905) effectively presents the varied moods of the sea in three "pictures." His last work for orchestra is a set of three unrelated pieces that he called *Images,* from which only the second, *Ibéria* (1908), is played with any frequency. Its three scenes present an intriguing Gallic distillation of the romantic substance of Spain.

Debussy's importance to twentieth-century composition as a piano composer is comparable to that of Chopin for the nineteenth century. His most significant impressionistic piano works, including the *Estampes,* two books of *Images,* and two books of Preludes, were written between 1903 and 1913. In these works he explored new sonorities, new pedal effects, colorful nuances, and a wealth of imaginative musical refinements which brought the expressive capabilities of the keyboard to undreamed-of heights. His best-known piano compositions include "Clair de lune" ("Moonlight"; 1890); "Reflets dan l'eau" ("Reflections in the Water"; 1905); and "La Cathédrale engloutie" ("The Sunken Cathedral"; 1910).

Together with Gabriel Fauré, Debussy liberated French chanson from the domination of the German lied; in fact, his significance as a writer of songs can hardly be overemphasized. Although their total number is relatively small—just sixty—they deeply influenced the greater part of twentieth-century vocal music.

In addition to his youthful cantata *L'Enfant prodigue,* Debussy composed three major works for voices and orchestra, each during a different period in his development. *La Demoiselle élue (The Blessed Damozel;* D. G. Rossetti; 1888) is an early work of singular beauty, which while stylistically unsettled, is nonetheless compelling in basic conception. His incidental music for Gabriele d'Annunzio's (1863–1938) dramatic mystery play *Le Martyre de Saint Sébastien (The Martyrdom of St. Sebastian;* 1911) is a late work from the same period that includes the *Études* for piano (dedicated to Chopin), the ballet *Jeux (Games),* and the sonatas for cello and piano, for violin and piano, and for flute, viola, and harp.

Debussy's only completed opera, *Pelléas et Mélisande* (1902), was written at the midpoint of his career. This remarkable realization of the ideals of musical impressionism is one of the significant landmarks in all operatic history. Debussy's perfect fusion of words and music in the most subtle of relationships enhances the timelessness of Maeterlinck's drama. It is as much a music-drama as *Tristan* by virtue of its continuous musical line, use of orchestral motives, and exclusion of ornamental details; yet, it is completely French in the implementation of its expression and idiom. The characters are frail, not heroic; for them musical bombast has no place in a fabric where even a whisper or a suggestion can be eloquent.

Debussy: *LA MER*

This is Debussy's most ambitious work for orchestra. Begun in 1903 and finished in 1905, its three symphonic sketches represent his impressions of the sea's beauty and majesty. The work has no recognizable form and no firmly established tonality in the traditional sense. Instead, Debussy establishes his discipline "in freedom" by constantly transforming thematic material throughout each sketch, and by establishing thematic connections among the three. Harmonically, rhythmically, and melodically *La Mer* is thoroughly representative of the impressionistic movement.

I. De l'aube à midi sur la mer (From Dawn to Noon at Sea). The quiet beginning of the first sketch suggests the gentle movement of waves as dawn's first light appears. The principal theme, first introduced by the trumpet and English horn, is used as source material throughout the entire work:

Example 16.

The tempo becomes more animated as the strings, harp, and woodwinds play various rhythmic figures and motives depicting the ceaseless motion of the sea. The motion continues as a new melody is introduced by the horns. Debussy then continues to depict the interplay of light and waves with a rhythmic complexity that includes, at times, as many as seven different patterns sounded simultaneously. Another tempo change introduces a new section that begins with the cellos, in a *divisi* of four groups, announcing a new idea rhythmically related to the opening of the movement. The tempo now gradually decreases and the main theme is heard once again in the horns and bassoons. The movement closes brilliantly, depicting the sun at high noon.

II. Jeux de vagues (Play of the Waves). This remarkable example of Debussy's compositional skill is a veritable textbook of impressionistic orchestral devices. The movement opens with a number of fragmentary motives and rhythms played by tremolo strings, muted brass, harp, and glockenspiel. A triplet passage, first played by the English horn and then repeated by the oboe, is heard subsequently, in various guises, throughout the movement. The tempo increases, and the main melodic material of the movement, whose theme is related melodically to the principal theme of the first sketch, is heard in a dancelike section:

Example 17.

Sections based on this material alternate with the purely atmospheric effects of harp glissandos, triple-tonguing by the woodwinds, muted trumpet rhythmic figures, and horns playing parallel ninth chords and augmented chords. A gradual *accelerando* builds to a climax whose tension slowly subsides. At the end of the movement the muted trumpet and flute, in its low register, whisper a melodic motive lightly accompanied by the harp, cymbal, and glockenspiel.

III. Dialogue du vent et de la mer (Dialogue of the Wind and the Sea). Rumblings in the bass and the sound of the rising wind in the woodwinds open the final sketch. The volume increases, punctuated by a muted trumpet loudly proclaiming the source theme. Suddenly the fury subsides as the oboe and bassoon sing a new, expressive chromatic idea:

Example 18.

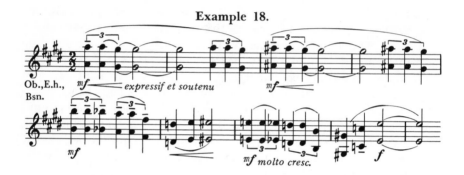

This theme and the source theme, interspersed with sections depicting the sea's stormy mood, effectively alternate throughout the remainder of the movement. These references to the source theme and to other melodic fragments from the first sketch strongly underline the cyclic nature of this work.

Debussy: *L'ÎLE JOYEUSE (THE HAPPY ISLAND)*

Debussy originally intended *L'île joyeuse* (1904) to be part of the *Suite Bergamasque* (1890–1905), the work that includes the popular "Clair de lune," but then he decided to have it published separately. This interpretation for piano solo of the Watteau painting, *Embarquement pour Cythère (Embarkation for Cythere)*, is technically one of Debussy's more difficult keyboard works, stylistically related, within the impressionistic development, to the Lisztian technique. Although the form follows the general outline of traditional sonata-form, the complex rhythmic structures and harmonic devices Debussy used are encyclopedic for his time.

Watteau—*Embarquement pour Cythère* (1717)

Editorial Photocolor Archives, Inc., New York.

A six-measure introductory cadenza in free improvisatory style leads to the dancelike opening theme of the first subject:

Example 19.

The theme is repeated and then its triplet figure serves as a background to a new theme based entirely on the whole-tone scale. A variant of the opening cadenza builds to a climax declaimed in the cadenza's original form; then a soft repetition of the first theme leads to the second subject. The tenderly expressive lyric quality of this subject gives the impression of having great rhythmic freedom through the use of a five-note pattern in the left hand:

Example 20.

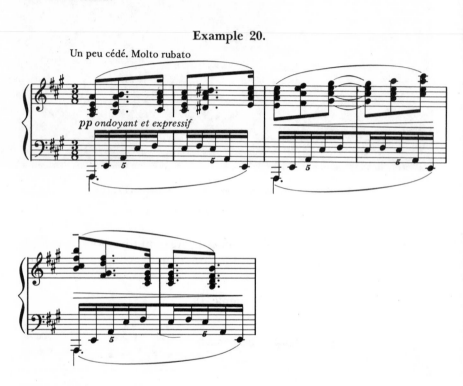

The exposition is generally oriented to the key of A major; the development, by contrast, begins in the dominant. The two subjects are developed alternately and simultaneously, and ultimately the section closes on a unison (E). The recapitulation's return to the tonic follows the normal convention of sonata-form; however, Debussy's treatment of his subjects departs considerably from the exposition. The first theme is now given a new accompaniment, the subsidiary theme of the first subject appears more quickly than before, and the first theme reappears in the form of a distant march over a muffled drumbeat effect. An exciting climax is reached and the second subject enters exultantly over a fanfare accompaniment. A gradual *accelerando* culminating in a loud, rhythmic return to the opening cadenza gives the close of *L'île joyeuse* the character of a wild bacchanal.

OTHER IMPRESSIONISTS

Though impressionism's only full-fledged exponent was its originator, its varied effects were reflected in the works of a large number of composers writing during the opening decades of the twentieth century. In France, it most influenced Jacques Ibert (1890–1962), whose impressionistic tendencies are best represented in his orchestral suite, *Escales* (*Ports of Call;* 1922); and Albert Roussel (1869–1937), particularly in his early works, the *Poème de la forêt* (*Poem of the Forest;* 1906) and *Le Festin de l'araignée* (*The Spider's Feast;* 1912).

In Italy, Ottorino Respighi (1879–1936) was influenced by impressionism to some degree, notably in his two most popular works, the tone poems *Fontane di Roma* (*Fountains of Rome;* 1917) and *Pini di Roma* (*Pines of Rome;* 1924). In both, his great gift for melody and his imaginative, colorful orchestration are fully realized. Poland's important composer Karol Szymanowski (1882–1937) and two Englishmen, Arnold Bax (1883–1953) and Cyril Scott (1879–1970), were also strongly influenced by Debussy's art.

The compositions of Spain's Manuel de Falla (1876–1946) combine impressionistic characteristics with significant nationalistic elements. His most thoroughly impressionistic work is a set of three impressions for piano and orchestra entitled *Noches en los jardines de España* (*Nights in the Gardens of Spain;* 1909–15).

In the United States as in France, impressionism was a reaction to the domination of German romanticism and pedagogy. Among the American impressionist composers, Charles Martin Loeffler (1861–1935) and Charles Tomlinson Griffes (1884–1920) are the most important. Loeffler, an Alsatian, came to the United States in 1881 to join the Boston Symphony Orchestra, but later, in 1903, he left the orchestra to devote himself entirely to composition. His style is basically impressionistic, although many other influences helped shape his music. Griffes, after returning home from his studies in Germany, became interested in Oriental music and the music of Mussorgsky. Later he came under the spell of impressionism and the music of Debussy, influences which are evident in his two finest works, *The Pleasure Dome of Kubla Khan* and the *Poem* for flute and orchestra. Unfortunately, he died at the early age of thirty-six, before he could fully realize his considerable potential.

POSTIMPRESSIONISM

The impressionist movement in painting had, by the end of the nineteenth century, generated a considerable diversity of experimentation among a new generation of painters that included Georges Seurat (1859–

Cézanne—*Les Joueurs de Cartes* (1892)

SCALA, New York/Florence.

Van Gogh—*La Maison de la Crau* (1888)

The Albright-Knox Art Gallery, Buffalo, New York.
Bequest of A. Conger Goodyear.

91), Paul Gauguin (1848–1903), Vincent Van Gogh (1853–90), and Paul Cézanne (1839–1906). While these *postimpressionist* painters continued the ideals and many of the techniques already established by the impressionists, they gave new expression to the idiom through the application of concepts gleaned from the past. They attempted, in the words of Cézanne, "to make something more solid and durable out of impressionism." The musical counterpart of this artistic movement is best exemplified in the works of Maurice Ravel.

Maurice Ravel (1875–1937)

Maurice Ravel began his career in Paris at a time when Claude Debussy was at the height of his fame. As a consequence, he was placed in the unfortunate situation of finding it difficult to establish his individuality. Naturally he was influenced by Debussy, but so was every young composer studying and composing in Paris at the time. He admittedly used many impressionistic effects and techniques, but his approach to form and his more precise and direct style have no counterpart in the music of Debussy. Ravel himself stated: "While I consider that Debussy may not have been altogether alien to my personal inheritance, I should identify also with the earlier phases of my evolution Gabriel Fauré, Emmanuel Chabrier, and Erik Satie." By contrast with Debussy, Ravel's harmonies are firmly rooted in tonality and are structurally conceived, his forms are classically oriented, and his music is more vigorous and brilliantly orchestrated. Furthermore, his rhythms are traditional, clear-cut; Debussy's are vague, irregular; he is a contrapuntalist; Debussy preferred block harmonies. Even the whole-tone scale is conspicuously absent in Ravel's music. If anything, Ravel can be accused of being too intellectual and sophisticated, of allowing his technique to interfere with his inspiration—Stravinsky called him a "Swiss watchmaker." Ravel's classical orientation is particularly noticeable among his post-1912 compositions, while his earlier works—the piano pieces *Pavane pour une Infante défunte (Pavane for a Deceased Infanta;* 1899), *Jeux d'eau (Play of the Water;* 1901), *Gaspard de la Nuit (Gaspard of the Night;* 1908), the orchestral work *Rapsodie espagnole (Spanish Rhapsody;* 1907); and the ballet *Daphnis et Chloé* (1912)—are more overtly impressionistic in their general aesthetic. The simplicity of the delightful *Ma Mère l'Oye (Mother Goose;* 1908) and the approach to form used by Ravel in many of these early works, particularly the String Quartet (1903) and Sonatina (1905), give early evidence of the stylistic path he was to follow in later years. The *Valses nobles et sentimentales* (1911) marks the beginning of a more rational, objective, "neoclassic" approach to his musical materials. *Le Tombeau de Couperin (In Memory of Couperin;* 1917), for instance, is a suite of dances that utilizes the harpsichord style of the eighteenth-

Maurice Ravel

The Bettmann Archive.

century composer François Couperin, and the Trio for Piano, Violin, and Cello (1914) is a masterpiece of form, whose second movement is based on a passacaglia theme. During this period, Ravel became increasingly interested in the use of the contrapuntal language of his twentieth-century contemporaries, an influence that is particularly prominent in the Sonata for Violin and Cello (1922). His later works include a Concerto for Piano (1931), a brilliant work that is almost Mozartian in style and texture (the form of the second movement is based on the slow movement of the Mozart Clarinet Quintet). The *Concerto for the Left Hand,* written the same year, is a dark, almost brutal work with strong jazz elements, considered by some critics to be one of his finest works.

Ravel's brilliant orchestrations place him, along with Berlioz, Rimsky-Korsakov, and Richard Strauss, among the great orchestrators of the past. His transcription of Mussorgsky's *Pictures at an Exhibition* and his ballets *La Valse* (1920) and *Bolero* (1928) are familiar examples of his mastery of the craft.

Ravel's stature and innovative genius are undoubtedly less than Debussy possessed; his unique and lasting significance lies instead in the fact that he perfectly represents the sophistication, logic, and sensibilité of the Gallic temperament in twentieth-century music.

Ravel: DAPHNIS ET CHLOÉ

During the years just preceding the first World War, that remarkable impresario of the Ballet Russe, Serge Diaghilev, "discovered" the genius of twentieth-century composers Stravinsky, De Falla, and Prokofiev, and utilized the talents of artists Picasso, Rouault, and Bakst while they were still struggling for recognition. He was also quick to recognize the importance of Ravel's talent and in 1910 commissioned him to write a ballet, *Daphnis et Chloé,* to follow a scenario written by the choreographer Michel Fokine. The first performance of the ballet took place in Paris, June 8, 1912, with Pierre Monteux conducting a sumptuous production that featured sets by Léon Bakst, choreography by Fokine, and the fabulous dancers Nijinsky and Karsavina. As a ballet, it was less than a complete success; performers found themselves having to adapt their movements to what is essentially a symphonically conceived work. Ravel himself later said of the ballet that "the work is constructed symphonically according to a strict tonal plan by the method of a few motifs, the development of which achieves a symphonic homogeneity of style." Reflecting upon this evaluation of the ballet, he fashioned two suites, or series, from the larger work, well suited to the concert hall.

The scenario was taken from a pastoral written by the Greek poet Longus, who lived about the beginning of the third century A.D. The tale is simple: Daphnis and Chloé have grown up together but become aware of their love for each other only when Chloé is abducted by pirates. Daphnis invokes the god Pan to rescue her, and she is returned amid general rejoicing. Ravel's score for this slight plot has an iridescent sheen and tonal splendor that requires an orchestra with a brilliant virtuoso technique. To increase the opulence of the whole, Ravel added music for a chorus instructed to sing without words and at times *a cappella.* Each of the two series has three sections intended to be played without pause, and the plot continuity for each has been indicated by Ravel in his score. Of the two series, the second, analyzed below, is the one most frequently performed.

I. Daybreak. "No sound except the murmur of brooklets fed by the dew running from the rocks. Daphnis lies stretched out in front of the nymphs' grotto. Day breaks gradually and the song of birds can be heard." Ravel's musical description is thoroughly convincing—shimmering scales by the woodwinds blended with the harp bring the dawn, and birds are imitated by the piccolo and violin. Gradually a broad arching theme rises from the depths of the orchestra. It begins as a repetitive motive with the double basses, ascends to the violins, and is then extended by the violas and clarinet:

Example 21.

The piccolo plays a florid phrase as "in the distance, a shepherd passes with his flock." A similar phrase is then played by the small E-flat clarinet as "Another shepherd crosses the back of the stage." Other instruments augmented by the wordless harmonies of the offstage chorus give the melody further intensity. "A group of herdsmen enter looking for Daphnis and Chloé. They discover Daphnis and awaken him. In torment he looks about for Chloé. At last she appears, surrounded by shepherdesses. They throw themselves into each other's arms." The music reaches a rapturous climax as the lovers embrace, but then quickly subsides to a *pianissimo* as "Daphnis perceives Chloé's crown. His dream was a prophetic vision: the intervention of Pan is manifest." The opening theme once more arises from the orchestra, this time moving rapidly to a climax in which the entire orchestra glitters with bells, triangles, celesta, harp glissandos, and woodwind figurations. There is a rapid *diminuendo* as "the old shepherd, Lammon, explains that if Pan has saved Chloé, it is in remembrance of the nymph Syrinx, whom the god once loved." The meter changes (to $\frac{6}{8}$) and the oboe plays a pastoral figure as the second scene begins without pause.

II. Pantomime. "Daphnis and Chloé mime the adventure of Pan and Syrinx: Chloé impersonates the young nymph wandering in the meadow." The oboes play a melodic phrase that is associated with Chloé in both this and the following scene:

Example 22.

"Daphnis, as Pan, appears and declares his love for her. The nymph repulses him and the god becomes more insistent. She disappears into the

44

reeds. Desperate, he plucks some stalks, fashions a flute, and plays a melancholy tune." The music has followed the text very closely, and so inevitably, accompanied by rhythmic pizzicatos from the strings and by soft harmonies from the horns and violas, the flute plays Pan's beautiful melody:

Example 23.

As the flute begins this long and languorous melody, "Chloé reappears and acts out, through her dance, the accents of the flute. The dance grows more and more animated and with an abandoned whirl, Chloé falls into the arms of Daphnis." The music once more resumes the original slow tempo, and the woodwinds and strings play an expressive variant of the Chloé theme. "Before the altar of the nymphs he swears his faith, upon two sheep." The movement is slow and stately, with the trumpets intoning the original cadenzalike motive from the First Series. The meter changes (to $\frac{5}{4}$) and the tempo changes abruptly as "A group of young girls enter dressed as Bacchantes, shaking their tambourines. Daphnis and Chloé embrace tenderly. A group of young men enter. Joyous tumult —general dance."

III. Danse générale. Ravel supplied no commentary, save for the entrance of Dorcon, to describe the wild dance that follows. It is based on two themes that alternate in close proximity as the music becomes increasingly frenetic. The first theme is introduced by the violas and clarinets against the steady $\frac{5}{4}$ background of the snare drum and basses:

Example 24.

The second, more animated theme is played by the E-flat clarinet with the timpani supplying the steady $\frac{5}{4}$ pulse:

Example 25.

Occasional musical references to Daphnis and Chloé are all that interrupt the headlong thrust of frenzied excitement engendered through this tour de force of Ravel's astounding orchestral wizardry.

part **II**

PRINCIPAL
EUROPEAN
COMPOSERS

chapter 4

Development of the New Music

INTELLECTUAL AND POLITICAL DEVELOPMENT

During the closing decades of the nineteenth century, there was among the nations of Europe and the United States a growing sense of confidence that the political and economic systems of Western man were the most effective the world had yet seen. To most people this was the Age of Progress, the Age of Optimism; dissenting voices of those who attempted to picture man in a futile struggle against an evil society were relatively few. Herbert Spencer, an important voice of the Victorian era, stated, "Progress is not an accident but a necessity . . . the ultimate development of the ideal man is certain. . . ."

By contrast, the opening decades of the twentieth century witnessed a deterioration of the general confidence that had characterized the Victorian era. Growing doubts and unrest reached a climax of intensity in the tragedy of World War I. Nothing was resolved, schisms widened, and pessimism festered. The unprecedented "progress" during the years following the war merely exaggerated man's growing loss of identity as he became engulfed in the dehumanizing process of mechanization brought about through the completion of the Industrial Revolution.

The rapidity with which these changes occurred created a cultural lag between twentieth-century society and the scientists and artists of the age. Contact between the artist and the public grew tenuous as the artist reacted to displacement within a society that was based on a material-istic and pragmatic philosophy. The arts soon became an important vehicle for social criticism: expressionists turned to tragedy, pathos, and despair; and existentialists proclaimed an extreme negativism, picturing the universe as an absurd and meaningless phenomenon.

The artist's alienation from society was further intensified because large masses of society contented themselves with the accepted "classics" of previous eras, despite the fact that highly advanced techniques useful in the production and dissemination of culture were being produced. The artist, in order to survive, sought to reestablish a kind of patronage sys-tem. Commissions for new works from either individuals or institutions were eagerly sought. Particularly in the United States, the university has been established as a special type of patron. Artists have become teachers not only to earn a livelihood but also to maintain contact with this highly responsive element of society.

Throughout history, the artist has alternated between interpreting the world as a part of himself and seeing it as apart from himself. Both views, the first expressed as subjectivity and emotion and the second as objectivity and the intellect, have found expression during the twentieth century. During the first quarter of this century, particularly in a number of German and Austrian centers, the artist, placing emphasis on emo-tion and content rather than form and structure, fostered the growth of the various movements classified under *expressionism*. The dark drives, hidden terrors, and hallucinatory visions of the realm of the subconscious explored by the founder of psychoanalysis, Sigmund Freud (1856–1939), became the dominant theme of expressionist writers August Strindberg (1849–1912) and Franz Kafka (1883–1924), painters Oskar Kokoschka (b. 1886) and Wassily Kandinsky (1866–1944), and the composers Arnold Schoenberg (1874–1951) and Alban Berg (1885–1935). Two notable paint-ings, Vincent Van Gogh's *The Starry Night* (1889) and Edvard Munch's *The Scream* (1893), anticipated the expressionistic view of the subcon-scious. In attempting to mirror the dark regions of the soul, the visual artist resorted to the use of distortion, new techniques and symbols, and violent exaggeration; the writer employed man's subjective self and his displays of psychotic behavior; and the composer used jagged melodic lines, clashing dissonances, and distorted rhythms.

Many expressionists embraced *primitivism,* a movement that grew from the many exhibitions of African sculpture and artifacts, and the displays of Polynesian crafts and East Indian arts at the Paris Exposition of 1889. The Tahitian paintings of Paul Gauguin and the publication of anthropologist Sir James Frazer's monumental work, *The Golden Bough* (1890), were also influential in this movement. Primitivism became popu-lar because it offered an escape from what to many were the offensive

Van Gogh—*The Starry Night* (1889)

Collection, The Museum of Modern Art, New York.
Acquired through the Lillie P. Bliss Bequest.

Munch—*The Scream* (1893)

Oslo Kommunes Kunstsamlinger.

Matisse—*Deux Negresses* (1909)

The Baltimore Museum of Art. The Cone Collection, formed by
Dr. Claribel Cone and Miss Etta Cone of Baltimore, Maryland.

wheels of progress. Fascinated by the anti-intellectual nature of African
art works, Pablo Picasso (1888–1973), particularly in his painting *Les
Demoiselles d'Avignon* (*Young Ladies of Avignon;* 1907), and Amedeo
Modigliani (1884–1920), through the use of elongated heads and bodies
in his paintings, reflected the influence of primitivism. Music of the non-
European cultures of Africa, India, China, and even southeastern Europe
and Asiatic Russia jolted traditional concepts of rhythm and meter in
Western music, particularly the overrefinement of the impressionists and
postimpressionists.

Expressionism also embraced the nihilistic movement called *Dadaism*
and its successor, *surrealism* (super-realism). These antirational developments were anticipated by the painters Giorgio de Chirico (1888–1978)
and Marc Chagall (b. 1887) in their pre-World War I paintings. Dadaism,
which grew out of the disillusion, despair, and world-weariness following
the first World War, was a protest led by Marcel Duchamp (1887–1968)
against all established values, moral and aesthetic. This anti-art movement
attracted many young artists of the time because of its anarchistic philosophy. Dadaism, as a defined movement, however, was short-lived
(c. 1916–22). Surrealism, on the other hand, was a stronger movement; in
fact, it still retains much of its early vitality. Taking its cue from Freud's
Interpretation of Dreams (1900), surrealism proclaimed the superior

Picasso—*Les Demoiselles d'Avignon* (1907)

Collection, The Museum of Modern Art, New York.
Acquired through the Lillie P. Bliss Bequest.

Chagall—*I and the Village* (1911)

Collection, The Museum of Modern Art, New York.
Mrs. Simon Guggenheim Fund.

Dali—*Illuminated Pleasures* (1929)

The Sidney and Harriet Janis Collection.
Gift to The Museum of Modern Art, New York.

reality of the dream state and soon created a language of its own with which it could present to the outer world of reality a symbolism from the inner world of the subconscious. Salvatore Dali (b. 1904), Max Ernst (b. 1891), and Joan Miró (b. 1893) are the principal surrealist painters; James Joyce (1882–1941) and Gertrude Stein (1887–1946) adapted its use of the subconscious to their literary works. It is interesting to note that surrealistic tendencies predating the period itself can be found in the iconoclastic piano works of Erik Satie (1866–1925) and in the strange symbolism used in the opera *Bluebeard's Castle* (1911) by Béla Bartók (1881–1945).

The final stage in the growth of pessimism during the twentieth century is represented in existentialist philosophy. Growing out of the work of Friedrich Nietzsche (1844–1900) and Søren Kierkegaard (1813–55), it is represented in this century mainly through the works of Jean-Paul Sartre (b. 1905) and Albert Camus (1913–60). To the existentialist, all forms of absolutism are anathema, whether they be political, literary, or musical. The influence of existentialism can be found in a substantial amount of literature, music, and drama written since 1940, including Samuel Beckett's (b. 1906) *Waiting for Godot,* Camus' *L'Etranger,* and the chance (*aleatoric*) music of John Cage (b. 1912) and Lukas Foss (b. 1922).

Coeval with the post-World War I expressionist movements, an objective, more intellectual approach to artistic expression, emphasizing form and structure rather than subjective content, exerted a considerable influence in the arts. This twentieth-century movement, known as *neo-classicism*, centered in Paris. It was first fostered by Picasso and Igor Stravinsky in their 1920 collaboration on the ballet *Pulcinella*, a stylized contemporary version of early eighteenth-century *commedia dell'arte*, using the music of Giovanni Battista Pergolesi (1710–36). Picasso's *Three Graces* and his illustrations for the new editions of Ovid's *Metamorphosis* and Aristophanes' *Lysistrata* further reflect neoclassicism. The movement also found expression in a number of Greek myths that were rewritten in contemporary language, including Franz Werfel's (1890–1945) *The Trojan Women*, Sartre's *The Flies*, and Joyce's *Ulysses*. The neoclassic movement in music was a conscious return to the pre-nineteenth-century forms and textures of the baroque and classic periods; the musical language was of the twentieth century, but expressiveness was far outweighed in importance by formal considerations.

Painters and sculptors continued the neoclassic emphasis upon form and structure in yet another school, *cubism*. They sought to reduce nature to its basic geometric patterns, and to view it both fragmentarily and simultaneously from a number of vantage points. Cézanne is credited with pointing the way toward cubism; his successors, Picasso and Georges Braque (1882–1963), are the principal painters usually associated with the development of this school. A modification of pure cubism is evident in

Picasso—*Les Amoureux* (1923)

National Gallery of Art, Washington, D.C.

Braque—*L'Homme au Guitare* (1911)

Collection, The Museum of Modern Art, New York.
Acquired through the Lillie P. Bliss Bequest.

the abstract sculptures of Constantin Brancusi (1876–1957). Cubism's simultaneity of view is reflected in music through the use of *polytonality* (two or more keys sounding simultaneously) and *polyrhythms* (two or more rhythms sounding simultaneously).

MUSICAL DEVELOPMENT

The highly subjective, often grandiose musical language of nineteenth-century romanticism, which found its way into the beginning of the twentieth century through the postromantics, was considered out of step with contemporary thought and the realities of contemporary existence by a growing number of twentieth-century artists. The impressionists had sought a new expression and to some extent they were successful, but the implications of the harmonic system and the subjectivism of the nineteenth century remained. Existing musical practices, rooted in the previous century, simply had been used too often and had as a consequence lost their spontaneity of meaning. For many the remedy was obvious: new styles and techniques must be developed to express contemporary purposes—overt change was in order. The resulting changes in traditional musical concepts that characterize the "New Music" were so significant that one cannot listen to the largest portion of music produced during this century through ears attuned to nineteenth-century practices.

Tonality

The functional major-minor concept of tonality, with its hierarchy of melodic and harmonic order, was for the two-hundred-year period beginning about 1700 the principal form of tonal organization in Western music. Particularly during the second half of the eighteenth century and the beginning of the nineteenth century, every note, every chord and chord progression, and every modulatory scheme stood in clearly defined relation to the central key, and through it, to every other note, chord, and scheme. After the time of Beethoven, however, traditional concepts of tonality were expanded through the use of chromaticism. The use of chromatic tones not found in the scale upon which a composition was based ultimately weakened the supreme dominance of the tonic and prepared the way in the twentieth century for the free use of all twelve notes within an octave around a tonal center rather than the seven used in the major-minor (*diatonic*) system. As a consequence, the distinctions between major and minor and between diatonic and chromatic soon disappeared, and traditional modulatory procedures were replaced by more abrupt shifts of tonal center.

In 1891, the American composer Charles Ives (1874–1954) achieved a startling interplay between two keys in his *Variations on "America"* by superimposing F major on A-flat major. The effect—*polytonality*—is defined as the simultaneous use of two or more tonalities. Frequently the term *bitonality* is used instead of polytonality when just two tonalities are used simultaneously. During the second decade of the twentieth century this practice gained common acceptance when Igor Stravinsky and Darius Milhaud (1892–1974) incorporated it into a number of their works. The following examples, from among the extensive possible applications of polytonality, illustrate the fascinating result of juxtaposing two key relationships:

Example 26. Stravinsky: *Petrouchka*

Example 27. Bartók: *Bagatelle No. 1*

The excessive use of chromaticism during the late nineteenth and early twentieth centuries precipitated the development of an interesting innovative technique: *pandiatonicism.* Rather than use the chromatic scale as their tonal basis of composition, a number of composers chose to use the diatonic scale, but without employing its traditional harmonic functions. In this technique strong harmonic movement and traditional cadences are replaced by greater emphasis upon rhythm and counterpoint. Examples can be found in much of Satie's piano music, in Debussy's *Children's Corner,* in large portions of Stravinsky's music, and in a considerable amount of twentieth-century American music, particularly that of Aaron Copland (b. 1900).

During the nineteenth century, composers sought out the folk music of their countries as resource material for nationalistic expression. Much of this music had as its tonal basis the medieval system of *church modes* whose use had preceded the development of the familiar major-minor system of more recent times. This system is reflected, within the context of the major-minor system, in music written by a substantial number of nineteenth-century composers, including Chopin, Liszt, Glinka, Mussorgsky, Dvořák, and Fauré. Twentieth-century composers, however, preferred not to accommodate modality (use of the church modes) to the major-minor system and strove instead for a more strict modal language. Seldom used today, modality was in vogue through the third decade of this century. Bartók and Ralph Vaughan Williams (1872–1958) in particular used the appealing sounds of modality to excellent advantage:

58

Example 28. Bartók: *Roumanian Folk Dances*, No. 2 (Dorian mode)

Example 29. Vaughan Williams: *Sir John in Love* (Phrygian mode)

By permission of Oxford University Press.

Atonality

In the opening decades of the twentieth century, a group of composers led by Arnold Schoenberg abandoned the use of a tonal center and the gravitational characteristics of key relationships. The term *atonality* was given to this new music in which all twelve tones within a given composition had equal importance. According to the noted composer-writer George Perle, "Atonality originates in an attempt to liberate the twelve notes of the chromatic scale from the diatonic functional associations they still retain in 'chromatic' music—to dissociate, so to speak, the chromatic scale from chromaticism." Schoenberg disliked the term *atonality* and preferred to call this technique *pantonality,* or the synthesis of all tonality. "I regard the expression *atonal* as meaningless. . . . A piece of music will necessarily always be tonal in so far as a relation exists from tone to tone." The term *atonality,* however, caught on and is now in universal use.

There is an almost constant feeling of tension in this music, largely because of the complete absence of any gravitational pull toward a tonal center. Furthermore, vertical intervallic relationships such as seconds and sevenths are not treated as requiring resolution. Vertical simultaneities have little structural function in atonality—they seem to just happen, without any harmonic significance. Thematic material is often based on a motivic cell of two or three intervals that is then expanded through transformation and combination. In the following example, the first three notes in the middle voice present a motivic cell of two intervals (Ab, G, Bb)—down a minor second and up a minor third—which is then presented in the other voices in inversion, diminution, and various transpositions. The motive is also developed through a varied rhythmic treatment and through imaginative transformations throughout the composition. At the beginning of the fourth measure, for instance, it is even stated vertically (C, B, D#):

Example 30. Schoenberg: Five Piano Pieces, Op. 23

Serial Technique

Schoenberg, realizing the aesthetic necessity of establishing an organizational congruence or coherence among the various elements of an atonal composition, developed a unifying and systematizing concept that he called "A Method of Composing with Twelve Tones Which Are Related Only with One Another." He applied this concept, sometimes known as *serial technique* or the *dodecaphonic* [*twelve-tone*] *system* to his works written after 1923. The basis of this new compositional method is a series, or set, of the twelve pitch classes (a note and any of its octave duplications), called a tone row. The disposition of the twelve tones and the resultant intervals between them determine the course of the entire composition. Certain principles are generally observed in the construction of a tone row: The composer may choose any order of the twelve tones he wishes but may not repeat a tone (except for an immediate repetition); no significance is attached to different spellings of enharmonic equivalent notes; groups of notes that present tonal implications are generally avoided. The following tone row, taken from Schoenberg's Fourth String Quartet, is typical (note his use of varied melodic intervals and avoidance of all tonal patterns):

Example 31.

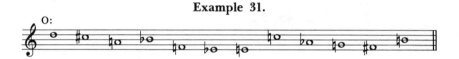

In addition to the original row, O, there are three other forms of the tone row that may be used: backwards (retrograde), R; upside down (inversion), I; and backwards and upside down (retrograde inversion), RI:

Example 32.

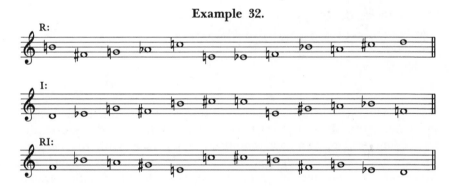

Since the twelve notes have equal importance, it is possible to begin the tone row on any note of the chromatic scale as long as the melodic intervals remain the same. There are, therefore, twelve transpositions possible for each of the four forms of the tone row, making a total of forty-eight possibilities that can serve as the basis for all melodic, harmonic, and contrapuntal material within a composition. The listener is not ordinarily aware of this fact since the appearances of the tone row are perpetually varied through rhythmic, melodic (because of octave transpositions and immediate repetition possibilities), harmonic, and contrapuntal means. The tone row, however, must not be confused with "theme" or "motive." As the basis of a composition it is used for both thematic and nonthematic material. The following example, based on the original tone row and its modifications shown in the previous two examples, shows a few of the row's endless possible variants:

Example 33.

Though the structure itself is not readily evident to the listener, there are other more obvious characteristics that result from the use of the twelve-tone system. First, by completely doing away with the need to prepare and resolve dissonance, Schoenberg's system totally emancipates dissonance. Second, melodic lines are likely to be filled with tension-building leaps made possible through octave transpositions of the tone row's pitches. As a consequence, melodies are not necessarily the subtly contoured entities they once were. Third, although vertical simultaneities are structurally significant, the system is primarily linear in concept, and therefore contrapuntal by nature.

A number of composers were quick to realize that within the total framework of the tone-row concept lay an extensive new means for individualized expression. Its greatest influence on contemporary musical creativity, however, has been relatively recent—since the early 1950s. It is interesting to note that many composers, including Schoenberg himself, have reconciled the system with other compositional procedures, including tonality.

Melody

The critic Henry Pleasants, in his well-known diatribe on modern music, writes that the contemporary composer has forgotten that the musician's primary duty is to sing. This view is far too narrow to accommodate the great diversity of twentieth-century melodic idioms, and even Webster's definition of melody as "an agreeable succession of sounds organized into an aesthetic whole" is simply no longer valid. The only definition broad enough to include all melodic styles of every period states that *melody is a meaningful succession of pitches*. Melody in this context is sufficiently flexible of interpretation to admit the notion that what is melodic to one person need not necessarily be melodic to another.

While twentieth-century melodies display a wide diversity of styles, they do hold a number of characteristics in common: greatly extended melodic and dynamic range; use of additional scale and tonal resources; use of wide leaps and irregular structures; and often, great rhythmic intricacy. Within the framework of these general characteristics, the following examples illustrate some among the vast diversity of melodic styles that have resulted from the experimental spirit of the age:

Example 34. Prokofiev: Violin Concerto No. 2

Example 35. Copland: *Appalachian Spring*

Example 36. Stravinsky: *The Rite of Spring*

Tempo guisto

Example 37. Webern: Variations for Orchestra, Op. 30

Example 34 is tonal (it is in the key of G minor). Example 35 illustrates the extraordinary range characteristic of many contemporary melodies; it is also a fine example of pandiatonicism. Example 36 is based on a five-tone scale (*pentatonic*); and the final melody, Example 37, demonstrates the extremes in range, dynamics, and rhythmic complexity so typical of atonal expressionistic music.

Rhythm

Undoubtedly one of the most striking aspects of the emerging New Music of the twentieth century is its greatly expanded concept of rhythm. A number of rhythmic practices were derived from identifiable sources of the near and distant past, including the savage rhythms of Asiatic and African music (*primitivism*), the subtle refinement of rhythmic structures used by the impressionists, the measure-free music of plainchant and Renaissance polyphony, and the complex syncopations of twentieth-century jazz. These means, however, served simply as resources for the fertile imagination of composers who ultimately produced rhythmic structures of unprecedented effect and complexity.

64

Through the use of dynamic stress marks, composers shifted accent patterns in conventional-appearing rhythmic structures to selected weak beats, completely transforming their character:

Example 38. Copland: *Billy the Kid*

Trp. *mf*

Shifting accent techniques were further extended through the imaginative use of syncopation:

Example 39. Stravinsky: *The Firebird*

Bsn.,Hrn.

These techniques, although useful, were limited in their capacity for giving expression to the great flexibility in metrical flow desired by composers. The folk music of eastern Europe provided the appropriate resource—changing meters (*multimetric* rhythmic organization). The implied stress organization created by a meter is used to advantage in multimetric music to implement rhythmic ambiguities and asymmetric inflections in a musical line:

Example 40. Stravinsky: *The Rite of Spring*

Bsn. *p*

Example 41. Bartók: Concerto for Orchestra, Fourth Movement

Asymmetric meters (those based on five, seven, eleven, and thirteen beats per measure) and asymmetric divisions of the measure have been used frequently throughout this century. Béla Bartók in particular found them useful in his attempts to capture the unique rhythmic structures of Balkan music in his composition. A bar with eight beats, for instance, he often divided into groups of 3–3–2—a common Bulgarian rhythm—rather than the symmetrical 2–2–2–2 arrangement. In the scherzo from his Fifth String Quartet he specifically indicates the nine beats per measure in the time signature as 4–2–3; the trio of the same movement adds another beat to give a pattern indicated as 3–2–2–3. Among the various asymmetric meters, $\frac{5}{4}$ is the one most commonly used. Note an early instance of its use in the second movement of Tchaikovsky's Sixth Symphony (1893), and later, in the final section of Ravel's *Daphnis et Chloé*.

The term *polyrhythm* can be used to refer to any situation in which simultaneous parts within a texture take on separate rhythmic identity. Normally, however, the term is used to identify a situation in which sharply contrasted rhythms occur either within the same meter, or, as is often the case, as a conflict of meters (sometimes designated as *polymetric* music). The use of this technique, now largely associated with contemporary music, has as its most famous example the Ballroom Scene from Mozart's *Don Giovanni*, written in 1787! Three orchestras play simultaneously, one in $\frac{3}{4}$ meter, one in $\frac{2}{4}$ meter, and another in $\frac{3}{8}$. One of the earliest twentieth-century examples of polyrhythm (polymetric music) occurs in *Putnam's Camp* from Charles Ives's *Three Places in New England* (1903–11). A trumpet plays the tune "The British Grenadiers," in $\frac{4}{4}$, the percussion instruments play in $\frac{2}{4}$ and $\frac{3}{4}$, and the remainder of the orchestra plays in $\frac{3}{8}$. Stravinsky used polyrhythms throughout a number of his early works, including *L'Histoire du soldat* (*The Soldier's Tale;* 1918).

Harmony

In general during the past, composers of a given era have shared a common harmonic language. During the twentieth century, however, harmony, like all other musical concepts, has become another important extension of a composer's individual style. As a consequence, identifying a generalized system of twentieth-century harmonic principles is impossible. All one can do is describe a few of the widely diverse and complex twentieth-century harmonic techniques. A number of these innovative harmonic procedures have already been noted in the sections of this chapter on tonality and atonality.

The major-minor system of tonality inherited by twentieth-century composers was based upon triadic chordal structures of from three to five tones—the *triad,* the *seventh* chord, and the *ninth* chord. In a natural extension of this concept of building chords by superimposing intervals of a third, twentieth-century composers added the *eleventh* chord and the *thirteenth* chord. Each successive addition of a third to a basic triad increases the degree of dissonance-generated tension until finally, as in the case of the thirteenth chord, all seven degrees of the scale have been presented (chromatic alterations of these notes are possible). The following example illustrates several of these chords in a musical context (note that the thirteenth chord, within the bracket, is both "broken" and, as is frequently the case, incomplete—the third is missing):

Example 42. Ravel: *Le tombeau de Couperin*

A remarkable example of the extended use of "skyscraper" chords is found in Darius Milhaud's opera *Christophe Columb* (1930):

Example 43.

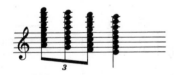

Having exhausted the structural possibilities of chords built on the interval of a third (*tertian* harmony), twentieth-century composers investigated the harmonic possibilities of chords built on the interval of a fourth (*quartal* harmony). The striking effect of quartal harmony normally is reserved for relatively short sections of a composition:

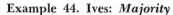

Example 44. Ives: *Majority*

There are also a number of isolated instances of chords built on fifths:

Example 45. Stravinsky: "Dance of the Adolescents" from *The Rite of Spring*

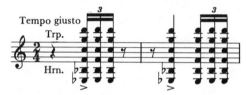

Superimposed seconds are essentially nonharmonic, and so their use is limited to coloristic and percussive effects. When three or more seconds occur simultaneously, without any octave separations, the resulting "chord" is called a *cluster*. Note the varied uses of superimposed seconds in the following example:

Example 46. Bartók: Piano Sonata

Extended passages of tone clusters are particularly idiomatic to the piano. The example quoted below by Ives is extraordinary for its time (1909):

Example 47. Ives: The *Concord* Sonata

Faster and faster

Texture

Subjective lyricism and expressive harmonic sonorities were the musical hallmarks of the nineteenth-century homophonic style. By contrast, most twentieth-century composers of the New Music found greater compatibility with polyphony than with homophony for achieving their aesthetic aims. As a consequence, vertical masses of sound and accompanied melody have been replaced in their music by cleanly etched linear contrapuntal writing, characterized by logic, order, and craftsmanship. Because contemporary composers have utilized all the imitative techniques and formal contrapuntal structures of the past, many refer to their music as being neoclassic or even "back to Bach." Their compositional method, however, has varied in one significant respect—the functional harmonic movement of traditional counterpoint (i.e., its vertical aspect) is now almost totally ignored in favor of underlining the independence of contrapuntal lines through the use of dissonance.

Twentieth-century composers such as Hindemith, Bartók, Schoenberg, and Stravinsky have found great compatibility with the purely musical, objective nature of fugal forms. The first example cited below illustrates the combining of two seemingly unrelated melodies; the second, by Frank Martin (1890–1974), is a fine example of imitative dissonant counterpoint:

Example 48. Hindemith: *Mathis der Mahler*, First Movement

69

Example 48. Continued

Example 49. Martin: Piano Prelude

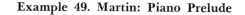

Form

Among the various concepts of musical organization expressed in contemporary music, form has undergone the least amount of change from practices of the past. It is true that a number of composers, particularly the avant-garde writers of chance (aleatoric) and electronic music, have attempted to break with the formalistic traditions of the past by creating musical expressions without form. Their creations, however, have not as yet reached the status of common practice. While the general outlines of traditional formal structures have remained largely intact in contemporary musical practice, the degree of ease with which they can be understood by the average listener has changed considerably.

Many traditional forms of absolute music, including sonata-form, theme and variations, and a number of baroque forms (passacaglia and chaconne, toccata, fugue, and suite) have all been given new life during the first half of this century through complete harmonic freedom and emphasis upon contemporary contrapuntal techniques for the manipulation of subject matter. Among them, the sonata-form has proved to be the most widely used of the absolute forms. Separately, or as part of a larger sonata cycle, it has accommodated twentieth-century expressions of the symphony, concerto, solo sonata, and chamber music, and has survived changing melodic and harmonic styles. Bartók, Hindemith, Schoenberg, and to a lesser extent, Stravinsky, have all used modified versions of sonata-form.

The theme-and-variations form has also held particular interest for twentieth-century composers. Although the binary sectional form of the classical variation principle is still used, it has largely been replaced by a new free variation form. Both the *Istar Variations* (1896) by d'Indy and *Don Quixote* (1897) by Richard Strauss are important forerunners of this free variation technique in which just one aspect of the theme is used in a variation while the remainder of the melodic, harmonic, and rhythmic elements may be entirely new. Aaron Copland's *Piano Variations* (1930) and Schoenberg's *Variations for Orchestra,* Op. 31 (1927–28) are significant compositions representing the use of this form in the twentieth century.

chapter 5

Arnold Schoenberg
(1874-1951)

Since the beginning of the Austro-German musical tradition in the seventeenth century, successive generations of Austrian and German composers have based their work and teaching largely on the study of music written by their own countrymen. By building on previous achievements, they developed a style that progressed logically to ever greater subtlety and complexity. This progression is particularly well defined in the long development of harmonic practices that, through the increased incidence of complex chromatic structures during the nineteenth century, gradually broke down traditional concepts of tonality. Ultimately, what could seem like a revolution in compositional techniques brought about by Arnold Schoenberg in the twentieth century was actually a continuation of this development. As was pointed out in the previous chapter, he brought to a culmination the gradual dissolution of traditional tonal relationships by completely abandoning tonality, and then developed a new technique of composition that organized the twelve tones of the chromatic scale into a new structural unity. In formulating a "Method of Composing with Twelve Tones Which Are Related Only with One Another," Schoenberg created a logical substitute for tonality by guaranteeing equal relevance for every note in a score, a procedure that affected the entire course of twentieth-century music.

Schoenberg was born in Vienna. At an early age he undertook his own musical education by teaching himself to play the violin and cello,

Arnold Schoenberg

and by studying compositions of the great composers of the Austro-German tradition. His only formal training was a few months of contrapuntal study with his close friend and champion, the composer and conductor Alexander Zemlinsky, who later, in 1901, became his brother-in-law. It was Zemlinsky, in fact, who, recognizing the youthful Schoenberg's remarkable talent, encouraged him to follow a career in music. It is particularly interesting to note that Schoenberg, who was largely self-taught, spent much of his life in the role of teacher. His pupils, including Alban Berg and Anton Webern, regarded him with an almost fanatical devotion and enthusiasm. They felt that he alone could lead them in the path to their musical salvation. For his own part, Schoenberg held an unswerving dedication to his unique path of musical development, sustained in part by a mystic belief in his own genius.

Schoenberg's musical development can be divided into four well-defined periods: the first (1895–1908) is post-Wagnerian and is identified with his ever-increasing use of chromaticism; the second period (1908–14) is atonal and expressionistic; the third (1923–33), his dodecaphonic period, begun after a nine-year period in which he formulated his twelve-tone method, is characterized by his gradual departure from the neurotic expressionism of the second period; the final period (1933–51) is his American period, a time when he effected a rapprochement between twelve-tone writing and tonality.

73

His first period includes a number of important works: *Verklärte Nacht (Transfigured Night;* Op.4, 1899), *Pelleas und Melisande,* Op.5 (1902–3), the String Quartet No.1, Op.7 (1904–5), Chamber Symphony, Op.9 (1906), String Quartet No. 2, Op.10 (1907–8), and *Gurrelieder (Songs of Gurre;* 1900–11). These are all highly romantic, expressive compositions whose intense chromaticism still relates to tonal functions. The tone poem *Verklärte Nacht,* based on a poem by Richard Dehmel, is scored for string sextet (later arranged for string orchestra by Schoenberg). The idiom of this most popular among Schoenberg's compositions is derived from Wagner's *Tristan und Isolde.* Passionate climaxes and sudden modulations in this descriptive work create an emotionally charged atmosphere of extraordinary intensity. The *Gurrelieder* is a cantata scored for an enormous orchestra, chorus, and soloists, whose kinship with the works of Wagner and Mahler is immediately evident. It is revealing to note that this work was much admired by Richard Strauss. It was during this first period that Schoenberg began his important role as a teacher, first at the Stern Conservatory in Berlin and then, in 1903, at the Schwarzwald School in Vienna. In 1904, Berg and Webern began their studies with him.

The Three Piano Pieces, Op.11 (1909) and *Das Buch der hängenden Gärten (The Book of the Hanging Gardens;* Op.15, 1908)—fifteen songs for voice and piano on poems by Stefan George—begin the atonal phase in Schoenberg's music, a period in which there is no longer a functional relationship between chords, and no one note or chord has dominance over the others. Schoenberg transferred the atonal idiom to the orchestra in the Five Orchestral Pieces, Op.16 (1909). He supplied a descriptive title for each: *Premonitions, Yesteryears, Summer Morning by the Lake, Peripetia,* and *Obligatory Recitative.* These extremely concentrated works are organized through constant motivic manipulation. The third, the most striking among them, is based on a five-note chord whose timbre is subjected to ever-changing instrumentation and dynamics (*Klangfarbenmelodie*). His next two compositions, *Erwartung (Expectation;* Op.17, 1909) and *Die glückliche Hand (The Lucky Hand;* Op.18, 1913), are expressionist dramatic works. Just as the increase in the use of chromaticism and nonfunctional harmonies in Schoenberg's music led to the dissolution of tonality, so his preoccupation with the expressionist dream world of the subconscious led to an increase in emotionalism and self-expression in his music. The expressionist movement, in fact, found its perfect musical representation of fear and tension through atonality. *Erwartung,* a surrealistic monodrama for female voice, describes the nightmarish inner world of a woman who, while searching for her lover in the forest at night, stumbles over his dead body. One of his finest works, the song cycle *Pierrot Lunaire,* Op.21 (1912), was written during this period.

The hostile criticism that had greeted many of Schoenberg's works previous to his atonal period had by now turned into almost complete alienation. Schoenberg, in breaking with the aesthetics of the past realized, however, that even those who had believed in him previously would not likely realize the need for his new development. It was not until he was nearly forty, in fact, that some measure of acceptance by a Viennese audience was given one of his works. Even then, however, the work was not of his atonal period, but rather, the first complete performance of *Gurrelieder.*

During the nine years (1914–23) Schoenberg spent formulating his twelve-tone method, he published nothing; then in 1923 his first experimental works in this idiom appeared: Five Piano Pieces, Op.23, and the Serenade for seven instruments and bass voice, Op.24. His use of the twelve-tone method is far more assured in other works of these formulative years; the Piano Suite, Op.25 (1924), the Woodwind Quintet, Op.26 (1924), the String Quartet No.3, Op.30 (1926), and the one-act opera *Von Heute auf Morgen (From One Day to the Next;* Op.32, 1929). All the possibilities of the technique he had so carefully formulated are crystallized for the first time in one of his most important works, the powerful Variations for Orchestra, Op.31 (1927–28), analyzed later in this chapter.

By this time, Schoenberg was recognized throughout Austria and Germany as an eminent teacher, and was honored in 1925 by being appointed professor of composition at the Prussian Academy of Fine Arts in Berlin. Unfortunately, his new-found recognition was short-lived. In 1933 Adolf Hitler was elected Chancellor, and shortly afterward all Jews holding civil service positions were removed. Schoenberg wrote his artist friend Kandinsky:

> For I have learned at last the lesson that was forced upon me during this year, and I shall never forget it. It is that I am not a German, not a European, indeed perhaps scarcely even a human being (at least, the Europeans prefer the worst of their race to me) but a Jew.

After a brief stay in Paris, Schoenberg emigrated to the United States, where he spent the remainder of his life teaching and composing. Most of that time was spent in Los Angeles, where until his retirement in 1944 he taught, first at the University of Southern California and then at the University of California, Los Angeles (UCLA).

During his "American" period, Schoenberg further refined his serial techniques and produced a number of distinguished compositions, including many in which tonal elements and serial techniques coexist. The

Kandinsky—*Improvisation No. 30* (Warlike Theme)

The Art Institute of Chicago.

Suite for String Orchestra (1934); *Kol Nidre,* Op.39 (1939) for reciter, chorus, and orchestra; the Organ Variations, Op.40 (1943); and the Variations for Wind Orchestra, Op.43 (1943) all show Schoenberg's continued interest in writing tonal music. He employed both techniques simultaneously in his *Ode to Napoleon,* Op.41 (1942) for reciter, string quartet, and piano. The twelve-tone Piano Concerto, Op.42 (1942) retains some of the characteristics of tonality and as a consequence is readily accessible to both the performer and the listener. His Violin Concerto, Op.36 (1936) and the String Quartet No.4, Op.37 (1936), on the other hand, are both written in strict serial style. When asked why he sometimes reverted to the use of tonal techniques, he answered: "Trying to return to the older style was always vigorous in me; and from time to time I had to yield to that urge."

The opera *Moses and Aron,* begun in 1931 but never completed, is one of Schoenberg's greatest compositions. He wrote the libretto himself and constructed the entire opera on a single tone row. The two acts that he did complete have been performed with great success. The third act, sometimes spoken in performance, consists of just one short scene and is not essential to the plot. The opera is scored for large orchestra, a singing chorus, and six soloists.

A number of consistent traits can be observed in the music of Schoenberg throughout all four periods of his creative life. His melodies are generally characterized by wide leaps, creating a line of great subjective expressiveness; he normally avoids regularly accented rhythms and never projects the sense of rhythmic propulsion that so frequently characterizes contemporary music; he places strong emphasis on contrapuntal procedures, particularly during his twelve-tone period; and he achieves transparency and constantly changing timbres through his orchestrations.

Whatever the final judgment may be concerning his music itself, Schoenberg's uncompromising single-mindedness as an innovator and teacher made him one of the most influential composers of this century.

PIERROT LUNAIRE, OP. 21

The full title of this work is "Three times seven poems from Albert Giraud's *Pierrot Lunaire.*" It is the last work of importance from Schoenberg's atonal period, a period that includes a number of his finest works. Although this highly original expressionist composition was not well received at its first performance in 1912, it ultimately became the work responsible for first carrying Schoenberg's name beyond his close circle of associates. Schoenberg included precisely twenty-one poems (divided into three groups of seven each) from among the fifty of Giraud's original, probably because the number corresponded with the opus number of the work. It is scored for a reciting voice *(Sprechstimme)* and five instrumentalists playing piano, flute (also piccolo), clarinet (also bass clarinet), violin (also viola), and violoncello. Schoenberg adds in brackets the subtitle "Melodramas," signifying the combination of the spoken word with music. Part I deals with Pierrot's youth and yearnings; in Part II Pierrot concentrates on materialism, crime, and punishment; and the final group is concerned with Pierrot's homesickness and his return to the frivolities of his youth.

Giraud's poems are in the Old French thirteen-line *rondeau* form. Lines seven and eight of its three-verse form are a repetition of lines one and two, and line thirteen is a repetition of line one. Schoenberg's musical forms, by contrast, exhibit great variety in their conception.

In his foreword to the score, Schoenberg explains how the *Sprechstimme* (indicated in Ex.50 with an X bisecting the stems of the notes) vocal part should be performed. He instructs the reciter to transform the exact note values and indicated pitches into a spoken melody, but he warns against a singsong type of speech. He defines the difference between a sung note and a spoken one by stating that the sung note keeps its pitch while the spoken note immediately rises or falls away from the given pitch. Against this strange, eerie, quasi recitative, the instruments weave a contrapuntal web of fantastic, unearthly beauty. He extends the idea of continuous variation to every aspect of *Pierrot Lunaire,* including the instrumentation, meter and rhythmic patterns, and even the length of the pauses between pieces. Two from among the twenty-one settings (Part II, No.8, Part III, No.18) are representative of the remarkably varied means Schoenberg used in this work.

    8. *Nacht (Night)*—for bass clarinet, cello, and piano. Night falls as giant moth wings blot out the brilliance of the sun, bringing terror to the hearts of men. The dark tones of the bass clarinet and cello create a somber, sinister timbre. *Nacht* is in the form of a passacaglia whose ostinato figure of three notes is used as the motivic cell of the piece. The following example demonstrates some of the ways in which the ostinato figure is continuously varied:

Example 50.

The ostinato appears in the piano part, measure one, as E–G–E♭ and then in measure two it appears both as the three eighth-note figures and also as the combined first notes from each of the three figures. The treble piano part includes the figure transposed and in augmentation, while the bass clarinet part indicates it transposed and in diminution in the first measure and then continues in canon with the cello. The same figure is also outlined in the voice part.

18. *Der Mondfleck* (*The Moonspot*)—for piccolo, clarinet in B-flat, violin, cello, and piano. It is night. Pierrot discovers a white spot on his black jacket. Furious, he rubs until morning trying to remove the spot of shining moonlight. This piece is the most contrapuntally complex of the entire work. It is a double mirror canon in which the piccolo and clarinet, and the violin and cello, each play a different canon. They then play the same music backwards. At the same time, the piano plays a three-part fugue based on the woodwind canon in augmentation. The middle of the second measure of the following example is the point at which the double canon reverses itself:

Example 51.

rich-tig ei-nen wei-ssen Fleck

des hel-len Mon - des auf dem

VARIATIONS FOR ORCHESTRA, OP. 31

Schoenberg completed the Variations for Orchestra in 1928. It is scored for a sizable orchestra that includes harp, celesta, mandolin, four each of the woodwinds, and a very large percussion section in addition to the usual brass and strings. The effects he achieves, however, are solo-istic, and the instrumental colors change constantly, giving one the im-pression of a chamber work for full orchestra. René Leibowitz, author of *Schoenberg and His School,* emphasizes the historic importance of this work:

> The twelve-tone technique culminates in Schoenberg's *Variations for Orchestra,* Op. 31. By this I mean that the principal devices of this tech-nique, after having been gradually and partially developed in the works preceding Op. 31, are for the first time completely used in this work, so that all twelve-tone works (of Schoenberg and also of his pupils) after the *Variations for Orchestra* merely apply or develop these devices according to the same principles.

This work alone could serve as a textbook for the student of serial techniques. The tone row on which the composition is built is the source of all thematic material, accompanying figures, and chordal structures. The only extraneous material is the motive on the notes B-A-C-H (Bb–A–C–B♮) that Schoenberg uses in the Introduction, the end of the second variation, and the Finale. There are four versions of the tone row:

Example 52.

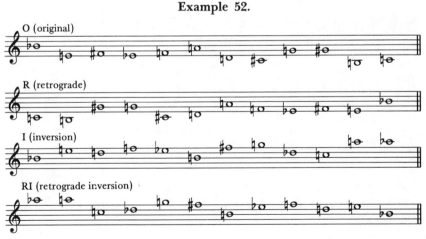

Transpositions of the row include one on G (a third below) and another on D-flat (a third above). He frequently achieves a measure of relaxation

81

in this work by combining a row with its transposition to produce a series of consonant thirds or sixths.

Introduction. Mysterious-sounding string tremolos begin the work. Gradually the first six notes of the row are heard in the flute, harp, and violin, while the first six notes of the row's inversion on G are played by the bassoon, bass, and bass clarinet. The row is then completed by the cello, bassoon, and bass clarinet while the inversion is completed by the horn. Fragments of the theme appear as more and more instruments are added to the texture and a *fortissimo* climax is reached. There is a hush as the B-A-C-H motive is played by the trombone and the music then fades away as mysteriously as it began.

Theme. The first half of the theme is played by the cellos, first in the O version, then in RI in the G transposition. There is an answering phrase using the R of the original followed by I in the transposition G:

Example 53.

Examples 53–57: Used by permission of Belmont Music Publishers, Los Angeles, California 90049.

The chordal accompaniment precisely reverses the sequence of rows used in the theme (i.e., I in transposition, R, RI in transposition, and O).

Variation I, Moderato. The theme is played by the bass clarinet and bassoons against a rhythmic accompaniment in thirds and sixths by the strings and oboes. The second part of the theme is played a measure at a time by various instruments.

Variation II, Langsam (slow). The slow-moving second variation is extremely complex contrapuntally. The solo cello and bassoon open with an inverted canon (a canon in which the second voice is an exact inversion of the first) and are joined by the bass clarinet and flute playing another inverted canon. The solo violin and oboe then enter canonically with the inversion of the theme. Variants of these two motives are heard imitatively throughout the variation. As the variation comes to an end, the trombone intones the B-A-C-H motive.

Variation III, Mässig (moderate). Although the pace of the third variation is slow, the piece is powerfully energetic. The theme, played by the horns, is subordinate to the main melodic material of this variation— the interval of an augmented fourth (the first two notes of the original row) heard in a dotted rhythm. The entire orchestra provides a strong conclusion for this variation.

Variation IV, Waltzer tempo. The theme played by the harp, mandolin, and celesta provides an expressive accompaniment to a new theme, played in waltz tempo by the flute with viola obbligato. The solo cello continues this theme with the English horn playing the obbligato, and then it is transferred to the woodwinds. Though this variation is scored for full orchestra, Schoenberg retains a delicate chamber music texture throughout.

Variation V, Bewegt (agitated). By contrast with the previous variations, the opening of this variation is for full orchestra. It is violent and strongly rhythmic, with the theme stated principally in the bass instruments. The rhythmic drive is relaxed for the middle section but then at the close, the opening mood returns.

Variation VI, Andante. The chamber music texture reappears. A solo cello plays the theme as one of the accompanying strands to the melody, played by the clarinet. More instruments are added, but Schoenberg maintains the original transparency.

Variation VII, Langsam (slow). This gentle but contrapuntally intricate variation first presents the theme with the piccolo, glockenspiel, celesta, and solo violin. Simultaneously, the bassoon introduces a new rhythmic structure in a florid melody that is soon extended, first by other woodwinds and then by the strings. The dynamics are hushed despite the use of the entire orchestra.

Variation VIII, Sehr rasch (very lively). This variation opens with
a strident conversation between the oboes and bassoons in which each
uses a different version of the tone row:

Example 54.

The numbers beneath the oboe part refer to the inversion of the tone row
beginning on G, while the numbers below the bassoon part refer to the
tone row in its original form. The cellos play an eighth-note ostinato
figure (the first measure presents the first six notes of O, a figure that is
then continued by the bassoon, while the second measure continues the
I form previously begun by the oboes) punctuated by string chords to
support this "conversation":

Example 55.

The melodic figures soon disappear as the ostinato and sharply accented
chords continue to create strong cross rhythms among the various sections
of the orchestra.

Variation IX, L'istesso tempo, aber etwas langsamer (the same tempo,
but somewhat slower). The oboe theme that opened the previous varia-

tion is now begun by the trumpet at a slightly slower tempo while the piccolo plays the original row in a new rhythmic design. Both themes are then imitated in inversion by the clarinet and bassoon. Bits of both themes are played throughout the orchestra, and the variation ends very quietly.

Finale.   According to Schoenberg, this finale is based on models such as the variation movement of the *Eroica Symphony* and the Brahms *Variations on a Theme by Haydn*. It opens quietly with a violin tremolo on the B-A-C-H motive reinforced by flutter-tonguing from the flute. The motive is repeated by the violins, and in succession by the horns, violas and cellos, and trumpet, as fragments of the main theme are played throughout the orchestra. An increase in tempo and dynamics leads to a *Grazioso* section in which the main theme is heard in various rhythmic forms with new countersubjects constantly appearing. An *accelerando* leads to a *Presto,* which begins with the theme in dotted rhythm against the B-A-C-H motive:

Example 56.

The B-A-C-H motive is then heard in rapid succession in various rhythmic guises:

Example 57.

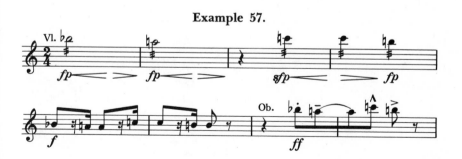

The tempo further quickens as both ideas are developed until a climax is reached with the B-A-C-H motive sounding *fortissimo* from the trumpets. An *Adagio* interrupts the breathless pace and the main theme is heard in a beautifully orchestrated passage of just six measures. The *Presto* returns and the work ends emphatically with a chord that contains all twelve notes of the chromatic scale!

chapter 6

Alban Berg (1885-1935) and Anton Webern (1883-1945)

These two composers are the most eminent among Schoenberg's disciples. Although they both came from the same background of Austro-German romanticism and shared in their formative student years the exploration of the ideas begun by their teacher Schoenberg, each later developed his own independent personalized expression. In the years following World War I, Webern chose to project the extreme facets of Schoenberg's work, while Berg attempted to link the newly developed twelve-tone idiom with the romantic past. As a consequence, Berg's works have become far more accessible than those of either his teacher Schoenberg or his friend Webern. Berg was essentially a lyricist who successfully linked the twelve-tone method with the implications of tonal music. Webern, by contrast, reduced music to a bare skeletal framework of essentials—overt expression and sentimentality are banished in his preoccupation with conciseness and purity of musical thought.

ALBAN BERG

Alban Berg was born in Vienna to a family with substantial artistic interests and better than adequate means. He showed an early enthusiasm for literature and by 1899 had developed an interest in music. Frail health, aggravated by the first in a succession of severe asthma attacks after the death of his father in 1900, plagued him the remainder of his life. In 1904, Berg began a six-year period of study with Arnold Schoenberg, marking both the turning point in his artistic career and the beginning of a lifelong friendship with his teacher.

Berg's compositions for voice occupy a central position in his entire output. One can, in fact, conveniently trace the significant stages in his musical development through these works. His first published songs, the *Sieben frühe Lieder (Seven Early Songs;* 1905–8), like his Opus 1 Piano Sonata (1906–8), closely reflect a Wagnerian chromatic style similar to that used by Schoenberg in *Verklärte Nacht.* The Four Songs, Op. 2 (1908–9) are transition works in which he experiments with expressionist procedures. It is in the Five Songs, Op. 4 (1912) for voice and orchestra, better known as the "Altenberg" songs, that the dramatic power and great lyricism characteristically associated with his personalized use of atonal procedures are in evidence for the first time. It is interesting to note that in the last of these songs, "Hier ist Friede" ("Here Is Joy"), Berg used a twelve-tone row, anticipating Schoenberg's formalization of the technique by eleven years! It is not at all surprising in light of the deference he consistently showed for the voice that his greatest masterpiece is another vocal work, the opera *Wozzeck.*

In 1914 Berg attended a performance of the Georg Büchner play *Wozzeck,* and was so affected by the experience that he immediately set to work arranging the twenty-nine scenes of the play into a workable opera libretto. Wartime duties for the War Ministry prolonged the completion of the libretto until 1917. By 1921 he had finished the score. The première, for which over a hundred rehearsals were necessary, took place in Berlin in 1925. Its triumphant success instantly catapulted Berg to international prominence. The reasons for the enormous success of the opera are not difficult to understand. The tragic story is universal in its human appeal, and Berg's intensely dramatic dissonant music expresses its emotional nuances with extraordinary insight. The story depicts an unfortunate soldier, tormented by his superiors and plagued by poverty, who is finally driven to murder and suicide as a result of his frustrations and the unfaithfulness of his mistress. Berg's imaginative exploitation of the varied potential of the human voice and his highly original orchestration are used with remarkable effectiveness in depicting the lust and violence, love and tenderness in this expressionist masterpiece. Undoubtedly this universally acclaimed work of the Viennese atonal school is one of the greatest operatic achievements of the twentieth century.

The Lyric Suite for String Quartet (1925–26) is deservedly one of Berg's most widely known works. Although Berg had completely mastered the twelve-tone method by the time he wrote the Lyric Suite, he decided to attempt a reconciliation, within the same work, of serial technique with atonality. He therefore completely serialized just the first and sixth

Alban Berg

Alban Berg posing at the window above a portrait of himself
painted by Arnold Schoenberg.

The Bettmann Archive.

movements and sections of the third and fifth movements; the remainder of the work is in free atonal style. The innovative new style and the past (including a quotation from Wagner's *Tristan und Isolde* in the last movement) are extraordinarily well met in this highly successful expressionist instrumental work.

Following the establishment of the Third Reich in Germany in 1933, the growing Nazification of Austria became a matter of great concern to Berg. His works, like those of Schoenberg and Webern, were branded "Bolshevik" art and were banned in Germany. A matter of even more immediate concern to him, however, was the fact of Schoenberg's exile. During these years of great disillusionment, Berg continued working on his opera *Lulu,* begun in 1928. He based his libretto on two tragedies by Frank Wedekind, both dealing with Lulu, the destructive, universal, "primal woman-spirit." Musically, *Lulu* rivals *Wozzeck* for originality, diversity, and imagination. Closed instrumental forms are used together with diversified vocal forms including the recitative, *cavatina, canzonetta,* hymn, arioso, and chorale. The harmonic texture of *Lulu* is sometimes tonal with clear triadic progressions, and at other times, atonal, bitonal, and atonal with tonal implications. Berg completed the piano score before he died in 1935 but orchestrated only the first two acts.

BERG: VIOLIN CONCERTO

In 1935, while Berg was attempting to finish his opera *Lulu,* he received a commission from the American violinist Louis Krasner to write a violin concerto. Uncertain about how he would proceed, he put off beginning the work; then the sudden death of Manon Gropius, the eighteen-year-old daughter of his intimate friend Alma Mahler, suggested the direction he would take. He shaped the concerto in the form of a requiem, and inscribed it "To the Memory of an Angel." This deeply moving, expressive concerto stands at the summit of Berg's achievements. While it is essentially a serial work, it has very strong tonal implications, presenting a rapprochement between twelve-tone procedures and tonal harmony. The tone row of the work, in fact, is constructed of four conjunct triads to which Berg has added four notes of the whole-tone scale:

Example 58.

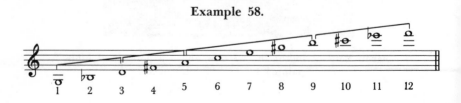

The concerto was written within a four-month period, an unusually short time for Berg, making it seem almost as if he had a premonition of his own death (he died just six months later of blood poisoning brought on by an infected insect bite). Great inspiration, remarkable craftsmanship, and deeply expressive lyricism characterize this masterpiece whose virtuoso aspects do not compromise the classic dialogue relationship between the solo part and the orchestra. It is in two movements, each divided into two sections.

First Movement: Section I, Andante. The improvisatory introduction that opens the concerto is constructed of arpeggios taken from the tone row. In alternation with the clarinets and harp, the solo violin first plays the notes 1–3–5–7, then 2–4–6–8, and finally 3–5–7–9 before ending the introduction with a cadence that gives one the impression of a dominant-tonic in G minor. The movement proper begins with an accompanying figure which, while based on the tone row, retains the illusion of G minor:

Example 59.

The solo violin then plays the original tone row and its inversion, and a bridge leads to the B section of this ABA form. The row now appears in a new guise—it is a graceful theme presented first by the solo violin and then by the cellos. Another bridge passage reintroduces the opening accompanying figure, and then the violin, in an embellished but abbreviated version of the first theme, ends the first section.

Section II, Allegretto. This section is a scherzo with two trios, in an arch-form with the pattern: Scherzo–Trio I–Trio II–Trio I–Scherzo. This section, apparently meant to represent Manon's love of life and her youthful spirit, incorporates elements of the Viennese waltz in the scherzo, and uses a Carinthian *ländler* (slow waltz) in the second trio. The theme of the scherzo, marked *Scherzando,* easily captures the spirit of Vienna within the twelve-tone idiom:

Example 60.

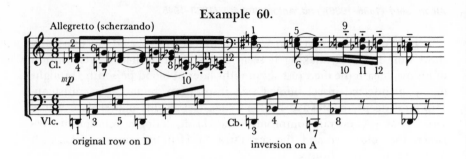

original row on D   inversion on A

The theme is then continued with phrases marked *wienerisch* (Viennese-like) and *rustico* (rustic), presenting a fine example of Berg's penchant for evoking poignant memories of the past in his romantically conceived serial idiom:

Example 61.

The first trio continues the exuberance of the scherzo. The theme is played first by the strings and then by the solo violin with a strong rhythmic emphasis provided by the brass. The second trio is more lyric than the first. Its attractive, gentle rocking theme is short-lived, however, and the first trio soon returns with the solo violin playing embellishments of the original accompanying figure. A bridge passage played by the violin leads to a return of the scherzo, now in $\frac{3}{8}$ instead of $\frac{6}{8}$. The coda opens with the horn playing the Carinthian *ländler* with the soloist adding a counterpoint based on material from the two trios:

Example 62.

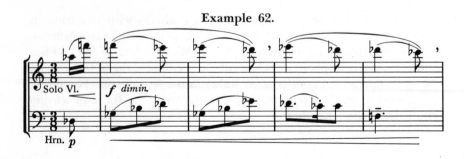

The tempo becomes more animated and the waltz rhythms more spirited, and finally the violin ascends the original tone row in waltz rhythm.

Second Movement: Section I, Allegro. This section is constructed precisely like the opening section of the first movement except that here the introduction is a solo violin cadenza accompanied by the orchestra. The dramatic opening telescopes the tone row into a strident, ominous chord that foreshadows the depiction of the tragedy of Manon's death. As the violin enters, hammerlike blows are struck on three timpani, outlining a G-minor chord that is continued in a fading roll. The *Allegro* proper is dominated by a dotted rhythm, designated by Berg as the *Hauptrhythmus* (principal rhythm), which is first heard in the orchestra accompanied by violin arabesques and then in the violin with a lyric orchestral accompaniment. The B section, somewhat lighter by comparison, makes references to the two trios of the previous movement. There is a long cadenzalike passage in which the solo violin plays a strict four-part canon, unaccompanied, based on the theme of Trio II. Because of its extreme difficulty, it is often played with the solo violin taking two lines and a solo viola the other two:

Example 63.

Immediately following the canon, a short bridge passage based on the opening arpeggio of the first movement leads to a return of the A section. There is a *crescendo* to a shattering climax, indicated by Berg in the score as the *Höhepunkt* (high point), which depicts the tragedy of Manon's death. The dominating rhythmic figure is powerfully asserted by the orchestra in chords consisting of the first nine notes of the row; the violin and a few solo instruments answer with the other three notes of the row, *fortississimo espressivo*. The tension gradually subsides as this climactic phrase is repeated six times, creating a beautiful transition to the final section.

Section II, Adagio. Religious consolation permeates this conclusion to the concerto. It is in a modified ABA form whose A section is based on the chorale *Es ist genug* (*It Is Enough*) used by Bach in his Cantata No. 60. The B section consists of two variations of the chorale, and the return is in the form of a coda. The soloist first announces the opening of the chorale, and then it is played in Bach's original harmonization by the clarinets:

Example 64.

Note that the opening phrase of four notes is a whole-tone sequence, analogous to the last four notes of the tone row. The violin and clarinets alternate until the chorale is ended with an echoed repetition of the notes corresponding to the words "es ist genug" of the chorale.

For the first variation, the chorale tune is begun by the cellos and imitated by the harp with a hushed woodwind accompaniment. The chorale is then continued by the trombone as the violin enters with a poignant lament. The second variation, contrapuntally more complex than the first, quotes the chorale in inversion in the bass. The brass section repeats the inversion, and another *Höhepunkt* is reached. A tranquil mood now prevails as the Carinthian *ländler* is recalled, "wie aus der Ferne" (as if from afar), in a synthesis with the whole-tone opening of the chorale. The musical allusion to Manon seems to reassure us.

The coda begins with a rich atonal harmonization of the chorale played by the entire woodwind section while the violin continues its statement from the second variation. The tempo slows to *Molto adagio* as the original tone row slowly emerges from the depths of the orchestra, played successively by the double basses, cellos, violas, violins, and finally by the solo violin ending on a high G. A final gentle arpeggio is played by the violins, the same arpeggio that opened the concerto, and so this beautiful elegiac work ends in a mood of gentle resignation.   ·

ANTON WEBERN

Webern became Schoenberg's first pupil in 1904, and like Berg, he continued to study with him until 1910. Meanwhile, he received his Ph.D. in musicology in 1906 from the University of Vienna, where he worked under the noted musicologist Guido Adler. Unlike Berg, Webern's almost complete obscurity as a composer during his lifetime necessitated his finding other means for earning a livelihood. Following World War I, he conducted two amateur groups (the Vienna Workers' Symphony and the Vienna Workers' Choral Union). In 1927, he was appointed conductor of the Austrian Radio Orchestra. Guest appearances abroad with other orchestras followed, but his income never rose significantly beyond the subsistence level. Toward the end of World War II he left Vienna to seek safety in Mittersill, a village near Salzburg. There, because of a tragic mistake, he was fatally shot by one of the American occupation troops.

It is difficult to reconcile Webern's great impact on the musical thinking of the third quarter of this century with his comparative obscurity during his lifetime. Since his death, many articles and books have been written about him and his music, and an international Webern "school" exists, but even now his music is still seldom performed. His total output is very small, just thirty-one compositions, none of which lasts more than ten minutes.

It is not so much the brevity of these works that serves as an identifying characteristic of Webern's music, but rather the remarkable concen-

Anton Webern

tration of musical thought that they display. "Consider," wrote Schoenberg, "what moderation is required to express oneself so briefly. You can stretch every glance out into a poem, every sigh into a novel. But to express a novel in a single gesture, a joy in a breath—such concentration can only be present in proportion to the absence of self-pity."

Webern's renunciation of tonality was far more complete and uncompromising than that of his teacher Schoenberg. Once committed to the twelve-tone system, he continued to explore its possibilities as a way of thinking rather than as one technique among many. Add to this the fact that Webern carried out the principle of continuous variation so completely within the complex contrapuntal web of his music that there are very few literal repetitions or clearly defined patterns, and one can begin to understand the problems of perception that confront the listener.

Rests take on a new significance in Webern's style, and become ends in themselves. The notes define no melodies or themes as such but are instead carefully assembled fragments separated by moments of thoughtfulness.

Within Webern's intensely concentrated style, linear continuity is achieved not only through pitch and durational differences but also to a very considerable extent through his providing a differentiation in timbre among the successive notes. This technique, known as *Klangfarbenmelodie*, attaches a new significance to each note and gives further evidence of the extent of Webern's economy of means. A particularly fine example of his use of *Klangfarbenmelodie* can be found in the first of his Five Pieces for Orchestra, Op.10 (1913). Webern's use of *Klangfarben-*

melodie has often been called *pointillism,* a reference to a technique used by a school of artists who constructed their paintings by using points of color.

If, as Schoenberg suggests, one surrenders himself to Webern's transcendent musical expression, he may "share the faith that music can say things which can only be expressed by music."

Webern's music can be conveniently divided into two periods; the first includes his two tonal works and fourteen atonal compositions; the second period consists of his last fifteen works, all based strictly on serial organization. Even his early works reveal his economy of utterance and usual avoidance of nineteenth-century romanticism, and unlike the early works of Schoenberg, they contain no trace of Wagnerian influence. His first work, the Passacaglia for orchestra, already contains the seeds of his future development. All of the works from this first period are notable for their originality, and remarkable brevity. They are so compressed, in fact, that the Six Bagatelles for String Orchestra, Op.9 (1913), for instance, have been characterized as "melodies in one breath"—every non-essential has been eliminated. Other works of the period include the Five Movements for String Quartet, Op.5 (1909), the Six Orchestral Pieces, Op.6 (1909), and the Five Pieces for Orchestra, Op.10 (1913), whose longest piece takes just one minute. They are further characterized by an extensive use of pointillism and an emphasis on the so-called dissonant intervals—the minor second, major seventh, and minor ninth. Since Webern's music at this time had no conventional harmonic basis and was predominantly athematic, these intervals were used solely for their sound characteristics and tone color. The following example, the fifth of the Six Bagatelles for String Quartet, illustrates his extreme brevity of expression (it is just thirteen measures long), his use of pointillism, and his athematic style. The second measure, containing one pizzicato note, is the only measure that does not include a minor second or major seventh:

Example 65.

Example 65. Continued

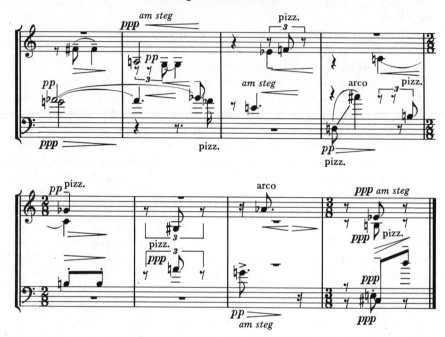

Though the Six Orchestral Pieces are scored for a large orchestra, the instruments are never all heard together and each piece has a different orchestration. In many of these early works, twelve-note series appear, foreshadowing Schoenberg's later systematization of the method.

Webern next explored the lyric side of his musical personality over a twelve-year period in which he concentrated exclusively on writing songs, at first with piano accompaniment and then with varied instrumental combinations.

Webern's last fifteen works, all based on the twelve-tone system, are more extended than his early works and depend more on contrapuntal devices for structural purposes. He seldom used conventional forms but instead allowed his music to develop in a continual variation entirely dependent on the tone row. Canonic devices provided him with his favorite method of achieving structural organization. To him, the canon represented the purest contrapuntal expression. The interval of the minor second continued to dominate his musical thought and became the basic interval in many of the tone rows of his early serial music. In the following tone rows, the minor seconds are bracketed to show their dominance:

Example 66.

In his late works, Webern began to stretch the concept of a structural organization based on pitch serialization to include a fixed series of dynamic gradations, rhythmic devices, and tone colors as well. However, it remained for his followers to extend these ideas and completely serialize rhythm, timbre, dynamics, articulation, and pitch.

The principal works of Webern's twelve-tone period are String Trio, Op.20 (1927); Symphony, Op.21 (1928); Quartet for Violin, Clarinet, Tenor Saxophone, and Piano, Op.22 (1930); Concerto for Nine Instruments, Op.24 (1934); String Quartet, Op.28 (1938); and Variations for Orchestra, Op.30 (1940).

Webern has been hailed by Igor Stravinsky as a great composer of "dazzling diamonds" and by Pierre Boulez as the "one and only threshold" to the music of today. The term "post-Webern" has come into as common usage among today's composers as "post-Wagner" was at the end of the nineteenth century.

SYMPHONY, OP. 21

Webern scored his only symphony for a small orchestra—clarinet, bass clarinet, two horns, harp, violins, violas, and cellos. Because the texture never exceeds four-part writing, the symphony has been called a quartet for nine instruments. It is not a conventional symphony by any means, although its two highly concentrated movements do approximate symphonic forms. The entire symphony takes less than ten minutes to play and is a model of Webern's condensed style. The first movement is a serialized variant of sonata-form and the second is a theme and variations. Because the retrograde form of the basic tone row is the same as the original row transposed up an augmented fourth, Webern has limited himself to just two forms of the row—the original and its inversion, together with their transpositions. The symphony is based on two musical concepts: imitation and variation. O and I (R and RI) represent imitation and are used exclusively in the first movement, while O and R (I and RI) represent variation and are used exclusively in the second movement. Only by carefully following the score during repeated hearings can one hope to fully appreciate the genius of Webern's intellectual creative process.

First Movement. The first movement is a large double canon in inversion (i.e., two voices are imitated by two other voices in inversion). The four parts also present the basic row imitated by its inversion and a transposition of the basic row imitated by its inversion (some analysts see this as all four forms of the row used simultaneously, since O is identical to R and I is identical to RI). These forms of the row are heard simultaneously throughout the movement. The movement is so orchestrated that each motive within the row receives its own delicate timbre, making the motive variation more accessible:

Example 67.

In the first canon (top two staves in Example 67), the tone row is composed of three motives played by the horn, clarinet, and cello, and imitated in inversion by the horn, bass clarinet, and viola. The *Klang-farbenmelodie* technique is more obvious in the second canon, a consequence of Webern's characteristic use of a different timbre for nearly every note. This canon (staves three and four of Example 67) is first played by the harp, cello, violin, harp, and horn in succession, imitated by the harp, viola, violin, harp, and horn. Note that the imitation is present in timbre as well as in tone row, further evidence of Webern's concentrated style and ability to "express a novel in a single gesture."

Each of the two sections of the movement is repeated. The hushed first section is treated as an exposition, and the second as the development and recapitulation. The second section begins with a sixteen-measure development whose second half is precisely the reverse of the first eight measures in pitch, note values, and dynamics. Because of the complexities of the development section, the dynamic indications characteristically range from *p* to *ppp*. The recapitulation is a repetition of the tone rows of the exposition even to the extent that they appear in the same voices as in the opening double canon; the note values and octave placements, however, are changed. The rhythmic movement is increased and the tone row now appears twice in each part as the passage reaches a *forte* climax. There is a short coda with a single canon continuing in inversion, and the movement ends *pianissimo*.

Second Movement. The eleven-measure theme of this theme-and-variations movement is played entirely by the clarinet (a continuity of tone color not often found in Webern's music) accompanied by the horn

101

and harp. It is composed of the inversion of the tone row starting on F. The theme is divided into two parts. Since its second half is a repetition of the first in retrograde, an augmented fourth higher, the theme played backward (transposed an augmented fourth) is the same as when played forward:

Example 68.

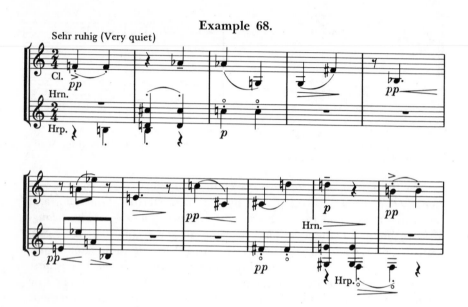

Note also the use of the tone row in the harmonization of the theme—it is the RI form of the theme.

    Each of the seven variations is eleven measures long and presents a symmetry similar to that of the theme. There is one important difference, however; in the theme, the second five and a half measures are a retrograde version of the first half of the theme at the interval of an augmented fourth. The second halves of the variations and the coda (except for the fourth variation) are also retrogrades of their first halves but at the same interval. In each variation the tone row is played twice, the second time in retrograde, to allow for this symmetry. The fourth variation is the keystone of an overall symmetry between the theme and the coda, Variations I and VII, II and VI, and III and V.

    The first variation, marked *lebhafter* (livelier), is a four-voice double canon in inversion played entirely by muted strings. The second variation, *sehr lebhaft* (very lively), is a dialogue between the clarinet and bass clarinet accompanied by a continuous eighth-note line in the horn and by occasional string pizzicatos. The horn line consists of alternating O and I forms of the tone row:

Example 69.

Var. II

Sehr lebhaft

The third variation is in a more moderate tempo, and in contrast to what has gone before, all of the instruments are used pointillistically. The entire fourth variation, the keystone of the movement, is played *pianissimo*. The instruments all play triplet figures in this complex variation, creating an unusually dense texture for a work of Webern. There are two O forms and two I versions, which could be considered all four forms of the tone row. The fifth variation corresponds to the third in its effect. Only strings and harp are used, the tempo is lively, and the dynamic level gradually increases from *pp* to *mf*. Webern concentrates on developing the harmonic structure of the tone row in this variation. Both the first four and last four notes of the row are grouped into chords whose intervals are exactly alike. They are played by the low strings and high strings, respectively, while the harp plays the middle four notes, creating a remarkable symmetrical structure. The marchlike sixth variation, like the second, is a canon between the clarinet and bass clarinet accompanied by the horn playing sustained notes derived alternately from the two forms of the tone row. The final variation is marked *etwas breiter* (somewhat broader) and, like the first variation, is a double canon in inversion. The coda consists of one simultaneous presentation of the O and I forms of the row, creating a perfect symmetry, both rhythmically and melodically:

Example 70.

Coda

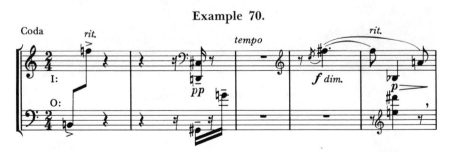

103

Example 70. Continued

René Leibowitz summed up the importance of this work for Webern's developing technique by saying: "On the one hand, Webern's musical thought is constantly enriched by the inclusion of new possibilities; on the other hand, it becomes ever more concentrated with each new acquisition. The result is that the language thus constituted attains, at one and the same time, the greatest complexity and the greatest simplicity."

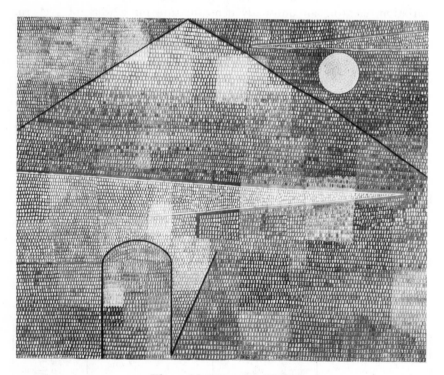

Klee—*Ad Parnassum* (1932)

104

chapter 7

Igor Stravinsky (1882-1971)

For over fifty years, Igor Stravinsky exerted a profound influence on the musical development of the twentieth century. While Stravinsky did not found a school of composition, he did explore the possibilities of nearly every important stage in the development of contemporary music. Each new work to him presented a problem requiring a unique solution, and as a consequence he seldom repeated himself. His lifetime of composition does, however, fall into a number of generalized periods. His first works emerged from the postromantic world of exotic composition of Rimsky-Korsakov; he then developed a powerful primitive style; next he entered a chamber music period, momentarily tinged by American ragtime; he then became austerely neoclassic for an extended period; and finally he embraced the principles of serialism.

Stravinsky was born near St. Petersburg (Leningrad). Although his father was a leading bass singer at the Imperial Opera, young Stravinsky was encouraged to study law, not music. It was in 1902 that he decided to explore his potential as a musician by submitting some of his work to Rimsky-Korsakov. Then, after working intermittently with Rimsky-Korsakov for three years, Stravinsky began to study music seriously in 1907. He soon produced two orchestral works, the *Scherzo Fantastique* (1908) and *Feu d'artifice* (*Fireworks;* 1908), which came to the attention of his

Igor Stravinsky

cousin Sergei Diaghilev, who was then in the process of organizing the
Ballet Russe. He was so impressed with Stravinsky's capabilities that he
commissioned him to orchestrate two Chopin compositions for the ballet
Les Sylphides. After their successful completion, Diaghilev immediately
commissioned Stravinsky to write the music for an entirely new ballet,
L'Oiseau de feu (*The Firebird*), which was produced in Paris in 1910.
Its overwhelming success made Stravinsky a musical celebrity overnight.
The orchestral suite he distilled from the complete score has since become
one of his most popular concert pieces.

 Petrushka, produced by Diaghilev in 1911, is Stravinsky's first significant departure from the nineteenth-century world of Rimsky-Korsakov. Its largely polytonal harmonic structure is based on two major
triads whose roots are an augmented fourth apart, C and F♯. Because
Petrushka was originally conceived as a piece for piano and orchestra,
Stravinsky was able through these particular choices of tonal relationships
to use the white keys of the piano for one tonal area and the black
keys for the other, greatly facilitating the execution of fast brilliant
passages. He also employed polyrhythms, including the simultaneous
use of $\frac{5}{8}$ and $\frac{2}{4}$ meters, and $\frac{7}{8}$ and $\frac{3}{4}$ meters. Instead of the romantic melodies and exotic harmonies of his earlier works, he used short motives

106

Benois's setting for *Petrushka*

The Bettmann Archive.

and clashing harmonies, and even his references to Russian folk song are far more sophisticated than in *The Firebird*. Folk music is, in fact, assimilated into the entire work, descriptively portraying every dramatic gesture. With *Petrushka*, Stravinsky for the first time began to assert his own remarkable musical personality.

His next ballet for Diaghilev, *Le Sacre du Printemps* (*The Rite of Spring;* 1913), is one of the most important works of the twentieth century. Its revolutionary score opened up a world of sound so new for its time that its first performance was the occasion of a near riot as the members of the audience reacted to this "blasphemous attempt to destroy music as an art." It must be understood, however, that this kind of reaction to music was not uncommon in Paris during the first decades of the twentieth century—this one was just better publicized than most. The following year, the ballet was performed in a concert version with considerable success. *Le Sacre du Printemps* is the musical counterpart to the early twentieth-century preoccupation with primitive art. It is a savage, brutal, and yet exhilarating work of primeval grandeur in which rhythm and clashing harmonies reign supreme. Harmonic clusters are used rhythmically, short fragmented motives are pounded out in staccato-

107

Igor Stravinsky (Drawing by Laszlo Krausz)

like fashion, and wild, irregular accent patterns, polyrhythms, and audacious harmonies are used by Stravinsky in his musical portrayal of the celebration of Nature's rebirth each spring.

Stravinsky also wrote a number of Russian-oriented works during this period, including the ballet-oratorio *Les Noces* (*The Wedding;* 1914–23), a stylized version of a Russian peasant wedding, scored for four pianos, seventeen percussion instruments, solo voices, chorus, and dancers. *Les Noces,* with its orgiastic exuberance, is a continuation of the primitivism of *The Rite of Spring.* Before he had completed it, however, Stravinsky had finished with his Russian orientation and was searching for a new means of expression. *L'Histoire du soldat* (*The Soldier's Tale;* 1918), *Ragtime for Eleven Instruments* (1918), and *Piano-rag Music* (1919) reveal a passing glance at American jazz. This is intimate music, whose scoring for small instrumental combinations represents a more objective approach to musical composition and is a reflection of the economic pressures imposed by World War I. It was with *Pulcinella* (1919), a work originally suggested by Diaghilev, that he reached the next important milestone in his career—his recognition of the musical forms and textures of the past. It is a ballet for orchestra and vocalists based on instrumental and vocal works by the important eighteenth-century composer Giovanni Battista Pergolesi (1710–36).

In conversations with his biographer, Robert Craft, Stravinsky said *"Pulcinella* was my discovery of the past, the epiphany through which the

108

whole of my later work became possible." Thus began his thirty-year love affair with the forms and styles of seventeenth- and eighteenth-century music, constructive principles which he consciously adopted. Neoclassicism provided him with an ideal means for attaining control and order in his problem solving.

After *Pulcinella,* he continued his neoclassic orientation in the Symphonies of Wind Instruments (1920), a noble, austere work written in memory of Debussy; the Octet for Wind Instruments (1922–23); the Concerto for Piano and Wind Instruments (1924); the Piano Sonata (1924); the ballet *Apollon Musagète (Apollo, Leader of the Muses;* 1928); and in two monumental choral works that climaxed the early part of his neoclassic period, *Oedipus Rex* (1927) and the *Symphony of Psalms* (1930). Stravinsky used the Latin version of the texts for both choral works because he preferred its detachment and objective dignity. Both are ranked among his greatest works.

Stravinsky composed comparatively little during the 1930s because of his concert tours and many guest conducting appearances. After writing

Picasso—*Woman with Blue Veil* (1923)

Los Angeles County Museum of Art: Museum Purchase with DeSylva Funds.

the *Symphony of Psalms,* he composed the Violin Concerto (1931), the *Duo Concertante* (1932) for violin and piano, and just three other works, the Concerto for Two Pianos (1935) written for a concert he performed with his son, and the ballets *Persephone* (1933) and *Jeux de cartes (A Card Game;* 1936), a ballet in three "deals." All of these compositions are well written and unquestionably clever, but they seem to be overconcerned with technique and too little concerned with content; as a consequence, they are seldom performed today.

In 1940, Stravinsky left Paris to make the United States his permanent home. During the next ten years, he created some of his finest neoclassic works, using large multi-movement forms. The Symphony in C (1940) is a genuine symphony in the classical sense of the word. It is written in a light, transparent texture that pays due homage to the spirit of Haydn and Mozart. The Symphony in Three Movements (1945), written while he was revising *The Rite of Spring,* recalls some aspects of his early primitivism through its use of a large orchestra and percussive rhythmic style. The Mass in G (1948), a deeply personal religious work, is one of the few compositions of this period that was commissioned. It took him four years to complete and was composed not for concert performance but to be part of the Roman Catholic service (it lasts just seventeen minutes, the time usually taken to celebrate the Catholic Mass). He also wrote a number of commercial works during this period: the *Circus Polka* (1942) for the Barnum and Bailey Circus, the *Four Norwegian Moods* (1942) for a film, and the *Ebony Concerto* (1946) for Woody Herman's jazz band. Throughout his long career, Stravinsky's interest in writing for the ballet never waned. During this period he wrote two abstract ballets, *Danses Concertantes* (1942) and *Scenes de Ballets* (1944), and the ballet *Orpheus* (1947), a work of disciplined but dramatic expressiveness. *The Rake's Progress* (1948–51) is the culminating work of Stravinsky's neoclassicism, and is undoubtedly among the greatest operas of the twentieth century. The libretto, written by W. H. Auden and Chester Kallman, is based on the series of William Hogarth (1697–1764) drawings of the same name. Classic form and content are here ideally combined within a twentieth-century idiom. Even the mannerisms and operatic forms of the seventeenth and eighteenth centuries are utilized in this intriguing synthesis of the past with the present.

During the 1940s, Stravinsky lived in California just a short distance from Arnold Schoenberg, the originator of the twelve-tone method; however, they never felt they had enough in common even to bother meeting each other. It was then a source of great amazement to his friends, critics, and imitators to find that following his seventieth birthday, Stravinsky turned to the serial techniques of the twelve-tone school. The death of

Schoenberg in 1951 may have had something to do with this about-face, although it is more probable that his objections to the twelve-tone method were largely overcome by his protégé and spokesman Robert Craft, a strong advocate of the music of Schoenberg and Webern. His first serial works were rather tentative. His *Three Songs from William Shakespeare* (1953) use a four-note row, the Septet (1952) is based on a six-note row, the *In Memoriam Dylan Thomas* (1954) uses a five-note row, and twelve-tone rows appear in much of the *Canticum Sacrum* (1955) and the ballet *Agon* (1956). His first work to be completely serialized, *Threni: id est lamentationes Jeremiae Prophetae* (*Threnodies: Being the Lamentations of the Prophet Jeremiah*), was completed in 1958. In this work, Stravinsky successfully assimilated the serial style, with all of its intricacies, into his own personal idiom. It has an austere dignity that affirms the deep religiosity already expressed in the *Symphony of Psalms* and the *Mass in G*. After *Threni* he wrote eleven more serial works including Movements for Piano and Orchestra (1959), *A Sermon, a Narrative, and a Prayer* (1961), *The Flood* (1962), Variations for Orchestra (1964), and *Requiem Canticles* (1966).

Throughout his long career, Stravinsky's most striking single stylistic characteristic was his rhythmic imagination. By breaking the chains of metrical consistency, he revived a rhythmic freedom that had been dormant for over four hundred years. His melodies are often short, have a narrow range, and are usually based on the notes of a diatonic scale or on the notes of a broken chord. His harmonic idiom (preceding the serial period) is essentially tonal and diatonic. Stravinsky's use of *polychords*—the addition of seconds to ordinary triads—and the simultaneous use of minor and major thirds result in a harmonic idiom that has been labeled *polydiatonic* or *pandiatonic*. The texture of his music, from 1914 on, is predominantly contrapuntal, with sharply defined melodic lines. His structural formats change with every work, although it is evident that he preferred the continuous "additive" forms of the sixteenth and seventeenth centuries to the closed developmental forms of the eighteenth and nineteenth centuries.

Stravinsky also constantly sought fresh means for expressing his musical ideas through imaginative orchestrations. Pure wind sonorities, chamber music effects, unusual instrumental combinations, percussive experimentation, and even seventeenth- and eighteenth-century textures extended his coloristic palette. When he later approached the use of pure counterpoint in his works, he demanded sharply etched articulations in order to achieve a dry, hard, objective sonority.

Stravinsky, in his Norton lectures at Harvard University, sums up his compositional creed:

My freedom consists in my moving about within the narrow framework that I have assigned myself for each one of my undertakings. . . . . my freedom will be so much the greater and more meaningful the more narrowly I limit my field of action and the more I surround myself with obstacles. . . . The more constraints one imposes, the more one frees one's self from the chains that shackle the spirit.

SYMPHONY OF PSALMS

Commissioned to write a symphony for the Boston Symphony Orchestra's fiftieth anniversary celebration, Stravinsky assigned himself the task of writing a "symphony" for chorus and instruments in which "the two elements should be on an equal footing." He then chose a text appropriate to his purpose—verses from the Psalms to be sung in Latin—and set them using a highly unusual but remarkably appropriate stark "biblical" orchestration. It includes two pianos, but no violins or violas, and draws a significant amount of its color from the woodwinds. The score, which he inscribed "to the glory of God," certainly ranks among the finest masterpieces of the twentieth century.

First Movement. The text of the opening movement is taken from verses 13–14, Psalm 38 of the Vulgate (verses 12–13, Psalm 39 in the King James Version):

Exaudi orationem meam, Domine,
  et depreciationem meam
  auribus percipe lacrymas meas.
Ne sileas, quoniam advena ego apud te,
  et peregrinus, sicut omnes patres mei.
Remitte mihi, ut refrigerer
Priusquam abeam, et amplius non ero.

Hear my prayer, O Lord,
  and give ear unto my cry:
  hold not Thy peace at my tears:
for I am a stranger with Thee,
  and a sojourner as all my fathers were.
O spare me, that I may recover strength,
  before I go hence, and be no more.

This brief movement opens with a short, detached chord (E minor), followed by an arpeggiated figure traced by the oboe and bassoon. The arpeggiated figure is continued by the pianos after an interjection of the opening chord. A solo cello and French horn then sing out the main motive, a lamentation confined to the repetition of two notes a second apart. The prayer itself is begun by the altos using the same motive:

Example 71.

Do - mi - ne

This motive of supplication is then woven into the homophonic choral sections of the movement, and sharp chords and dry, non-legato arpeggiated figures give strong contrast to the supplicating tone of the voices.

Second Movement. The text of the second movement uses verses 2, 3, and 4, Psalm 39 of the Vulgate (verses 1, 2, and 3, Psalm 40 in the King James Version):

Expectans expectavi Dominum,	I waited patiently for the Lord,
et intendit mihi.	and He inclined to me,
Et exaudivit preces meas;	and heard my cry.
et eduxit me de lacu miseriae,	He brought me up also out of an horrible pit, out of the miry clay,
et de luto faecis.	And set my feet upon a rock,
Et statuit super petram pedes meos,	and established my goings.
et direxit gressus meos.	And He hath put a new song in my
Et immisit in os meum canticum novum,	mouth, even praise unto our God.
carmen Deo nostro.	And many shall see it, and fear,
Videbunt multi et timebunt:	and shall trust in the Lord.
et sperabunt in Domino.	

The movement is in the form of a large double fugue. The oboe announces the first subject; it is then imitated by the flutes:

Example 72.

The first exposition ends with the four flutes and piccolo in their low and middle registers, producing an organlike timbre. The sopranos now enter with the chorus subject while the orchestra continues the first subject:

The choral fugue continues as the altos, tenors, and basses enter successively while the orchestra develops the first subject contrapuntally. There is a climax on a rhythmic variant of both themes, and then a sudden *piano* on the words *Et sperabunt in Domino* ("And shall trust in the Lord"), sung on a unison choral E♭, ends the movement. The orchestral fugue is almost entirely in C minor while the chorus is generally in the relative major (E-flat major). Stravinsky frequently made use of simultaneous relative keys with similar success.

Third Movement. The final movement, the longest of the work, is a setting of the entire Psalm 150 of the Vulgate (also Psalm 150 in the King James Version):

Alleluia.	Praise ye the Lord.
Laudate Dominum in sanctis ejus,	Praise God in His sanctuary:
laudate eum in firmamento virtutis ejus:	praise Him in the firmament of His power.
Laudate eum in virtutibus ejus,	Praise Him for His mighty acts:
laudate eum secundum multitudinem magnitudinis ejus.	praise Him according to His excellent greatness.
Laudate eum in sono tubae:	Praise Him with the sound of the trumpet:
Laudate eum in timpano et choro,	Praise Him with the timbrel and dance:
laudate eum in cordis et organo,	praise Him with stringed instruments and organs.
Laudate eum in cymbalis, bene sonantibus:	Praise Him upon the loud cymbals:
laudate eum in cymbalis jubilationibus.	praise Him upon the high sounding cymbals.
Omnis spiritus laudet eum,	Let everyone that hath breath, praise the Lord.
Laudate Dominum.	Praise ye the Lord.

After an opening chord, the chorus sings the opening line, *Alleluia, laudate,* with great simplicity and directness of religious expression:

114

Example 74.

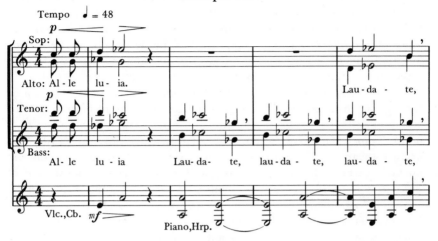

The orchestra strongly establishes the tonality of C while the chorus sings principally in E-flat. The conflict of affinities is appropriately resolved for phrase endings for the words *Dominum* ("Lord") and *Ejus* ("His") on C. Stravinsky returns to the music of these lines both in the middle and the close of the movement. Following this solemn introduction, the orchestra begins the *Allegro* proper with short staccato phrases filled with rhythmic energy. The chorus intones a *Laudate* derived from the introduction and then continues the rhythmic motive begun by the orchestra but now shifted to a different beat of the measure. The music rises to a forceful climax on the words *Laudate eum in sono tubae* ("Praise Him with the sound of the trumpet") and is then suddenly interrupted briefly for a return to the opening *Alleluia* before continuing its relentless drive. Multimetric sections, shifting accent patterns, and a throbbing pulse all add to the exultant spirit. The tempo then broadens as Stravinsky enters a brief canonic section climaxed by the words *laudate eum in cordis et organo* ("praise Him with stringed instruments and organs"). The coda begins *subito piano e ben cantabile* (suddenly soft and very singing) as the piano and harp play a four-note ostinato, moving in fourths, over which the chorus sings with serene dignity. The movement then closes with a repetition of the opening eight measures, cadencing in C major on the word *Dominum*.

THE RAKE'S PROGRESS

Stravinsky had been considering the idea of writing an opera in English for some time when he saw William Hogarth's drawings titled *The Rake's Progress.* They suggested a series of operatic scenes to him and so, at his request, his publisher commissioned W. H. Auden to write a libretto. Auden asked Chester Kallman to collaborate with him and together they wrote a masterful text for the eighteenth-century morality tale depicted by the drawings. To Hogarth's simple fable of a rake's downfall, they added three mythological ingredients—the character of Mephistopheles, the fable of the three wishes, and the card game in which the Devil is defeated. Traces of *Don Giovanni* and *Faust* can be found throughout the libretto: Nick Shadow is a combination of Mephistopheles and Leporello (Don Giovanni's procurer-valet), and the hero (or anti-hero), Tom Rakewell, is a composite of Don Giovanni and Faust. Ann, his sweetheart, is the epitome of every true, innocent, naïve heroine in operatic literature. The opera, like the drawings, has a moral, and in presenting it, Stravinsky satirizes many of the social customs of the period.

The *Rake's Progress* is divided into three acts of three scenes each. The first act is a comedy of manners, the second is a farce, and the third is a melodrama. It is interesting to note that the three scenes of the first act follow the same plan. Stravinsky has adopted a number of thoroughly traditional classical procedures in writing this opera: he uses separate arias, recitatives, and ensembles; the *secco* recitatives are all accompanied by the harpsichord; the texture of the orchestration is of a chamber music transparency; and even the melodic and harmonic idiom is neo-Mozartian. While it is certainly true that the work is basically derived from the stylistic models of Mozart's *Don Giovanni* and *Così fan tutti,* there are a number of features that can be traced to Gluck, Rossini, Donizetti, and even Verdi. It is a technically demanding work, filled with musical and dramatic variety ranging from scenes of coarse humor to tender scenes of great pathos. Many rank *The Rake's Progress* as "the greatest and most important neoclassic work that has been produced."

Act I: Scene 1.   The opera opens with a flourish of the trumpets and horns as the curtains part. The scene is set in the garden of Trulove's estate. Ann, Trulove's daughter, and Tom Rakewell sing a duet in extravagant eighteenth-century prose, extolling the joys of spring. Trulove joins them and offers Tom a position in a countinghouse; Tom, however, declines. Left alone, Tom, in a recitative and aria, reveals his more ambitious plans—he desires to achieve fame and fortune by trusting to his luck and his wits. At the end of the aria, in a speaking voice, he wishes for money. There is a flourish on the harpsichord and Nick Shadow appears at the gate to inform Tom that he has received a large inheritance from a forgotten uncle. The conversation is in classical *secco* recitative. Even the harmony is Mozartian; only the flourishes exhibit Stravinsky's characteristic pandiatonicism. Nick's recitative is quick and assured; Tom, startled at first, quickly regains his composure:

Example 75.

Example 75. Continued

Ann and Trulove are called out to hear the good news, and in the quartet that follows, Tom exults in the remarkable quick answer to his wish. Nick suggests that he become Tom's servant, although when asked about recompense for his services, he answers evasively, saying that at the end of a year and a day they will settle their account. Tom agrees. As Nick

The Rake's Progress (Quartet)

Copyright © Beth Bergman.

and Trulove go off to get a coach, Tom and Ann sing a touching duet of farewell. The final ensemble is a farewell trio in which Ann, Trulove, and Tom reveal their true feelings in asides to the audience—Tom eagerly anticipates the joys of London, Ann is rather apprehensive without knowing why, and Trulove is fearful that Tom's sudden fortune will turn his head:

Example 76.

Hogarth—*The Orgy* (1735) from *The Rake's Progress*

Act I: Scene 2. The scene takes place in London, in Mother Goose's brothel. The curtain rises on a chorus of "whores and gay young blades" singing and drinking to Mars and Venus. Tom, sitting with Nick and Mother Goose, dutifully recites Nick's epicurean philosophy but refuses to discuss the question of true love. Nick introduces Tom to the gathering, and Tom, in a moment of repentance, sings a moving cavatina of classic simplicity and directness, lamenting his betrayal of true love and imploring the Goddess of Love to aid him:

Example 77.

fre - quent - ly be - trayed For

some plau - si - ble de - sire

Or the world's en - chant - ed

Example 77. Continued

fire

The girls gather around Tom to comfort him, but Mother Goose, exercising her seniority, claims Tom for herself. The whores and young men form a double line through which Tom and Mother Goose walk slowly offstage. Nick watches sardonically as the scene ends.

Act I: Scene 3. It is an autumn night in Trulove's garden; there is a full moon. Ann enters, and in a recitative and aria, sings of her sorrow at not hearing from Tom. Stravinsky has ingeniously combined a number of standard melodic patterns and rhythmic formulas in the aria to create a deeply moving expression of great emotion. The accompaniment is appropriately classic in style with tinges of more contemporary dissonance to enhance the feeling of melancholy:

Example 78.

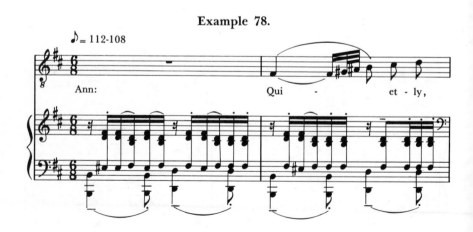

Ann: Qui -   et - ly,

Ann reveals in a short recitative that she feels Tom is weak and needs a helping hand. Stravinsky dramatizes her resolve to go to London to help Tom by making a sudden key change from B minor to C major to begin

the introduction of her cabaletta "I Go, I Go to Him." Ann's opening
measures develop a typically classic motif:

Example 79.

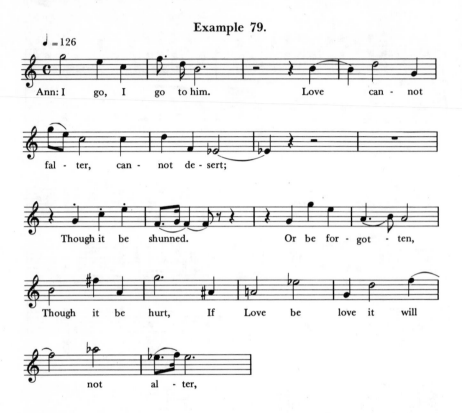

Synopsis of Acts II and III: Tom, bored of pleasure, wishes for
happiness, which, he is persuaded by Nick, lies in complete freedom to
choose one's actions without thought of society's pressures. Tom asserts
his freedom by marrying Baba the Turk, a bearded lady. Soon bored with
Baba, Tom's third wish is to be the Savior of the Human Race by invent-
ing a machine to turn stones into bread. This also fails and Nick now
claims Tom's immortal soul. Tom begs for mercy, and Nick agrees to a
card game, which Tom wins with the aid of Ann's love. Cursing, Nick
sinks into flames. Before he disappears, however, he takes away Tom's
reason, for although Tom has regained his immortal soul, he is not allowed to go unpunished for his sins. Tom finally dies in Bedlam, forgiven
by Ann. The final curtain falls, and the principals all return to sing an
epilogue proclaiming the moral of the play—"for idle hands, and hearts,
and minds, the Devil finds a work to do, a work, dear Sir, fair Madam,
for you and you."

AGON

Stravinsky began work on the ballet *Agon* in 1953 but then inter-rupted his work to write the *Canticum Sacrum*. He did not complete the ballet until 1957. During the comparatively long period of time in which he worked sporadically on *Agon*, Stravinsky became increasingly involved with serial music, particularly that of Anton Webern; *Agon*, conse-quently, is a work of varied harmonic idioms. It is diatonic, modal, poly-tonal, atonal, and serial—presenting in one work the stages of his development from the eighteenth-century classicism of *The Rake's Prog-ress* to the tonal serialism of *Threni*. In *Agon* the neoclassic idiom be-comes almost ascetic in its abstract objectivism as Stravinsky successfully combines neoclassicism with serial technique. The work follows no plot; it consists instead of a series of French court-dance sequences described in a French seventeenth-century dance manual. The Greek word *agon* is used by Stravinsky to denote a contest, an abstract choreographic contest calling for various combinations among the four male and eight female dancers.

Agon

Martha Swope, New York City.

The rather large orchestra Stravinsky uses for *Agon* is augmented by a harp, piano, mandolin, and large percussion section. He seldom uses it in tutti, however, preferring instead a highly varied orchestration for small groups of chamber music proportions. A number of unusual timbres are created by the instrumental combinations: solo violin, xylophone, and two trombones; two flutes, two bassoons, harp, and castanets; two trumpets, mandolin, harp, and solo cello; etc. All of the instruments are used with great imagination and their potentialities are fully exploited. Double-bass harmonics, flute harmonics, trumpet tremolos (flutter-tongue), and single notes on the piano for pointillistic effects all contribute to the creation of a remarkable variety of sonorities.

The ballet consists of seventeen short dances divided into four groups. It opens with a fanfare during which the curtain rises, disclosing four male dancers with their backs to the audience. They advance for the first *Pas de quatre*. Stravinsky uses a pandiatonic harmonic idiom, and divides the dance into three sections, each with its individual orchestral timbre. The next dance is a *Double Pas de quatre,* seemingly tonal, but all twelve tones are introduced in order by the oboe, bassoon, and violin. The third dance is a *Triple Pas de quatre* in which all of the dancers participate. The music is a variation of the *Double Pas de quatre.*

The second group of dances, called the *First Pas de trois,* opens diatonically with a Prelude whose tonal center is B♭. The first dance is a *Saraband-step* for solo male dancer accompanied by a solo violin, xylophone, and trombones. This is followed by a *Gaillarde* for two female dancers. The music is in the form of a canon for harp and mandolin supported by three flutes, solo viola, three solo cellos, and three solo basses. The second group ends with a Coda for the three dancers. The first of the three tone rows on which the ballet is based is heard here for the first time, played by the harp and solo cello:

Example 80.

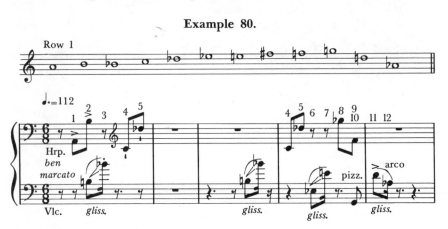

Examples 80–83: Copyright 1957 by Boosey & Hawkes, Inc. Reprinted by permission.

The row is repeated nine times by single notes in the piano and trombones as an accompaniment to the solo violin. The flutes and mandolin play the inversion of the row in various melodic patterns, and at the end of the Coda, the retrograde and retrograde-inversion forms are heard.

The third group of dances, called the *Second Pas de trois,* is introduced by an Interlude that is a reprise of the previous Prelude. This group consists of three *Bransles:* a *Bransle simple* for two male dancers, a *Bransle gay* for solo ballerina, and a *Bransle de poitou* for all three dancers. The first dance is in the form of a strict canon based on a six-note row; the second *Bransle* is based on a different six-note row; and in the third dance, the two six-note rows are joined and transposed to produce the second of the twelve-note tone rows:

Example 81.

A delightful polyrhythmic effect is achieved in the second *Bransle* by the castanets' playing a continuous $\frac{3}{8}$ meter while the other instruments alternate $\frac{3}{8}$, $\frac{7}{16}$, and $\frac{5}{16}$.

Another repetition of the Prelude as an Interlude introduces the final group of dances. The opening *Pas de deux* is divided into an *Adagio,* two variations, and a Coda. The ballet ends with Four Duos (four pairs of male and female dancers), Four Trios (four groups of three dancers), and a Coda (all dancers), followed without interruption by a repeat of the opening fanfare. The serial writing in this final section is very strict, based on a third tone row consisting of seconds and thirds:

Example 82.

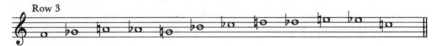

During the Four Duos this row is heard six times in various forms, with a complete absence of counterpoint and harmony. The uniform rhythmic beat is relieved only occasionally by syncopations in the trombones:

Example 83.

During the final fanfare, the female dancers leave the stage and the four male dancers conclude the ballet by turning their backs to the audience.

chapter 8

Béla Bartók (1881-1945)

Béla Bartók was one of the most remarkable geniuses in the history of twentieth-century music. His path was his own. He followed neither the established neoclassicism of Stravinsky nor the serialism of Schoenberg; instead, his highly personalized musical language includes a wide spectrum of contemporary techniques and practices encompassing the most extensive rhythmic, harmonic, and structural vocabulary of any twentieth-century composer.

Bartók was born in the provincial Hungarian town of Nagyszentmiklós. At that time it was a part of the Austro-Hungarian monarchy; later, at the time of the separation of Hungary from Austria after World War I, it became a part of Rumania. Bartók's mother, widowed when young Béla was just seven years old, gave him his first instruction in piano. In 1899, he entered the Royal Academy of Music in Budapest, where he excelled as a pianist. It was during these years at the Academy that his strong nationalist convictions developed. "I shall serve just one purpose in my entire life with every means at my disposal," he wrote, "that which is in the best interest of the Hungarian nation." It was this impulse that induced him as early as 1904 to do what he could to preserve the folk-music heritage of his country. Realizing that what passed for "Hungarian" music was actually the music played by gypsy bands, he made countless trips into the various provinces of Hungary with his friend, the composer Zoltán Kodály, recording and setting down the in-

Bartók supervising the recording of a folk song in a Hungarian
peasant village (Photo probably taken by Zoltán Kodály, 1908)

Copyright G. D. Hackett, New York.

digenous folk music of his country. This was the beginning of a lifelong
preoccupation with folk music that, in his words, "was of decisive influence upon my work because it freed me from the tyrannical rule of the
major and minor keys." He wrote five books and many articles on the
subject and published almost two thousand folk melodies of Hungary
and other countries of Eastern Europe. During his researches into ethnomusicology, he developed a system of cataloguing ethnic music that is
widely used today. In 1907, Bartók was appointed professor of piano at
the Budapest Conservatory, a position that he held for the next thirty
years. During these years, particularly those following World War I, he
developed an international reputation as a concert pianist, frequently
performing his own works. It was a matter of great disappointment to
him, however, to find his acclaim as a composer far greater abroad than
it was in his own country.

In the years preceding the outbreak of World War II, Bartók became
an outspoken critic of fascism, particularly of Hungary's Horthy regime
for its collaboration with Nazi Germany. He even banned the performance of his works in Germany and Italy. Such a stance made it
imperative that he leave Hungary before it was too late, and so in October, 1940, he arrived in New York, an exile in bad health, practically
destitute. For a brief time he held an appointment at Columbia University to do research in ethnomusicology, and he and his wife occasionally

Béla Bartók

The Bettmann Archive.

played concerts, but his existence was precarious at best. Unfortunately, his health grew worse, and in 1945, still a voluntary exile from his beloved Hungary, he died of leukemia.

Bartók's music is usually divided into three periods, characterized by marked changes in his approach to composition: the First Period (1903–26)—the formulative stage of his harmonic-melodic style, exhibits the considerable influence of others; the Second Period (1926–37)—the folk idiom has been completely assimilated and he experiments with expressionism as his music becomes increasingly contrapuntal; the Third Period (1937–45)—his music displays a new-found lyric quality in a final universal synthesis of his past and present. Similarities between Bartók and Beethoven have often been noted. Both composers have three style periods, both subdued their explosive inspirations through architectonic means, both expressed their most personal ideas in their string quartets, and both showed an increased interest in counterpoint as they matured.

The works of Bartók's first period, which covers twenty-three years, are not too numerous, largely because it was during these years that he devoted much of his time to collecting folk music. His first important work, the *Kossuth* Symphony (1903), is a large patriotic tone poem strongly influenced by Liszt and Richard Strauss. His first String Quartet (1908) reveals his knowledge of the late Beethoven string quartets, although there are also strong Wagnerian influences and traces of Brahms and

Debussy—influences that he later acknowledged in an autobiographical article. Bartók's three stage works written at this time—*Bluebeard's Castle* (1911), *The Wooden Prince* (1914–16), and *The Miraculous Mandarin* (1919)—were received with such resistance that he never again wrote in this medium. The ballet, *The Miraculous Mandarin*, because of the censors' disapproval of its lurid, fantastic story, was not performed in Budapest until 1946, although it was staged in Cologne in 1926. The music's primitivism indicates the likely influence of Stravinsky, while its propulsive expressionism is pure Bartók. Its driving rhythms and brilliant orchestration alone make it a successful work. The Second Quartet (1915–17) displays his complete mastery of the form and a substantial assimilation of folk-music elements. The possible influence of Schoenberg can be seen in the two expressionistic sonatas for violin and piano (1921–22). Both are intensely rhapsodic works characterized by wide melodic leaps and extensive use of polymeters. Bartók first used the pounding, frenetic rhythms found in *The Miraculous Mandarin* in his important piano work the *Allegro Barbaro* (1911). In this work, he exploits the piano's percussive potentialities through the use of savage rhythms and *martellato* (hammerlike) tone clusters. Because of this work, the term *barbarism* came to be used for Bartók's brand of primitivism.

Bartók reached the peak of his creativity during his second period. It was at this time that he wrote the *Mikrokosmos* (1926–37), a set of 153 piano pieces in six volumes that comprise a complete catalogue of contemporary keyboard procedures. The first two volumes were written for his son Peter's musical education and were dedicated to him. Like the pedagogical works of Bach, they have transcended their original purpose and are often heard on the concert stage. Many, in fact, have been transcribed for both string quartet and orchestra.

It was in 1926, the year that marked the beginning of Bartók's career as an international piano virtuoso, that he composed several important piano works for his concerts: the Piano Concerto No. 1, the Piano Sonata, and the *Out of Doors* suite. The five pieces of the *Out of Doors* suite, while employing many of the same percussive techniques as the Sonata, are far more accessible to the listener. The fourth, "Musiques nocturnes" ("The Night's Music"), creates a nocturnal atmosphere of nature that frequently recurs in his later works. The Piano Concerto No. 2 (1930–31) reminds one of Bach's concertos through its use of unflagging rhythm and continuous melodic expansion.

Among the string quartets written during the twentieth century, only those of Bartók possess a stature comparable to the quartets of Beethoven and Mozart. Distributed as they are throughout his career, his six quartets present a remarkably complete view of the various stages of his musical development. Bartók wrote three quartets during his middle period. The

Quartet No. 3 (1927) is basically expressionistic in effect and is in one movement, divided into four sections in the form ABAB. The arch form that became so important in Bartók's later works was used with great success in his Quartet No. 4 (1928), one of his most profound achievements. In addition to the *col legno* (playing with wood of the bow), *sul ponticello* (drawing bow close to bridge), *pizzicato* (plucking of strings), and *glissando* (sliding finger up or down string) effects used in the Third Quartet, Bartók further expanded his coloristic vocabulary by including pizzicatos in which the string strikes the fingerboard, glissando pizzicatos, and the alternation of vibrato and nonvibrato in this quartet. The Fifth Quartet (1934) will be analyzed later in this chapter. Two of Bartók's most important works were written at the end of this period; the Sonata for Two Pianos and Percussion (1937), and the Music for String Instruments, Percussion and Celesta (1936), which many critics consider his greatest work.

A great stylistic change took place in Bartók's music during his final period. The savage expressionism and the harmonic and rhythmic complexities characteristic of his previous works were gradually replaced by a greater lyricism, clearer textures, and more strongly affirmed tonalities. His most significant works of this period include the String Quartet No. 6 (1939), Divertimento for Strings (1939), Concerto for Orchestra (1943), Piano Concerto No. 3 (1945), and the Viola Concerto (1945).

Bartók completed his String Quartet No. 6 just before he left Hungary to live in the United States. His harmonic and structural means are much simplified in this work. It has been described by the music critic and author Everett Helm as "the crowning glory of the quartets and the apotheosis of what has gone before . . . one of the most moving commentaries on our century so far . . . one of its most searching expressions." The Divertimento for Strings was commissioned by the Basel Chamber Orchestra and was written in the incredibly short space of fifteen days. In spite of its being written during a most trying period in Bartók's life, just before his going into voluntary exile, it is a very happy work, spontaneous and free from all complexity. The harmonic idiom is quite simple and diatonic, the counterpoint is straightforward, and the structure is uncomplicated. The style is based on the early eighteenth-century concerto grosso form, which he expressed by using a solo string quartet in contrast to the rest of the string orchestra. This is one of his most easily accessible works, full of humor, and written at the height of his creative powers.

The Concerto for Orchestra, Bartók's first American work, was commissioned by the Koussevitsky Foundation. The conductor George Szell has called it the greatest symphonic work of the twentieth century; some critics, however, decry its lack of the inner tension and concentrated strength found in the earlier works. Tonality is strongly affirmed, rhythms are easy to follow, and the forms are classically functional. It is in five movements, representing, in Bartók's words, "a gradual transition from the sternness of the first movement and the lugubrious death-song of the third movement, to the life-assertion of the last one." The Third Piano Concerto achieves a lovely serenity unique among his larger works. Together with the Concerto for Orchestra it has become Bartók's most performed work.

The writer-musicologist William Austin sums up Béla Bartók's importance by saying: "More than Schoenberg or Stravinsky, Bartók left a source of possibly pervasive influence, unsystematic, open to every direction, rooted in the many-layered past, always fresh, energetic, precise, and personal."

STRING QUARTET NO. 5

The Fifth Quartet was commissioned by the Elizabeth Sprague Coolidge Foundation in 1934 and was completed that summer within the remarkably short space of one month. Its structural design is quite similar to that of the Fourth Quartet except that its five movements fit an even more structured arch form. The first and fifth movements share the same motivic material, form, and tonal center (Bb). The second and fourth movements are both slow and structurally similar, and the fourth movement is a variation of the second. The keystone movement is a scherzo with trio. The contrapuntal texture of this quartet is less complex and more transparent than that of his previous quartets.

First Movement. The quartet opens with a repeated Bb, announcing the tonal center of this movement and of the quartet. It leads directly to the first subject, played first by the viola and cello, then imitated canonically by the violins:

Example 84.

Examples 84–89: Copyright 1936 by Universal Edition; Renewed 1963. Copyright and Renewal assigned to Boosey & Hawkes, Inc., for the USA. Reprinted by permission.

After a few measures of tentative expansion, the theme returns, builds to a climax, relaxes into a slower tempo, and then the second subject, an expansion of the last measures of the opening theme, appears:

Example 85.

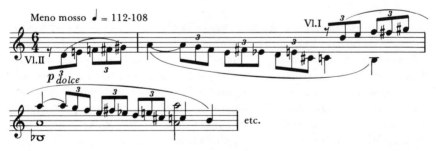

The second subject is extended slightly and the exposition comes to a quiet close. The development section is at once assertive. E is its tonal center, establishing E as the dominant of B♭ in a tritone relationship (augmented fourth). This tritone relationship between tonic and dominant is a prominent feature in much of Bartók's music. The first subject

135

is fragmented and developed during frequent tempo changes. Gradually a climax is reached on the opening rhythmic figuration. The development section is separated from both the exposition and the recapitulation by a general pause, making the sectionalization quite obvious. Since the movement is in arch form, the recapitulation content is reversed; it begins with the second subject, which is now inverted. By the time the first subject returns (also in inversion), the original tonal center of B♭ has been reached. The coda begins in a faster tempo and consists of a five-note motive derived from the first subject. Near the close of the movement the original tempo returns with repeated unison B-flats played *fortissimo*. The final three measures illustrate a contrapuntal procedure that Bartók exploited more fully in his Music for String Instruments, Percussion and Celesta—the five-note motive is imitated in inversion, and then the motive and its inversion are sounded simultaneously:

Example 86.

Second Movement. Marked *Adagio molto,* this movement is in ABA form. It is related to the mood-producing "night music" found in many of Bartók's slow movements. There is no thematic material; instead, fragmentary motives are played by various instruments. In the middle section, while the second violin plays an open G-string tremolo and the viola plays pizzicato glissandos, one of the motives comes into prominence, slowly taking form as the tempo becomes slower. The motive is developed canonically, rises in intensity to a climax, and then dies away. The opening mood returns and the movement ends with the cello playing a descending quasi glissando that slowly disappears.

Third Movement. The scherzo, marked *Alla bulgarese,* has a typical indigenous asymmetrical meter of $\left(\frac{4+2+3}{8}\right)$. In spite of its seeming complexity, the consistency and simplicity of its use by Bartók make this meter seem quite regular after a few measures:

Example 87.

Following this quiet *legato* opening, the middle section of the scherzo, by contrast, is more dancelike and ultimately rises to a frantic climax before subsiding for a repetition of the opening *legato* mood. The meter changes to $\frac{(3+2+2+3)}{8}$ for the trio, and the tempo increases to a *Vivacissimo*. The muted violin plays a ten-note ostinato over a simple folk tune played by the viola. While the other quartet members join the ostinato, the cello holds to the rhythm of the folk tune. Following a climax, the mood changes for a return of the scherzo in the original tempo. The A return is not a literal repetition but a variation of the original scherzo. The coda momentarily becomes faster and more agitated; however, at the very end, the texture thins out and the movement ends quietly. The tonal center of this, the keystone movement of the quartet, is C#. However, the trio—the central section—has F as its tonal center, marking a definite move in the tonal scheme of the quartet from Bb to F and then back to Bb. At the climactic measures of the trio, the cello plays an ostinato on the notes Bb, D, C#, the tonal centers of the first three movements.

Fourth Movement. The *Andante* is a counterpart of the second movement: opening pizzicato glissandos and short motivic fragments once more create a night-music atmosphere. The introduction is longer than that of the second movement. For the middle section of this movement,

137

Bartók returns to the motive of the middle section of the second movement. It is expanded and beautifully ornamented in a canonic imitation
between the first violin and the cello. The mood becomes more agitated
and intense as the viola and cello play thirty-second-note runs and the
violins continue to elaborate the motive from the second movement. The
coda begins *tranquillo* with an almost unrecognizable variant of the introduction. The movement ends with a series of pizzicato glissando chords
played by the cello.

Fifth Movement. After a short introduction, the first subject of the
finale is heard in a rather freely constructed inversion of the first subject
from the first movement:

Example 88.

The interval of an augmented fourth (Bb–E) is again prominent in this
predominantly canonic texture. After a general pause, the second subject
enters at a faster tempo and with more frequent use of canonic imitation.
The second subject features a falling seventh that Bartók uses to suggest
the entire subject. After two general pauses and a repetition of the introductory material, the development section begins *Prestissimo* with a
fugato based on the first subject, inverted so as to be nearly identical
with the first subject of the first movement:

Example 89.

The tritone Bᵇ–E is heard almost continuously throughout this section as a pair of pedal tones, first in the cello part and then in the viola. The entrances of the four voices are also at the interval of an augmented fourth, bringing this intervallic relationship into even greater prominence. The development section concludes with the four-note motive from the introduction played *fortissimo*. The recapitulation of this arch-form movement begins with the second subject, now abbreviated to the falling seventh in glissando. The interval of the seventh is also heard in its rising form, capriciously humorous in mood. The first subject returns in a compressed version and the tempo gradually increases. The *accelerando* is interrupted by a broad, tonal *Allegretto*. The cello holds to the tonic in A major while the viola plays an Alberti bass figuration in the same key; however, before the music becomes self-consciously naïve, the coda breaks in *prestissimo* and the movement ends on a unison Bᵇ, the keynote.

MUSIC FOR STRING INSTRUMENTS, PERCUSSION, AND CELESTA

The Music for String Instruments, Percussion, and Celesta (1936) was commissioned by the Basel Chamber Orchestra on the occasion of its tenth anniversary. It is in four movements and is scored for two string orchestras, celesta, harp, piano, timpani, side drums, tam-tam, bass drum, cymbals, and xylophone. It is probably the most highly organized and concentrated among Bartók's orchestral works and reflects the organic, generative methods of his fourth and fifth string quartets. The entire work exploits the subject of its opening fugue in a manner reminiscent of Beethoven. The subject is so varied and transformed throughout the work that each transformation breathes new life into the germinal idea. By relating the entire work to a central idea, Bartók has succeeded in creating a remarkably unified work.

The instrumentation, chosen for its sonorous possibilities, is imaginatively exploited by Bartók. He creates highly original sounds and sound combinations in ways never before utilized. Bartók gave explicit directions for the placement of the instruments on stage, so that full advantage could be taken of the directional aspects of various sound combinations. The strings are divided into two groups, one on each side of the percussion, basses are at the rear, and the piano and harp are in front.

The music is basically contrapuntal: the first and last movements utilize linear counterpoint; the second movement contains extremely complex rhythmic counterpoint; and the third movement features tone-color counterpoint. The tonal center of the work is A: the first and last movements are based on A; the second movement uses C (a minor third higher); and the third movement is based on F♯ (a minor third lower). The climactic points in both the first and last movements occur on an E♭, further evidence of Bartók's frequent use of the interval of an augmented fourth.

First Movement. The opening movement is a slow sinuous fugue whose highly chromatic subject is nearly arhythmic in structure. This is the germinal idea of the entire work:

Example 90.

Examples 90–96: Copyright 1937 by Universal Edition; Renewed 1964. Copyright and Renewal assigned to Boosey & Hawkes, Inc., for the USA. Reprinted by permission.

After its opening on A, successive entries of the subject appear alternately a fifth higher and then a fifth lower until the climax is gradually reached with an E♭ entry. Following the climax, the subject is inverted and the movement eventually returns to the tonic (A). A coda brings the movement to a quiet, mysterious close in which the original subject and its inversion are heard alternately in a stretto-like fashion and finally appear simultaneously, ending the movement on a unison A.

Example 91.

Second Movement. The second movement is a vigorous *Allegro* based on a sonata-form structure that uses two subjects in addition to a variety of small motives combined into passages of extremely complex rhythmic counterpoint. The first subject is obviously related to the germ theme, whose rising motive is emphasized by repetition:

Example 92.

The idea is developed, increasing in intensity until a *fortissimo* is reached. After a general pause, the dancelike, slightly impertinent second subject enters:

Example 93.

In addition to these two themes, a number of other motives enter and are developed and combined as the exposition rises to a climax. The section ends on a unison C♯ followed by a series of G major chords (the augmented fourth once more). The development begins quietly with pizzicato glissandos that recall the beginning of the movement. A climax is reached with one string group playing a five-note ostinato in eighth notes, producing constantly displaced accents as a result of the $\frac{2}{4}$ meter in which it is cast, while the piano and the other strings play a variant of the germ theme in an irregular rhythm. The string players create a percussive sonority by plucking their strings so hard that they rebound loudly against the fingerboard. The development continues with a rhythmically complex fugato based on the bowed half of the first subject. There is a complete recapitulation that opens with the first subject; however, the second subject is now in a $\frac{3}{8}$ meter. The tempo increases in anticipation of the coda (*Allegro molto*). The coda begins with the first subject played antiphonally by the two string groups and ends emphatically on C, the tonal center of the movement.

Third Movement. The slow movement is a sectional arch-type form —Introduction–A-B-C-D-C-B-A–Epilogue. All of the melodic material of the movement is derived from the opening fugue subject, while the connecting passages between sections use the germ theme almost literally. The introduction evokes a typically Bartók night-music atmosphere as the xylophone plays a repeated note and the timpani accompanies with a roll glissando. The A section is highlighted by a florid Hungarian folk-style song, played by the viola, which ends with a return of the xylophone-timpani duet.

Example 94.

The B section provides a counterpoint of timbres as an impressionistic background to a variant of the germ theme played by the first violins and celesta. The C section introduces new impressionistic sonorities. The celesta, harp, and piano play whispering glissandos while the strings play a tremolo figure, derived from the germ motive, in canon. The tempo has slowly increased and the dynamics have reached a *forte* as the D section opens. A *fortissimo* climax in an *Allegretto* tempo is reached at the midpoint of the arch form. The tempo and dynamics then slowly relax and the piano, celesta, and harp are heard in tremolo arpeggiated figures similar to those of the C section while the strings play the melodic material of section B in canon. In the final section, the violins play an abbreviated version of the opening viola theme and the movement ends mysteriously with a repetition of the sounds of the xylophone and timpani.

Fourth Movement. The finale is a rondo-like movement whose principal theme is a modal scale (Lydian) propelled by a Bulgarian rhythmic pattern (2+3+3):

Example 95.

The piano plays the first subsidiary theme *marcato* against pizzicato strings and a timpani ostinato. This chromatic theme is heard only briefly before the main theme returns *fortissimo*. Following a sudden pause, a broad Hungarian folklike dance theme enters at a slightly slower tempo. A relaxed variant of the main theme follows, but the tempo soon increases as a new vigorous dance theme is heard, with the piano and harp providing a steady pounding beat. Another variant of the opening theme is heard and then a new dance theme begins; however, it is soon overpowered by the piano hammering out the first subsidiary theme (in major sevenths). The strings then provide a canonic imitation to the piano, and a climax is reached as the tempo accelerates first to a *Vivacissimo* and then to *Presto strepitoso* (very fast, boisterous). The tempo suddenly changes to a *Molto moderato,* and the opening fugue theme of the first movement reappears, now diatonic and broad, *molto espressivo:*

Example 96.

It is treated contrapuntally first, together with its inversion, and then in a ten-part fugue. A three-measure *Adagio* serves as a transition to an *Allegro* in which the Bulgarian rhythmic figure of the rondo theme returns in an ascending line. A broad statement of the rondo theme, now in triplet quarter notes, leads to an exciting coda that ends majestically on an A

143

major chord. A fascinating alternative approach to this analysis of the *Music for String Instruments, Percussion, and Celesta,* utilizing the implications of the Fibonacci numeral system, appears in Ernö Lendvai's book *Béla Bartók, An Analysis of His Music* (London: Kahn & Averill, 1971).

PIANO CONCERTO NO. 3

During the final year of his terminal illness, Bartók accepted a commission from William Primrose to write a viola concerto, and he also promised Bartlett and Robertson a two-piano concerto. He put both aside, however, to work on his Third Piano Concerto. He knew he was dying and, according to his close friend and compatriot, Tibor Serly (who completed the Viola Concerto from sketches), he wished to leave an artistic legacy for his wife and pupil, Ditta Pásztory Bartók. Fortunately, he was able to complete the entire concerto (except for the orchestration of the last seventeen bars) before he died.

The concerto displays Bartók's complete mastery of his material. The music is refined, serene, and tranquil; it contains little conflict and has a remarkably transparent contrapuntal texture. Because of its lack of propulsive energy and inner tension and because of its mild tonal quality, a number of critics have misjudged this work, stating that it represents a decline in his creative ability and inspiration. Actually it represents an extension of his progressive movement toward a more lucid texture and a harmonic and structural simplicity. He abandoned the arch form in this work to return to the forms of the classical concerto: sonata-form, ABA form, and rondo.

First Movement. The opening *Allegretto* is in sonata-form, oriented to E as a tonal center. The first subject is a highly ornamented Magyar theme, played in single lines two octaves apart by the piano with a minimal accompaniment by the strings:

Example 97.

The strings repeat the subject, varied slightly, and the piano then enters with some brilliant passage work leading to the more lyric second subject, which consists of two themes, one *grazioso,* the other *scherzando.* A short codetta leads directly to the development section.

The development section features a *legato* transformation of the first subject; fragments of the second subject are played by the piano preceding the recapitulation. The return of the first subject is now fully harmonized by the piano. The strings begin a fugato whose compressed entries generate some excitement before a new connecting passage leads to the second subject. The movement ends very quietly shortly after the statement of the second subject.

Second Movement. The slow movement is a large ABA form, marked *Andante religioso.* It opens with a simple contrapuntal string passage. The piano then enters with a diatonic chorale of five verses, each punctuated by a shortened version of the string opening. The contrast is one of texture, with the chorale in block harmonies and the string interludes in close imitation:

Example 98.

145

The middle section is a superb example of Bartók's impressionistic night-music style. The strings shimmer in the background with constant *pianissimo* tremolo, trill, and occasional ponticello effects. The wood-winds and the xylophone twitter with birdcalls evoking the sounds of the night, to which the piano adds arpeggio and scale passages and birdcall imitations. There are no themes, just fragments of melody and rhythm.

The last section is similar to the first, except that now the woodwinds play the chorale accompanied by the piano playing a two-part invention that dissolves into a cadenza-like passage between verses. The strings enter in the final verse, and an emotional climax is reached as the gong is sounded. The piano ends the movement quietly on an E major chord.

Third Movement. The finale, marked *Allegro vivace,* is in rondo form with two subsidiary themes and an extended coda. The main theme, based on a characteristic Hungarian rhythm, is introduced by a flourish from the piano:

Example 99.

The piano repeats the theme and then expands it, emphasizing its basic rhythmic pattern. The orchestral tutti that follows ends with the solo timpani pounding its statement before gradually fading out. The piano begins the first subsidiary theme in fuguelike fashion, continued by the strings. The theme is presented in stretto and inversion and finally in unison by all the strings. The rondo theme reappears, now considerably shortened. It ends much like its first appearance, with the rhythmic sound of the solo timpani.

The second episode is an ABA form, all of whose sections are treated fugally. The theme of the B section is derived from that of the first section:

Example 100.

Of the two, the theme of the A section is more subdued and graceful (*grazioso*), presented by the strings with the piano playing a countertheme. The B section begins quietly but soon increases in intensity as the piano provides a brilliant background of passage work. The piano ends the B section playing the theme together with its inversion. The orchestra leads quietly back to the A section and the piano returns with the *grazioso* theme while the woodwinds play its countertheme. A *crescendo* leads to a return of the orchestral tutti. It is repeated and varied and reaches a *fortissimo* climax before coming to an abrupt halt. The tempo changes to *Presto* in a $\frac{3}{4}$ meter and the piano plays some brilliant passage work before returning to the original $\frac{3}{8}$ meter and its Hungarian rhythm, bringing the concerto to an exciting close.

chapter 9

Paul Hindemith (1895-1963)

BACKGROUND

The close cultural and linguistic ties between the German states and the Austrian Empire traditionally have made any distinction between the musical thought of the two extremely vague. Certain "Viennese" characteristics, for instance, which can be observed in the music of the Austrians Haydn, Schubert, Bruckner, and Mahler, can also be found in the music of the Germans Beethoven, Brahms, and Richard Strauss. After World War I, however, distinct differences in the musical thought between these two countries began to appear, notably in the works of the German Paul Hindemith on the one hand, and the works of the Austrians Arnold Schoenberg and his followers on the other.

German music, during the pre-World War I years of the twentieth century, was almost completely dominated by the postromantic Richard Strauss. Many came to realize, however, that by 1914 the one-time enfant terrible of music had little to say that was new. Then the war came, along with the disillusionment of the unsettled period that followed it. The viability of a life style and art expression rooted in the nineteenth century was openly challenged, and soon a strongly antiromantic movement took shape. An important point of reference in this movement was a 1907 publication by Ferrucio Busoni (1866–1924) in which he proclaimed that the renewal of music depended upon the understanding and use of the spirit and forms of the past, particularly those of the seventeenth and eighteenth centuries. This new aesthetic—neoclassicism—quickly found support throughout Europe, particularly in Paris with Stravinsky and in Germany with Hindemith.

This was an extremely exciting period in the cultural life of Germany. In spite of inflation, widespread unemployment, and general insecurity, opera houses and symphony orchestras were established in over a hundred cities. Music schools and art schools were reopened throughout the country, and theatre production was being revolutionized by Max Reinhardt. The Bauhaus, a school of architecture and design established under the leadership of the architect Walter Gropius (1883–1969), had as its guiding philosophy a return to austere simplicity and honesty of expression, a tenet that led to a utilitarian approach to form and design. Artist George Grosz (1893–1959), among others, also gave important expression to this new objectivity.

Grosz—*Republican Automatons* (1920)

Collection, The Museum of Modern Art, New York.
Advisory Committee Fund.

LIFE AND WORKS

Paul Hindemith's preeminence among post-World War I German composers is unquestioned. This extraordinarily versatile musician was a virtuoso violist, experienced in playing nearly every instrument in the orchestra; in his role as a composer, he wrote in all forms and for all media; and as a teacher, theorist, and music educator, he influenced an entire generation of composers through his teaching and textbooks.

Hindemith was born in Hanau, near Frankfurt, Germany. By the time he was eleven, he was playing in jazz bands for a livelihood. A wealthy businessman recognized the boy's talent, and sponsored his education at the Conservatory of Frankfurt. There he majored in violin, viola, and composition, and became so proficient as a performer that he was appointed concertmaster and later conductor of the Frankfurt Opera. Gradually, his interests centered in composition, and by the time he was twenty-six, his reputation as a composer was already established throughout Germany.

Paul Hindemith

Music Division, The New York Public Library at Lincoln
Center. Astor, Lenox and Tilden Foundations.

His earliest works were strongly influenced by the scholastic tradition so ardently championed by Reger and his followers, and by those who followed the romantic leanings of the Brahms tradition. As we have seen, however, the psychological atmosphere of the 1920s did not look kindly on introspection and *Weltschmerz* (nineteenth-century German romantic idealism). Hindemith, searching for his own identity in this time of change, experimented with the contrapuntal practices of pre-1750 music and gradually developed the element which is so basic to his style and to neoclassicism itself—*linear counterpoint.* Largely disregarding the vertical aspects of traditional counterpoint, he became preoccupied with the linear, horizontal independence of each line and, except in his late works, permitted dissonance to occur with little restriction. Furthermore, by using the principle of twelve tones around a center, he, unlike Schoenberg, never denied the principle of tonality; in fact, tension in his music is frequently ingeniously relieved with a simple triad. He borrowed the contrapuntal formal structures of the baroque for much of his work, and emphasized technique and workmanship as the foundation of music. He stated that personal expression and style develop from technique, and all are subordinate to ideas. He felt no "rage to be modern"; as a true neoclassicist, he found artistic fulfillment in reinterpreting the past in terms of the present.

During his experimentation period, Hindemith wrote a number of distinguished works, including three string quartets (1921–24); the profoundly moving song cycle *Das Marienleben* (*The Life of Mary;* 1923), based on the poetry of Rilke; and the opera *Cardillac* (1926), based on a tale by E. T. A. Hoffmann. In 1927 he was appointed professor of composition at the Berlin *Hochschule für Musik.* In this position, he soon became aware of the growing separation between composer and public and set about writing a body of *Spielmusik* (instrumental music) and *Singmusik* (vocal music) suitable for amateurs and students. Often designated *Gebrauchsmusik* (useful music; Hindemith himself grew to dislike the term), these compositions were designed for specific functional purposes, such as children's choruses and games, community singing, and education.

His growing concern with the creative artist's relationship to the social issues of his time is directly reflected in his most significant work for the lyric theatre, *Mathis der Maler* (*Matthias the Painter;* 1932–34). His music of this period is less dissonant, more tonally oriented than that of the preceding decade. He next turned his attention to writing quantities of *Gebrauchsmusik* and two works that have become part of the standard ballet repertoire—*Nobilissima Visione* (1938), based on the

Hindemith conducting

The Bettmann Archive.

life of St. Francis of Assisi, and the *Four Temperaments* (1940), a theme
and variations for piano and strings.

Hindemith presented his acoustically based system for applying tonal
organization to contemporary harmonic and melodic structures in his
important text *Unterweisung im Tonsatz* (*The Craft of Musical Composition;* two volumes: 1937, 1939). Later, he summed up the essence of
his viewpoint in his book *A Composer's World* (1952):

> We cannot escape the . . . effect of tonal unification, of tonality. The
> intervals which constitute the building material of melodies and harmonies
> fall into tonal groupments, necessitated by their own physical structure
> and without our consent. Have we not heard many times of tendencies in
> modern music to avoid these tonal effects? It seems to me that attempts at
> avoiding them are as promising as attempts at avoiding the effects of
> gravitation.

Seeing no future for himself in Germany (his music had been banned
by the Nazi government for what is called "musical Bolshevism"), he came
to America in 1940 to take the post of professor of composition at Yale

152

University. In 1942 he wrote *Ludus Tonalis* for piano, subtitled *Studies in Counterpoint, Tonal Organization and Piano Playing.* It consists of a Prelude, twelve fugues divided by Interludes, and a Postlude. The fugues are arranged according to the basic scheme of tonal relationships that he had outlined in the *Unterweisung im Tonsatz.* His familiar *Symphonic Metamorphoses on Themes by Weber* was completed in 1943. In 1953 he left the United States to live in Zurich, where in 1957 he completed a large five-act opera entitled *Die Harmonie der Welt* (*The Harmony of the Universe*), based on the life of the German astronomer Johann Kepler (1571–1630). Parts of this opera had appeared previously in 1951 as a three-movement symphony. Prophetically, his last work, written in 1963, was a Requiem for *a cappella* chorus.

MATHIS DER MALER (MATTHIAS THE PAINTER)

Very little is known about the personal life of Matthias Grünewald (c. 1470–1528), the painter hero of Hindemith's opera. Hindemith, therefore, drew upon his imagination to construct a libretto portraying Grünewald as an important participant in the Peasants' War of 1524. Mathis seeks to resolve the moral dilemma of the artist when faced with the oppression and suffering of his fellow men. Should he participate in the struggle or seek to illuminate it through his art? Hindemith, through Mathis, asks himself if he has fulfilled his duty to God and his fellow man. As an active participant in the struggle, Mathis becomes disillusioned, and in the climactic scene of the opera, his soul-searchings are transformed into a reenactment of the subject of one of his greatest paintings, the *Temptations of St. Anthony,* a panel from the altarpiece at Isenheim.

The authorities banned the opera over the strong objections of Wilhelm Furtwängler, the music director of the Berlin State Opera. For the Nazis, peasants rising against authority was hardly a fit subject for presentation. Frustrated for some time in his attempts to have the opera staged, Hindemith decided to extract three scenes from the opera for presentation in concert form as a symphony. Each of the three movements represents a panel from Grünewald's Isenheim altarpiece. This musical triptych contains some of Hindemith's most inspired music, and has become his best-known work.

I. Engelkonzert (Concert of the Angels). The introduction to the first movement opens brightly with a G major chord. Soon the theme of the introduction, the medieval tune "Es sungen drei Engel" ("Three Angels Were Singing"), is intoned by the trombones:

Grunewald—Isenheim Altarpiece (c. 1510–1515)

Musée Unterlinden, Colmar. Photographie Giraudon.

Temptation of St. Anthony

The Crucifixion

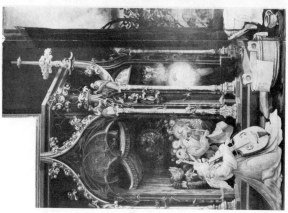

Concert of Angels

Example 101.

Ruhig bewegt (Quietly moving) (♩.etwa 66)

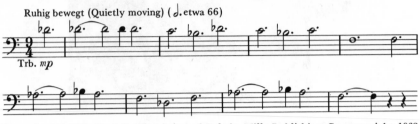

Trb. *mp*

Examples 101–105: Used by permission of Belwin Mills Publishing Co., copyright 1962 by B. Schott's Sohne.

More instruments then join in as the tune is repeated and soon the volume decreases while the opening chords are heard once more, ending the introduction. The tempo changes to a brisk $\frac{2}{2}$ and the principal subject of a modified sonata-form is heard (note the characteristic Hindemith use of the skip of a fifth in measure three):

Example 102.

Ziemlich lebhafte Halbe
(Quite lively half-notes) (♩ =108-112)

Fl., *mf*
Vl.

This idea is expanded slightly, and then the lyric second subject appears (note the skip of a fifth in measure two):

Example 103.

Ruhig (Quietly)

Vl. *p*

mp

After being repeated and heard in augmentation, the second subject is followed by a gay, dancelike closing subject played by the flutes. The opening measures of the principal subject reappear and the exposition ends quietly.

The two themes are combined and treated imitatively in the development section. A climax is reached when the trombones and trumpets enter, intoning the medieval tune of the introduction against a dissonant linear contrapuntal treatment of the two subjects. The tempo gradually decreases as the development section comes to a quiet close. The recapitulation opens with the closing subject but then the opening measures of the principal subject are heard before a sudden *crescendo* leads to a strong, staccato appearance of the second subject. The movement ends with the opening measures of the first subject.

II. Grablegung (The Entombment). The slow movement, just forty-five measures long, is in ABA form with a coda. The first theme is marchlike and somber, with the muted violins playing the first phrase, answered by the woodwinds:

Example 104.

The B section is a tender lament sung by the oboe over pizzicato strings. This is imitated by the flute as the oboe continues with a plaintive counterpoint. The music becomes more intense as the full orchestra returns to the opening theme; a sixteenth-note counterpoint is provided by the violins and violas. The second theme is heard in a transformed version in the short coda. Soon the throbbing dotted rhythm returns and the movement ends serenely on a C♯ major chord.

III. The Temptation of St. Anthony. Beneath the title of the last movement, Hindemith wrote the words St. Anthony cried out during his ordeal, "Where wert Thou, good Jesus, where wert Thou, why wert Thou not present to heal my wounds?" The movement opens with a rhapsodic declamation, undoubtedly referring to the outcry, played by unison strings punctuated by crashing dissonances from the full orchestra. This recitative-like introduction, having reached a climax with all the wood-

winds and strings in unison, quickly subsides as the opening notes of the
outcry fade away. Grünewald's painting depicts the saint, prostrate and
helpless before an onslaught of horrible demons that swarm upon him
from all sides. This struggle is suggested by the sinuous line of the main
theme:

Example 105.

This theme, played next by all the brass, rises to a climax. A flowing
oboe theme over a repeated *legato* string figure follows. Tension builds
steadily until a climax is reached with the full orchestra playing a four-
note descending figure that is repeated and expanded before the first
section ends on a sustained violin trill. The next section is slower, played
entirely by the strings. The theme, played first by the cellos against the
violin trill, is then repeated by the violins with the other string groups
subdivided to create an extremely thick, "sensuous" texture. The fast
tempo returns with the brass playing the four-note motive. After the
violas play a quiet interlude based on the sensuous theme of the second
section, the main idea of the movement returns, now rhythmically altered
and augmented, played by the trombones. The coda begins *subito piano*
(suddenly soft) with a *fugato,* to which an ostinato based on the introductory declamation is added by the clarinets and horns. Out of this
contrapuntal web emerges the hymn "Lauda Sion Salvatorum" suggesting
the deliverance of the saint. The movement ends impressively with a
mighty "Alleluia" played by the brass *mit aller Kraft* (with full strength),
signifying the victory of the St. Anthony–Grünewald–Hindemith combination over all temptation.

chapter 10

Sergei Prokofiev (1891-1953) and Dmitri Shostakovich (1906-1975)

SOVIET RUSSIA

In the years before the October Revolution of 1917, there were two principal schools of composition in Russia: the Moscow Group, headed by Taneiev and Rachmaninoff, which continued in the Tchaikovsky tradition by seeking closer integration with German romanticism; and the St. Petersburg Group, headed by Rimsky-Korsakov and his pupils Liadov and Glazounov, which was intensely nationalistic. After the Revolution, however, two new groups were formed, implementing Lenin's words, "Art belongs to the people. Its deepest roots must lie among the very thick of the working masses. . . . It must voice the feelings, thoughts and will of these masses, must uplift them." The first of these groups, the Russian Association of Proletarian Musicians, attempted to create an entirely new working-class art. Its members rejected contemporary trends, considered most classics bourgeois, and even frowned on nationalism. Music, for them, had to be immediately comprehensible to the working-man or simple peasant.

By contrast, the second group, known as the Association for Contemporary Music, encouraged experimentation and performances of the new music from western Europe. In Leningrad, from 1925 to 1928, Russians heard Berg's *Wozzeck,* Krenek's *Jonny spielt auf,* and Stravinsky's

Oedipus Rex among other works, and in Moscow a conductorless orchestra (an attempt at a musical collective) played works by Bartók, Stravinsky, Ravel, Falla, and Honegger. In 1932, the Union of Soviet Composers was formed to bring together all of the various factions that had developed since the Revolution. The Union assumed responsibility for the economic welfare of its members, the promotion of performances of Soviet music, and the publishing of the music of its members. It adopted the principle of socialist realism as proclaimed by Maxim Gorky, giving emphasis to socially significant communication: "bringing into being," as Shostakovich said, "a work that must be permeated with great ideas and great passions." The Union also took upon itself the interpretation and implementation of this principle by reevaluating earlier Russian music and stimulating composition in the more remote Soviet Socialist Republics. All music that did not follow the aesthetic principle of socialist realism and was therefore considered lacking in ideas and content, having instead "a complete concentration on form," was labeled *bourgeois formalism* and was anathematized by the Union. As a consequence, the music of composers such as Schoenberg and his school, Stravinsky, Hindemith, and Bartók was banned.

The ban against foreign influences became even more pronounced when in 1936, *Pravda,* the newspaper serving as the official voice of the Communist Party, severely condemned Shostakovich's opera *Lady Macbeth of Mzensk* principally because of its "decadent" subject matter and "formalistic" style (i.e., violence and dissonance). Later, during World War II, Soviet composers dutifully expressed their love of country and confidence in its triumph; however, in 1948, the Central Committee of the Communist Party once again violently criticized most of the leading Soviet composers for straying into "formalistic" means of expression. The Committee of the Union of Soviet Composers, consisting of Russia's leading composers, was accused of autocratic methods and of being interested in performances only of their own works. The result of this attack was a rash of second-rate compositions based on folk songs, written in a nineteenth-century style. Fortunately, after Stalin's death the official line relaxed, and in 1958 the Central Committee admitted that the 1948 criticism had been unfounded and unjust, the result of Stalin's limited artistic views. Shostakovich and Prokofiev, among others, were absolved of any wrongdoing, and the ban on performances of works by so-called "formalist" composers, including Hindemith, Bartók, Milhaud, and Stravinsky, was lifted. The measure of this liberalization must be judged, however, within the context of the Soviet government's continued ban on serialist works.

SERGEI PROKOFIEV

Among those Russian composers who had reached their maturity at the time of the Revolution, Sergei Prokofiev was undoubtedly the most gifted. When he entered the St. Petersburg Conservatory at the age of thirteen, he came with scores of four operas, two sonatas, a symphony, and a great variety of piano music. He wrote his first two piano concertos while still a student at the Conservatory and soon acquired a reputation as one of Russia's leading virtuosos. Prokofiev was considered a rebel and extreme musical leftist by his fellow students and teachers because of his percussive style of piano playing and the satirical and grotesque character of his music. Nevertheless, he received the first prize in piano when he graduated in 1914. During this first phase of his musical career he wrote the *Sarcasms* (1912) and *Visions Fugitives* (1915–17) for piano, the First Violin Concerto (1914), the *Scythian Suite* (1914), the Piano Concerto No. 3 (1917–21), and the *Classical Symphony* (1917). The last three works have remained among his most popular compositions. The *Scythian Suite* was taken from a ballet commissioned by Diaghilev. A fine example of primitivism, it displays propulsive rhythms and mass sonorities that probably found their inspiration in Stravinsky's *The Rite*

Sergei Prokofiev

Cleveland Public Library.

of Spring, which Prokofiev heard in London in 1914. The Piano Concerto No. 3 is characterized by emphases on form, rhythmic drive, and the sardonic. The *Classical Symphony,* composed as if by Haydn, were he living today, is an affirmation of Prokofiev's belief in the classical principles of clarity and form.

Searching for a better situation in which to work, Prokofiev left Russia in 1918 and came to the United States, where he received acclaim for his piano playing but was sharply criticized by a conservative public for his compositions. Disappointed, he moved to Paris in 1921, making it his headquarters for the next eleven years. In December of 1921, he returned to the United States to conduct the première of his opera *The Love for Three Oranges,* which he had completed in 1919. During his Paris years—his middle period—he composed three symphonies, and two ballets for Diaghilev, *Le Pas d'acier (The Age of Steel;* 1925), and *L'Enfant prodigue (The Prodigal Son;* 1929). These works, written outside his native environment, seem to lack the inspiration, the spontaneity and drive of his other compositions. Realizing this, and longing for the atmosphere of his native soil, he returned to Russia in 1932 to stay. During the years that followed his return, he produced some of his finest works: the film scores to *Lieutenant Kijé* (1934) and *Alexander Nevsky* (1938); his Violin Concerto No. 2 (1935); *Peter and the Wolf* (1936); the ballets *Romeo and Juliet* (1935) and *Cinderella* (1941–44); his Symphony No. 5 (1944) and Symphony No. 7 (1952); the opera *War and Peace* (1941–42); and the Piano Sonata No. 7 (1943), for which he won the Stalin Prize.

The music Prokofiev wrote before he left Russia was representative of the new antiromanticism, a revolt against the cloying mysticism of Scriabin and the extremely subjective romanticism of Rachmaninoff. In spite of his use of extreme dissonance in these early works, the music is basically tonal and has a great melodic emphasis. During his middle period, he came under the influence of the Stravinskian constructivist approach that dominated the Parisian scene during the twenties. His move back to Russia was also a move toward romanticism and nationalism. His early satiric musical characterizations and percussive style were now joined with a mature lyricism and more conventional harmonic orientation, possibly because of the restraints of socialist realism, but more than likely simply as a result of his own inclinations. Certainly these late works show neither any diminution of his powers nor any watering down of his artistic integrity.

Prokofiev: PIANO CONCERTO NO. 3 IN C MAJOR

First Movement. The ten-measure introduction is begun by an unaccompanied clarinet playing a gentle, lyric theme:

Example 106.

The *Allegro* section opens with a rising sixteenth-note passage over a pedal C that leads to a statement by the piano of the principal subject. The opening three notes of this theme are the reverse of the opening three notes of the introduction. The sudden shift in tonality in the third measure is a harmonic characteristic found in many of Prokofiev's works:

Example 107.

This theme is discussed by the piano and orchestra in a technically brilliant interplay that ends with the entrance of the second subject, an engaging theme played by the oboe accompanied by pizzicato strings and castanets:

Example 108.

163

The piano then takes up the theme, adding embellishments and elaborating on the idea in an increasingly bravura manner. The tempo increases (*più mosso*) and a triplet passage ends the exposition with a flourish.

The development section, by contrast, opens *Andante* with the violins expressively singing the theme of the introduction. The piano then enters with this theme and the woodwinds answer canonically, first at the interval of a measure, then at a two-beat interval. The piano now plays a hushed chromatic passage over tremolo strings, bringing the development section to a close. The recapitulation returns to the rising sixteenth-note passage of the exposition, once more over a pedal C, but now extended for twenty-five measures in a mounting *crescendo*. The principal subject returns with little change; the second subject, however, now introduced by a series of brilliant chromatic scales on the piano, is played by the piano with *fortissimo* chords, very dissonant and grotesque, accompanied by the strings *col legno*. The coda reintroduces the rising sixteenth-note passage over a pedal C in a *crescendo* that ends the movement.

Second Movement.   The slow movement is in the form of a theme and five variations. The flute and clarinet present the theme, a lyric melody with a slightly wistful character:

Example 109.

The piano begins the first variation alone in a very lush, colorful harmonization; the flute and clarinet complete the variation accompanied by piano figurations. The second variation is a tempestuous *Allegro* in which the piano plays bravura scales and brilliant passage work while the trumpet plays fragments of the theme, always in a key different from that of the piano. The next variation, still bravura but slightly slower, matches the piano in $\frac{12}{8}$ meter against the $\frac{4}{4}$ meter of the orchestra. The melodic accents in the piano part fall on the eighth note before the beat, creating an interesting cross rhythm. In the fourth variation, the original *Andante* tempo returns, and the piano and orchestra discourse on the theme in a quiet, contemplative mood. The final variation, *Allegro giusto,* is strong and energetic. It leads without pause to the coda, where the theme is restated in a tempo now marked *Allegro* but with note values indicated in augmentation. The orchestration, similar to the opening, includes a series of staccato eighth-note passages by the piano. The cadence is extended to bring the movement to a quiet close.

Third Movement. The finale is based on two strongly contrasting themes and two subsidiary themes that fill out a large ABA form. The opening theme is angular and rhythmically irregular, displaying Prokofiev in a brittle, jesting mood. It is announced by the bassoon and pizzicato strings:

Example 110.

The piano immediately answers with a sprightly, minuetlike theme. The orchestra repeats the first theme, again answered by the minuet from the piano, which this time dissolves into a series of scale passages. A *poco più mosso* brings back the opening theme very softly, with considerable use of imitation. A climax is reached with both themes combined, but soon subsides as a new *legato* theme is introduced by the woodwinds, a broad singing melody in a slightly slower tempo:

Example 111.

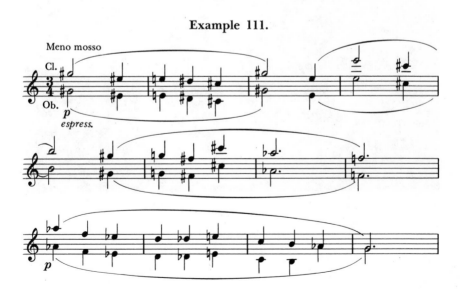

The piano answers, unaccompanied, with a quiet, almost mocking theme, as if Prokofiev were embarrassed by the emotional content of the lovely B melody. The lyric theme does return, however, and is developed by the piano and lower strings in a grand, Tchaikovsky-like manner. The opening theme is restated as in the beginning and soon builds to a furious climax that leads to a strongly rhythmic coda.

DMITRI SHOSTAKOVICH

Dmitri Shostakovich, by contrast with the cosmopolitan Prokofiev, was very closely associated with Soviet culture throughout his entire career. At the age of thirteen, he entered the Leningrad Conservatory, where his talent was immediately recognized and encouraged by Glazounov, the director at that time. He wrote his First Symphony as a graduation composition in 1925. Performed in Russia and abroad, it quickly focused international attention on the exceptional talent of this nineteen-year-old. The Soviet government was anxious to encourage such talent, particularly at a time when so many prominent musicians had chosen to leave the

Dmitri Shostakovich

The Bettmann Archive.

country. Eager to please, he wrote two new symphonies (1927; 1929) subtitled "October" and "May Day." The results were less than successful artistically. His only genuine success from this period was the opera *Lady Macbeth of Mzensk* (1932), written on a theme of adultery, murder, and corruption in an earlier Russian bourgeois society. Its musical style was strongly influenced by Viennese expressionism and Western standards of dissonance. First produced in Moscow and Leningrad in 1934, it ran for two years to capacity audiences before *Pravda,* the official newspaper of the government, denounced it in a scathing attack. The contrite Shostakovich accepted their verdict and withdrew both the opera and his newly completed Fourth Symphony, feeling that it too would be unacceptable. He then set about writing his Fifth Symphony (1937), to which he gave the subtitle: "A Soviet Artist's Practical and Creative Reply to Just Criticism." The success of the symphony was immediate and lasting; in fact, over the years since its composition it has become his most popular work. For the Soviets, the Fifth Symphony marked Shostakovich's coming of age as an "artist-realist," a status fully affirmed when in 1940 he received his first Stalin Prize ($25,000) for his Piano Quintet.

Mahler's influence, already evident in some of his earlier works, now became even more apparent in the symphonies that followed, although it was Beethoven whose epic quality of victory through struggle he consciously tried most to emulate. Shostakovich, unlike Prokofiev, displayed a considerable interest in using counterpoint in his works. He was also a masterful orchestral colorist. In his fifteen symphonies we find the confident hand of a composer whose resourcefulness and technical mastery may be much admired. Too often, however, pretentiousness, excessive sentimentality, and an unfortunate unevenness of quality mar his works.

Shostakovich: SYMPHONY NO. 5

The fact that Shostakovich's Fifth Symphony satisfied all of the tenets of socialist realism seems to bear little relationship to its more universal value as a significant twentieth-century composition. Among his symphonies, this work seems to approach the epic quality of Beethoven. The best of Shostakovich's style characteristics are found here: driving rhythms, brilliant orchestration, and jesting parody coupled with deeply emotional, long-breathed lyricism and delicately scored counterpoint.

First Movement. The opening movement is in an expansively conceived sonata-form. The opening rhythmic theme of the first subject is announced antiphonally between the lower and higher strings:

Example 112.

The more lyric second theme of the opening subject follows immediately, played by the violins:

Example 113.

These themes are expanded both separately and together, clearly delineated through Shostakovich's characteristically transparent orchestration.

The second subject presents a fine illustration of Shostakovich's ability to spin out an idea to remarkable lengths. It is a slow, arching melody, full of wide expressive leaps, sung by the violins over a throbbing rhythmic figure played by the other strings. It is in E-flat, a semitone higher than the first subject:

Example 114.

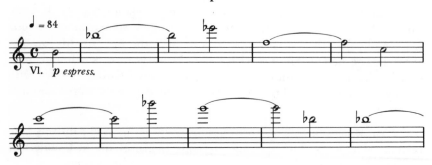

168

A three-note rhythmic figure from the close of the second subject is expanded upon, and then the second subject is repeated by the violas. The three-note figure then becomes a background to the closing subject, a rhythmic transformation of the second theme of the first subject.

The development section is marked by a steady increase in tempo. The opening measures of the second theme of the first subject now take on a martial air, played first by the low brasses and then by the woodwinds. The tension mounts as Shostakovitch manipulates all of the themes contrapuntally and makes use of antiphonal effects among the various orchestral choirs. A climax is reached as the strings and woodwinds. The tension mounts as Shostakovich manipulates all of the brass blare out the second subject. At the very height of the climax, the recapitulation begins with a very strong unison statement of the first subject, now considerably shortened. A canonic treatment of the second subject by the flute and French horn follows. The tempo slackens for the coda, with the rhythm of the opening subject serving as a background for a soaring, introspective version of the first subject by the solo violin. The sound then fades away as delicate scales from the celesta close the movement.

Second Movement. The scherzo is a boisterous movement in the style of a Mahler ländler. A satiric mood is set immediately with the E-flat clarinet playing the first, rather whimsical tune that is then extended by the bassoon:

Example 115.

The entire orchestra then enters with a deliberately vulgar dance tune in waltz time. After a repetition followed by a fanfare from the horns, the sharply contrasting trio begins. The first theme is played by the solo violin accompanied by pizzicato cellos and harp. Shostakovich's debt to Mahler is immediately evident:

Example 116.

The theme is repeated by the flute and extended. A *legato* theme is then added before the scherzo returns, precisely as at the beginning, except that the roles of the strings and woodwinds are now reversed. There is a short coda in which the oboe plays the theme of the trio briefly. The entire orchestra then ends the movement emphatically.

Third Movement. The slow movement is a deeply moving, tragic piece, skillfully orchestrated for divided strings, woodwinds, two harps, piano, xylophone, and celesta. There are three themes arranged in a modified arch form to which Shostakovich adds a considerable amount of subsidiary material derived from the themes. The movement opens tentatively with the first theme played by the strings alone:

Example 117.

Much of the material of the movement is derived from this theme. The second theme, also played by the strings, follows immediately:

Example 118.

170

The flutes now enter and, accompanied only by the harp, develop this idea. The strings and woodwinds, using the second and third measures of the opening theme, gradually develop an impressive climax. The tempo increases slightly, there is a *decrescendo,* and a tremolo in the violins leads to the statement of the third theme:

Example 119.

The clarinet and flute successively repeat the theme, and then an *agitato* section, heightened by a gradual *crescendo,* leads to a *fortissimo* section in which the second and third themes are restated emphatically. Following a series of massive chords, a cello passage moves swiftly from *fortissimo* to *pianissimo* for the hushed ethereal coda. Material from the first theme appears, and then the harp and celesta play a reminiscence of the third theme before the strings bring the movement to a serene close.

Fourth Movement. The finale is an energetic, almost satanic movement whose marchlike rhythms recall the uninhibited vitality of the Rimsky-Korsakov and Tchaikovsky heritage. The form is that of a rondo, although references to themes from the earlier movement recall the cyclical finales of Dvořák and Franck. The opening theme is blared out by the brass against a savage pounding by the timpani:

Example 120.

A frantic dancelike tune by the violins that follows is repeated by the woodwinds. The opening theme returns, played now by the bass instruments of the orchestra, and both themes are then developed as the tempo increases. Against a series of continuous sixteenth notes from the strings and woodwinds, the solo trumpet enters with a new theme:

Example 121.

The volume continues to increase, and soon all the strings and woodwinds play this theme *fortissimo* against a rhythmic accompaniment by the trumpets. A shattering climax is reached as the timpani beat an eighth-note rhythm while the brass again blare the opening notes of the main theme. Gradually the drama subsides, and a long calm section presents theme fragments in augmentation. It is concluded by the opening theme, also in augmentation, played quietly by the clarinet and bassoon. The imposing coda presents the brass section, rhythmically reinforced by the rest of the orchestra, in a triumphant major key version of the main theme.

chapter 11

Ralph Vaughan Williams (1872-1958) and Benjamin Britten (1913-1976)

RALPH VAUGHAN WILLIAMS

The importance of Elgar and Delius in reestablishing England's position of prominence in musical composition during the early years of this century has already been discussed in the chapter on postromanticism. During these same years, a younger generation of composers established the direction for a twentieth-century national school of composition. Using England's rich national heritage of folk song and sixteenth- and early seventeenth-century vocal polyphony as resource materials, they produced music with a characteristic "English" flavor. Among them, Ralph Vaughan Williams and, to a lesser extent, his friend Gustav Holst (1874–1934) were the most significant.

Vaughan Williams was born in Down Ampney, Gloucester. He received his early musical training at the Royal College of Music, where, under the guidance of Sir Charles Hubert Parry and Sir Charles Stanford, he was first introduced to the great English choral tradition. He then went on to Trinity College, Cambridge, where he received both a musical and a general degree. After a short stay in Berlin, where he studied with Max Bruch, he returned to Cambridge and received a doctorate in music in 1901. He joined the English Folk Music Society and soon became strongly involved with the then current folk-song revival. He served as musical editor of the new English Hymnal from 1904 to 1906, an associa-

Ralph Vaughan Williams

tion that left a lasting impression on his music. Later, "stodgy" evidences of German romanticism in his work made him decide, at the age of thirty-six, to study with Ravel to add "a little French polish." He came to the United States in 1932 to give a series of lectures at Bryn Mawr College, which were later published in a book titled *National Music*. In 1954, at the age of eighty-three, he returned to the United States to deliver a lecture series at Cornell University, which he later published as *The Making of Music*.

One of the reasons for the complete acceptance by the English public of Vaughan Williams as their foremost composer was his recognition of the importance of the amateur in British society. From 1909 to 1953 he directed the annual Leith Hill Music Festivals in Surrey and also wrote a considerable amount of music for local amateur singing groups. His works for amateurs include the *Benedicite* (1930), the *Household Music* (1941) for "almost any combinations of instruments," a Concerto Grosso for triple string orchestra (1950) in which the third group is for those who prefer to play only on the open strings, and the choral cycle *Folk-Songs of the Four Seasons* (1950).

Vaughan Williams's identification with his country and its rich musical heritage permeated every aspect of his musical life and creation. It is not merely a resurrection of the past or an imitation of a previous style but the emergence of an extremely personal style. Although he seldom actually quoted folk-song material in his works, its influence is evident in the character of his melodic orientation. Modal harmonies

174

and 'transparent counterpoint, derived from his thorough acquaintance with the practices of sixteenth- and seventeenth-century polyphonists, give his works much of their characteristic flavor. He shunned romantic chromaticism; his orientation, by contrast, was basically diatonic. Dissonance, however, was an important expressive element in his musical vocabulary. In common with most of his English colleagues, he was a conservative and had little sympathy for either the neoclassicism of Stravinsky or the expressionism of the Viennese atonalists.

Vaughan Williams's active creative life extended over an incredibly long span of time. His first published work was written when he was nineteen; he finished his Ninth Symphony when he was eighty-five. Although his huge musical output encompasses works in a wide variety of forms, his symphonies, the masque *Job* (1930), and the *Fantasia on a Theme by Thomas Tallis* (1910) are the works that have established his fame throughout the world. His first three symphonies—The *Sea Symphony* (1905–1910), the *London Symphony* (1914), and the *Pastoral Symphony* (1922)—are written in a gentle descriptive style; Vaughan Williams explains, however, that the title of his Second Symphony should not be taken too literally. "A better title would perhaps be *Symphony by a Londoner*, that is to say the life of London (including its various sights and sounds) has suggested to the composer an attempt at musical expression; but it would be no help to the hearer to describe these in words. The music is intended to be self-impressive, and must stand or fall as 'absolute' music. Therefore if listeners recognize suggestions of such things as the Westminster chimes or the *Lavender Cry*, they are asked to consider these as accidents, not essentials of the music." It is from this same period that the *Fantasia on a Theme by Thomas Tallis* was composed. Thomas Tallis was a sixteenth-century English composer who served as organist of the Chapel Royal during the reigns of Edward VI, Mary, and Elizabeth. Vaughan Williams adapted the third of Tallis's tunes written for the Metrical Psalter of the Archbishop of Canterbury for the *Fantasia*. To emphasize the sixteenth-century antiphonal style, he divided the strings into two orchestras and a quartet of soloists. Parallel triads within a modal framework create a rich tapestry of sound that can also be found in many of his later works. The impressionist-influenced song cycle *On Wenlock Edge* (1909), for tenor, string quartet, and piano, and the beautiful romance for violin and orchestra, *The Lark Ascending* (1914), are also representative works from this period.

Vaughan Williams made an abrupt departure from the folk-song-influenced idiom of his previous works in his Symphony No. 4 in 1935. It is a violent, dramatic work, strongly dissonant and somber, as if protesting the English "sense of propriety which brakes the most powerful impulses." He later remarked, "I don't even know if I like it—but that is what I meant when I wrote it." The Symphony No. 5 (1943) is a return to his more accustomed folk idiom. Gentle and pastoral in mood, it is considered by many critics to be his orchestral masterpiece. The Sixth, Seventh, and Eighth symphonies are all unconventional in form and contain an ever-increasing use of dissonance and harmonic tension. The Symphony No. 9 (1957–58) is a retrospective work in which nationalism has been sublimated into a deeply moving personal expression.

The choral style adopted by Vaughan Williams reflects the art of the sixteenth-century English masters. His most successful liturgical works include the Mass in G minor (1922)—two movements of which were performed at the coronation of Queen Elizabeth II—*Benedicite, Magnificat* (1932), and *Festival Te Deum* (1937). While his operas are an important part of his output, their strongly nationalistic character has considerably diminished their popularity outside of England. They include *Hugh the Drover* (1914), a folk ballad opera; *Sir John in Love* (1929), based on Shakespeare's *Merry Wives of Windsor;* and *Riders to the Sea* (1937)— likely his best work in this form—based on the play by Synge.

Vaughan Williams: SYMPHONY NO. 4

The romantic introspection of Vaughan Williams's first three symphonies offers no precedent for the startlingly harsh dramatic expressiveness of this symphony. We must look instead to his stage work *Job,* produced during the interim of twelve years between his Third and Fourth symphonies, in order to find evidence of the kind of musical conflict expressed in this work.

Vaughan Williams derived much of the thematic material for each of the four movements of his Fourth Symphony from two basic four-note mottoes:

First Movement. The principal subject is presented immediately by the full orchestra:

Example 122.

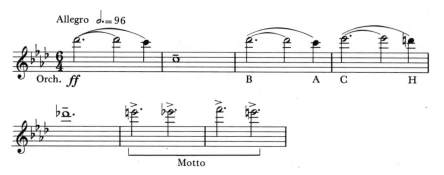

Motto

Examples 122–126: Copyright 1935 by Oxford University Press. Used by permission.

Measures three and four of this subject are derived from the motto by raising the third and fourth notes one half step. The result is actually a transposed version of the familiar B-A-C-H (B♭-A-C-B♮) motive. The motto itself is stated in this opening subject as measures six and seven. A *subito piano* begins a chromatic ascent to another *fortissimo* capped by the B motto from the brass. The opening theme and A motto then appear in a higher register, and A is repeated insistently. The second subject follows immediately. It is played passionately by the strings in unison against a rhythmic, harmonic background alternated between the woodwinds and brass:

Example 123.

This idea, after being extended with great intensity, leads to a closing subject, much slower in tempo.

The short development section opens with a forceful statement of the principal subject and a working out of the A motto. The conflict

177

between $\frac{3}{2}$ and $\frac{6}{4}$ meter constantly reminds one of the use of hemiola during the sixteenth and seventeenth centuries. There is a sudden *piano* and then a rapid *crescendo* as the B motto is heard in the trombones, leading to the recapitulation. The first subject's statement is now considerably shortened; the expressive second subject returns in a low register with a countersubject played by the violins and high woodwinds. The closing subject precedes a gentle coda played by muted strings.

Second Movement. The slow movement is in sonata-form. Vaughan Williams's interest in the contrapuntal practices found in sixteenth- and seventeenth-century polyphony is reflected in much of this movement. It opens with the brass playing the B motto, which is then repeated an octave higher by the woodwinds. An ostinatolike figure, played pizzicato by the cellos and basses, serves as an accompaniment to the first subject, played by the violins:

Example 124.

This theme and much of the movement is based on a scale devised by Vaughan Williams:

F G A B C Db Eb F. The oboe introduces the second subject, which is then contrapuntally imitated by a number of other instruments. The ostinato figure is finally added to the texture as the strings continue the imitation. The brass enter with the B motto, and musical activity subsides as the flute plays a cadential figure to end the exposition. An extensive development of both themes is climaxed with a return to the opening subject. The rather free recapitulation ends as the cadence figure in the flute leads to a quiet coda, *molto tranquillo,* in which the A motto is played by the trombones as the flute ends the movement with a cadenza-like passage.

Third Movement. The intervals of the fourth and fifth are very prominent in this movement. Their continuous use imparts a feeling of modality, intentionally reminiscent of early English music. Following a four-measure introduction that opens the scherzo, the A motto is played by the trumpets, is repeated in diminution by the woodwinds, and is then taken over by the strings as an accompaniment for the main scherzo theme. It is a forceful idea, based on the B motto and introduced by the bassoon:

Example 125.

This theme is developed at considerable length, alternating between humor and a violence seldom present in his works. The A motto returns, and it too is developed before a quiet return to the opening of the movement ends the scherzo section. The trio is in *fugato* style. With exaggerated humor, it opens with a theme based on rising fourths, an expansion of B, played by the tuba, bassoon, and contrabassoon unaccompanied. Successive imitations of this theme build to a climax before the return to the scherzo. The scherzo, now shortened considerably, ends with a long, quiet *legato* coda over a pedal G. The B motto is heard contrapuntally in the orchestra together with the first theme of the first movement. A sudden *crescendo* leads directly to the finale.

Fourth Movement.   The last movement of the symphony is subtitled "Finale with Fugal Epilogue." It opens aggressively, *Allegro molto,* featuring a broad theme that alternates with a marchlike rhythmic idea:

Example 126.

Example 126. Continued

The second subject is based on the same scale that was used in the second movement. After an extensive contrapuntal treatment, the second subject is transformed into a choralelike version played by the brass. The opening subject returns and it too is developed as the march rhythm gradually dissipates into a *Lento* interlude based on the closing subject of the first movement. With a resumption of the *Allegro molto,* the two mottoes are played quietly and mysteriously. A *crescendo* leads to the recapitulation, where the first subject, slightly varied rhythmically, is played while the march rhythm continues inexorably. The second subject is now more emphatic than at the beginning. The movement builds to a brilliant climax as if coming to the end, but instead, a remarkable summation of the work is introduced in the form of a fugal epilogue based on the A motto. The exposition of the fugue features the A motto stated with rhythmic variety throughout the orchestra, punctuated occasionally by appearances of the B motto. Both mottoes are then ingeniously combined with the various themes of the movement. A final climax is reached as the opening theme is stated by the bass instruments against the A motto in the upper instruments, and then the entire orchestra ends the movement with the principal subject of the first movement.

BENJAMIN BRITTEN

Benjamin Britten, undoubtedly the best-known and most distinguished English composer of his generation, also built an enviable reputation as a pianist, conductor, and founder of both the English Opera Group and the Aldeburgh Festival. Britten's considerable interest in the English folk-song and choral tradition and English baroque music, particularly that of Purcell, accounts in part for his predilection toward writing in short sectionalized forms such as the song cycle and variation form. These factors also help explain the fact that opera, another sectionalized form, became his preferred and most successful means of expression.

Benjamin Britten was born in Lowestoft, Suffolk, on St. Cecilia's Day. By the time he was sixteen he had written a symphony, six string quartets, ten piano sonatas, and over fifty songs. For the next four years he studied at the Royal College of Music in London, where he studied composition with John Ireland and piano with Arthur Benjamin. On leaving the College, Britten worked for four years at the G.P.O. Film Unit, writing scores for documentary films. It was during this time that he wrote

the first work to bring him international recognition, the *Variations on a Theme of Frank Bridge* (1937).

In 1939, shortly before the war began, Britten came to the United States to live. During the three years he remained in America, he wrote the *Sinfonia da Requiem* (1940), the Violin Concerto, the First String Quartet, and two song cycles, *Les Illuminations* (1939) in French and the *Seven Sonnets of Michelangelo* (1940) in Italian. As the war progressed, Britten felt that his proper place was in England. It was in 1942 while waiting for the opportunity to return to England that Britten met the conductor Serge Koussevitsky at a performance of his *Sinfonia da Requiem* by the Boston Symphony Orchestra. Their meeting led to his receiving a commission from Koussevitsky to write an opera. It took him three years to complete the work, *Peter Grimes*.

Britten returned to England with two choral scores he had written on the boat: *Ode to St. Cecilia* for unaccompanied voices and *Ceremony of Carols* for treble voices and harp. During the three years he spent completing *Peter Grimes* (1945), Britten also wrote the Serenade for Tenor, Horn, and Strings (1943), the String Quartet No. 2 (1945), commemorating the two hundred fiftieth anniversary of Purcell's death, and the *Young Person's Guide to the Orchestra* (1945), a cleverly designed set of variations and a fugue, based on a theme by Purcell, which was commissioned by the Ministry of Education in England for an educational film describing the various instruments of the orchestra.

Peter Grimes quickly established Britten's reputation throughout the musical world as an important musical dramatist, and reactivated an English operatic tradition that had lain dormant since Purcell. He followed this success by writing three chamber operas: *The Rape of Lucretia* (1946); *Albert Herring* (1947), his only comic opera; a new arrangement of the *Beggar's Opera* (1948); and an "entertainment for young people," *The Chimney Sweep* or *Let's Make an Opera* (1949). These works were followed by a full-scale opera in 1951, *Billy Budd*, based on Melville's story, in which Britten returned to the style of *Peter Grimes*. *Gloriana* (1953), closer to a masque than an opera, is based on the love between Elizabeth I and Essex, and was written for the coronation of Elizabeth II. He returned to the chamber opera concept with *The Turn of the Screw* (1954), a "musical ghost story" based on the Henry James novel.

A Midsummer Night's Dream (1960) is a happy score, the most successful of Britten's operas written after *Peter Grimes*. In it he captured all of the color and vitality of Shakespeare's comedy. Quite different are the three "Parables for Church Performance"—*Curlew River* (1964), *The Burning Fiery Furnace* (1966), and *The Prodigal Son* (1968)—written for the Orford church as part of the Aldeburgh Festivals. They were inspired by the traditions of the Japanese No-play, which Britten had seen on a visit to Tokyo in 1956. "Whereas in Tokyo the music was the ancient Japanese music, jealously preserved by successive generations, here I have started the work with that wonderful plainsong hymn 'Te lucis ante terminum,' and from it the whole piece may be said to have grown." The three Parables represent Hope, Faith, and Charity.

His last operas were the television opera *Owen Wingrave* (1971), a study in pacifism based on the Henry James story, and the very successful *Death in Venice* (1973) based on the novel by Thomas Mann.

Britten has proved that effective, original opera can still be written in a basically conservative, classical style. His means are substantially eclectic, derived from sources as diverse as Mahler and Berg, Purcell and Stravinsky. The result, however, is uniquely his own. It is sophisticated, elegant, and charged with great sensitivity for a lyricism that accommodates the natural inflection of the English language. "One of my chief aims is to try and restore to the musical setting of the English language a brilliance, freedom and vitality that have been curiously rare since the death of Purcell."

Following his writing the *Young Person's Guide to the Orchestra*, the only purely instrumental works Britten composed were for individual performers. The best of these are the cello works he wrote for the great Soviet virtuoso, Mstislav Rostropovitch: a sonata, two suites, and the Symphony for Cello and Orchestra (1963). The Symphony, a welcome addition to the limited contemporary literature for cello and orchestra, is classical in structure.

In general, Britten's most successful nonoperatic works have been those in which he has combined instruments with voices. These works include the Serenade; the *Spring Symphony* (1949) for soloists, chorus, and orchestra, which is actually a suite of songs with orchestral accompaniment, on the general topic of spring; and the moving *War Requiem* (1962), written for the dedication of the rebuilt Coventry Cathedral. It is based, with some embellishments, on the traditional oratorio structure and is Britten's personal stand against the "violence and tyranny of the twentieth century."

Britten: *PETER GRIMES*

In 1941 the Boston Symphony Orchestra under Serge Koussevitsky performed Britten's *Sinfonia da Requiem* (1940). Impressed with the dramatic quality of the work, Koussevitsky commissioned Britten to write an opera. The idea for the libretto came to Britten from a poem by George Crabbe entitled *The Borough*. The poem depicts life in the Borough, a little fishing village in Suffolk, during the early part of the nineteenth century. The central figure is a brutal, callous fisherman, Peter Grimes, who, because two of his maltreated apprentices have died, is isolated from society by the hatred of his neighbors. The subject appealed to Britten because he saw in it the potential for portraying an individual's struggle against an unreasoning society. The character of Peter was therefore changed by Britten's librettist, Montagu Slater, to a more sympathetic character, who, although actually innocent of any crime, is doomed by the vindictive fury of his fellow villagers. In creating the Borough as protagonist, Britten and Slater carefully delineated the opera's characters, giving special attention to their varied psychological conflicts.

Britten established a role for the orchestra in this opera similar to that created by Verdi for *Otello;* in each, it is used both to accompany the voices and to create a fatalistic atmosphere of impending disaster. Six descriptive orchestral interludes are used to connect the various scenes and acts of the opera by providing an appropriate atmosphere and musical commentary on the action. Four from among them have been formed into an effective suite for separate concert performance.

Prologue. The Prologue is set in Moot Hall, where a coroner's inquest is in progress. Peter is questioned about the death of his apprentice by the presiding officer, Swallow, a lawyer overly impressed with his own importance. The scene is illustrative of Britten's masterful capacity for setting narrative speech. It is in *secco* recitative accompanied by the orchestra. Peter tells about his last voyage and of his making a large catch. He goes on to explain that as he was heading for London, a storm blew his boat off course, and that his apprentice died when their supply of drinking water was exhausted:

Example 127.

Peter is absolved of guilt, but ugly suspicions by the villagers persist, so much so that he is requested not to take on another apprentice unless he finds a woman who can care for the boy. The village characters, including the lawyer, the overly officious bailiff Hobson, the gossipy Mrs. Sedley, and the widowed schoolmistress Ellen Orford, who loves Peter, are all portrayed with remarkable insight through Britten's music. The first interlude, "Dawn," descriptive of the gray atmosphere of the little fishing town, becomes the background for the opening music of the first scene.

Act I.   The opening scene of Act I takes place on a street faced by the Borough's Moot Hall, the Boar Inn, Keene's shop, and the church porch. The beach and the bleak seascape beyond form a backdrop for the action. The villagers move about their everyday work quietly singing the opening lines of Crabbe's poem. First the audience is introduced to Balstrode, a retired merchant skipper. Auntie, the landlady of the village pub and her two "nieces," and Ned Keene, "apothecary and quack," are then introduced into the scene. When Peter pulls his boat in to dock, the villagers refuse to help him; only Balstrode and Keene give him a hand. Keene informs Peter that he has found another boy at the workhouse who could serve as Peter's apprentice. The carter, Hobson, refuses to go after the boy but Ellen volunteers to bring him, and in a beautiful aria, she remonstrates with the villagers for their cruelty to Peter. The meter changes constantly to fit her speech patterns:

Example 128.

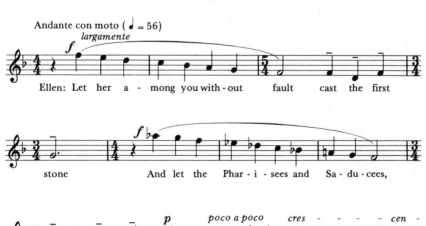

Example 128. Continued

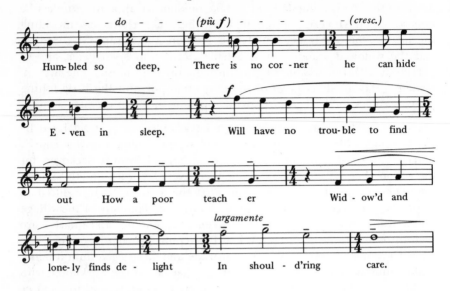

An approaching storm is announced, first by the orchestra, then by Balstrode, and the villagers (chorus and soloists) scurry about making everything secure as they sing a fast, agitated fugue. Seeking shelter in their homes and in the Boar, they leave Peter and Balstrode alone on the stage. Asked why he continues to stay in the village, Peter tells Balstrode that his roots are in the Borough and he could not even consider leaving. As the fury of the storm continues, he sorrowfully recalls the death of his apprentice. The characteristic leap of a ninth from this arioso is associated with Peter repeatedly throughout the opera:

Example 129.

Balstrode tells Peter to ask Ellen to marry him, but Peter says he does not want her pity; rather, he feels that he can ask her only when he has money and position. Balstrode goes into the inn and Peter, alone, dreams of the future in a continuation (half as fast) of the previous arioso:

186

Example 130.

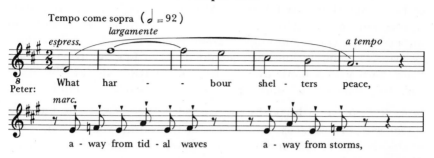

The second interlude, "The Storm," depicts the raging fury of the growing storm; trumpets in parallel fifths and trombones in biting seconds are furiously answered by the horns. Toward the end of the interlude, the broad singing phrase of the previous example is heard, but it is quickly swallowed by the storm music as the second scene begins.

The second scene takes place inside the Boar Inn. Each time the door is opened momentarily to admit more fisherman, the gale is heard in its full fury, and then just the rumble of the timpani is heard to remind one

Peter Grimes (Just after Grimes enters Boar Inn. Grimes—Jon Vickers)

187

of the storm outside. As the villagers drink and sing, the characteristics of Boles, the Methodist fisherman, Mrs. Sedley, the virtuous pill-taker, Auntie and her two frivolous "nieces," and Balstrode are carefully delineated. Peter enters and sings an arioso about the stars and their effect on man. Thinking he must be mad, the drunken Boles is about to quiet Peter down with a bottle over his head when Balstrode restrains Boles and asks someone to start up a song. A round, containing three tunes in $\frac{7}{4}$ meter, is begun by the villagers. Peter joins them, but consistent with his character, he does not fit in, and his voice is soon overwhelmed as the round continues in full force. The door opens once more, Ellen and Hobson enter bringing with them Peter's new apprentice, and Peter takes the boy out into the howling storm as he heads for home.

Synopsis of Acts II and III.   Ellen soon discovers that Peter is mistreating the boy. She tries to reason with him, but Peter, losing his temper, strikes her in frustration and rushes off with the boy. Having observed the scene, some of the village men indignantly go off in search of Peter. Back at his hut, Peter orders the terrified boy to don his boots and jersey and drag the nets to the boat. The boy slips on the cliff and falls to his death. In the final scene, Peter, half-crazed with despair, is urged by Balstrode to get in his boat, sail out to sea, and sink it.

Dawn comes to the Borough, and as the music of the first interlude is heard, the villagers, unaware of Peter's fate, gradually go about their day's work, quietly singing the concluding verses of Crabbe's poem. Life goes on, and the opera ends much as it began.

part III

OTHER EUROPEAN COMPOSERS

chapter 12

France

Albert Roussel (1869–1937)

Albert Roussel fell under the pervasive spell of impressionism in his early works, but by 1918 he was completely committed to neoclassicism and the large multimovement forms. As an officer in the French navy during his early twenties, he had made a number of trips to the Far East. He was so intrigued with his experience there that after he had completed his formal musical studies at the Schola Cantorum under Vincent d'Indy, he made an extended trip to the Orient and India. He drew from this experience in two works, the *Évocations* (1912) for orchestra, solo voices, and chorus, and his ballet-opera *Padmâvatî* (1918), based on an Indian legend. His most successful work at this time, however, was the concert suite taken from his ballet *Le Festin de l'araignée* (*The Spider's Feast;* 1912). By the time he wrote his Second Symphony (1921), he had arrived at a mature, personal style that was predominantly classical. His finest symphonic works of this period include Suite in F (1926), the Symphony No. 3 (1930), Sinfonietta for String Orchestra (1934), and the Symphony No. 4 (1935). In addition to these works, he also wrote a large amount of chamber music and two highly successful ballets, *Bacchus et Ariane* (1930) and *Aeneas* (1935).

Erik Satie (1866–1925)

In 1888 Erik Alfred Leslie Satie published the hauntingly beautiful *Gymnopédies* and the *Sarabandes,* the first works to reveal his genius. These were followed in 1890 by the three *Gnossiennes.* In these early piano works, the compositions through which he is best known to the public, Satie anticipated much of the harmonic language later adapted and developed by Debussy and Ravel. They create an atmosphere of simplicity and chasteness that was completely at variance with the pretentious, overblown romanticism of his time.

It was at this time that he became attached to the Rosicrucian Society. He was offered the post of official composer of the organization, and because he had been attracted to ritualistic music and mystic, pseudo-religious organizations for many years, he accepted gladly. For the Society, he wrote three Preludes for *Le Fils des étoiles* (*The Son of the Stars,* 1891), a play written by the High Priest of the Society, and the three *Sonneries de la Rose-Croix* (1892). In these works and in the *Gnossiennes,* he followed a highly unorthodox procedure for the time by dispensing with bar lines and key signatures. Moreover, in *Le Fils des étoiles* he explored the use of chords constructed in fourths. Much in this work evokes the spirit of Gregorian chant, whose remoteness and impersonality is noticeable in many of Satie's compositions.

As early as 1890, Satie began writing mysterious directions for the performer in his piano music. Though the comments he included in his earlier works were certainly unusual, they were intelligible and did bear some relation to the music. After 1908, however, his comments became more and more fanciful and bizarre, presenting a running commentary of purposeful nonsense. He gave many of these piano works fantastic titles, parodying the overly fanciful titles used by the impressionists. Pieces with the titles "Dessicated Embryos" (1913), "Flabby Preludes for a Dog" (1912), and "Sketches and Annoyances of a Wooden Man" (1913), for instance, also contain the following directions for the performer: "like a nightingale with a toothache," "with astonishment," "from the top of the teeth," "a little bloodily." His self-protective parody and nonsense (one critic called it "the method of protective irony"), however, are no more than superficial aspects of his music, and are unrelated to the content. These unpretentious but important piano pieces have an objectivity and basic seriousness that foreshadowed the neoclassicism of the twenties.

During the early years of World War I, Satie became friendly with a number of creative artists with whom he soon collaborated in writing the ballet *Parade* (1916). Diaghilev produced it, Cocteau wrote the book, décor and costumes were by Picasso, and Massine created the choreography. The music was performed by a conventional dance band aug-

Erik Satie

The Bettmann Archive.

mented by a number of highly unconventional noisemakers, including a typewriter and a steam whistle, which combined completely incongruous musical styles to create a musical mélange as cubist as the costumes and décor. The audience at its first performance in 1917 was scandalized, but the English critic David Drew wrote that the music of *Parade* was the equal of anything Debussy had written, and was superior to anything of Ravel's. While this was certainly an exaggeration, the work did inspire a manifesto by Jean Cocteau, *Le Coq et l'Arlequin* (*The Rooster and the Clown*) attacking Wagnerianism, impressionism, and Russian nationalism, as well as all romantic affectation. ". . . Satie teaches what, in our age, is the greatest audacity, simplicity." Cocteau's statements became the guiding aesthetic of a group of young composers in Paris who considered Satie their spiritual leader and Cocteau their spokesman. Dubbed affectionately by Satie as "Les Nouveaux Jeunes," they later became famous as "Les Six."

Satie's most important work, according to most critics, is *Socrate*, a "symphonic drama" written in 1918. It is a musical setting of three of Plato's dialogues, the last of which deals with the death of Socrates. It is scored for four sopranos accompanied by a small chamber orchestra. The music is calm and gentle, with a complete absence of any dramatic qualities. Paul Collaer, the French writer and critic, calls this the "masterpiece of its composer," a judgment with which other critics have concurred. However, the monotony of mood, rhythm, and melodic content have not endeared it to the public. The first-night audience hissed and tittered, and even present-day audiences may find it incomprehensible. It possesses a timelessness that makes it "contemporary" in any age. *Socrate's* importance lies in Satie's avowed denial of Wagnerianism, impressionism, and romanticism in its composition. It is a work of calm objectivity and economy of means, values that were to become more and more important as the century progressed.

Melody is always of primary importance in Satie's music; thematic lines are direct, simple, and vocal. Rhythmic structures and harmonizations are usually kept simple in order not to detract from the melody. In Satie's words, the rhythm "is peculiar because the melody is peculiar, 'singing' as only the piano 'sings', wandering over the twelve notes of the keyboard with little regard for scales, yet often suggesting various diatonic modes." Georges Auric, in his critique of *Parade,* writes of Satie's having anticipated styles and tastes with astonishing precision while ignoring the prevailing taste and style of his day. His influence on later composers was probably Satie's most important contribution to the music of the twentieth century. Debussy, Ravel, Poulenc, Virgil Thomson, and Stravinsky, have all readily acknowledged the debt they owed Satie.

"Les Six"

The "Les Six" designation was originated by the French critic Henri Collet in an article published in 1920 titled, "The Russian Five, the French Six, and Erik Satie." Actually, the group of six composers to

Les Six with Cocteau

The Bettmann Archive.

which he referred formed no "school" held together through common stylistic similarities; what they shared instead was their mutual friendship, their association with the writer Jean Cocteau and with Erik Satie, and in general, an irreverence for impressionism and romanticism. Among the six, Louis Durey (b. 1888) and Germaine Tailleferre (b. 1892) wrote very little, and Georges Auric (b. 1899) became known principally as a writer of movie scores. Darius Milhaud (1892–1974), Arthur Honegger (1892–1955), and Francis Poulenc (1899–1963), by contrast, became the leading French composers of the period between the two wars.

Darius Milhaud (1892–1974)

Darius Milhaud, one of the twentieth century's most prolific composers, has over four hundred works to his credit, representative of nearly every division of musical literature. By his own admission, his style is derived from Mediterranean lyricism. Just as characteristic, however, is his penchant for polytonality achieved both by combining melodies of different keys and by combining several planes of harmony in support of his basically diatonic melodies.

Following his studies at the Paris Conservatory, Milhaud accepted a position in 1917 as secretary to the French Ambassador to Brazil—his friend Paul Claudel—a gifted poet and dramatist as well as diplomat. During the two years he spent there, he collaborated with Claudel in writing the ballet *L'Homme et son désir (Man and His Desire;* 1918) and continued to work on the incidental music for Claudel's translation of the

Darius Milhaud

Music Division, The New York Public Library at Lincoln Center. Astor, Lenox and Tilden Foundations.

Orestes trilogy (1913–22), in which he successfully experimented with polytonal and metrical resources. He also expressed his delight with Brazilian music through his whimsical Cocteau ballet *Boeuf sur le toit* (*The Bull on the Roof;* 1919) and through two volumes of piano pieces, *Saudades do Brasil* (*Souvenirs of Brazil;* 1921).

When Milhaud visited the United States on a professional tour in 1922, he took the opportunity to spend many hours in Harlem, listening to the music of the Negro jazz bands. The experience was such a revelation to him that he stated, "I was resolved to use jazz for a chamber-music work." On his return to France the occasion soon presented itself and he wrote the jazz ballet *La Création du monde* (*The Creation of the World;* 1923). This work, like a number of other compositions Milhaud wrote for the stage, shows his considerable abilities to best advantage. Particularly notable among the sixteen operas, fifteen ballets, and incidental music for over fifty plays and films he wrote are the operas *Christophe Colomb* (1928), based on Claudel's libretto; *Les Malheurs d'Orphée* (*The Misfortunes of Orpheus;* 1924); and *Le Pauvre Matelot* (*The Poor Sailor;* 1926) on a libretto by Cocteau. Among his varied instrumental works, the charming lyric *Suite provençale* (1936) has achieved lasting popularity. During World War II, Milhaud taught composition in the United States at Mills College in California; then after 1947, he divided his teaching duties between Paris and the United States.

Milhaud: *LA CRÉATION DU MONDE (THE CREATION OF THE WORLD)*

When in 1923 Milhaud was asked to write a ballet to a scenario by Blaise Cendrars based on African folk legends about the creation of the world, he seized the opportunity to utilize the jazz idiom and instrumental combinations he had heard in Harlem the previous year. While comparisons may be drawn between this scenario and that of Stravinsky's *The Rite of Spring*, that is where all similarity between the two works ends. Fernand Léger's settings and costumes were childlike and stylized compared to Roerich's bizarre scenery and costumes for *The Rite*. The savage primitivism of Stravinsky's score called for an orchestra of over one hundred players; Milhaud's diminutive, elegant score calls for just seventeen players, an expansion of the jazz ensembles Milhaud had heard in Harlem. The instrumentation includes two flutes, oboe, two clarinets, bassoon, horn, two trumpets, trombone, piano, two violins, cello, bass, saxophone, and a large percussion section. It is interesting to note that it was not until a year after *The Creation of the World* was produced that George Gershwin also successfully transferred the jazz idiom to the concert stage in his *Rhapsody in Blue.*

Milhaud's score includes an overture and five sections played without pause; all are easily marked by their contrasting tempos. Section I depicts the three giant African deities of creation—Nzamé, Mébère, and N'Kwa— moving about the darkened stage casting spells over an amorphous mass of bodies. In Section II, the darkness lifts, the mass begins to move, and slowly the birds, beasts, insects, plants, and trees of creation take form. In Section III each in turn takes a place in a dance circle about the deities. Finally, two more bodies gradually emerge from the central mass. Man and Woman (Sékoumé and Mbongwé) stand gazing at each other. In Section IV the pair dances the primal Dance of Desire while the remaining figures in the mass disentangle themselves and join the growing frenzy of the dance. The excitement subsides in the final section, and all but Man and Woman gradually leave the stage. They embrace in a lasting kiss.

The overture begins with a pensive lyric blues theme played by the saxophone against an ostinato figure in the piano and strings. The saxophone solo, which continues throughout the overture, is in the key of D minor, but the accompanying figures and the interjections by the trumpets in syncopated rhythm are often in D major and a number of other keys. Section I is a jazz fugue whose theme first appears in the double bass accompanied by the piano and a percussion group:

Example 131.

Examples 131–133: Used by permission of Associated Music Publishers.

This theme is played successively by the trombone, saxophone, and trumpet, and then gradually a *fortississimo (fff)* climax is reached as the theme is developed by the entire ensemble. A sudden *pianissimo* with descending scales in the woodwinds leads to Section II. Its quiet opening features the flute playing the saxophone theme of the overture while the violins play the ostinato figure and the cello states the fugue theme in augmentation. A new blues theme, played by the oboe, vaguely reminiscent of the fugue theme, sounds almost as if it had been written by Gershwin:

Example 132.

As the theme is repeated, the tempo increases, and the section ends with a flutter-tongue passage by the flute. Section III, the dance of the plants and animals, is a lively cakewalk which features a jaunty tune in the violins (a) that alternates with a syncopated figure (b) first introduced by the bassoon:

Example 133.

The music reaches a frenetic *fortissimo* climax, there is a sudden *pianississimo* (*ppp*), and the dance theme, played by the flutes with the blues theme of the second dance in the violins, is used to depict Man and Woman as they emerge from the mass of plants and animals. Section IV is the most completely jazz-oriented part of the work. The clarinet plays in an improvisatory style accompanied by an ostinato-like rhythmic figure in the strings, piano, and percussion. The oboe then enters with the blues theme of the introduction. The music increases in intensity, gradually rising to a *fortississimo* (*fff*) climax, with the clarinet, trumpet, and saxophone indulging in improvisatory style "breaks" over typical jazz chord progressions. The final dance, gently reminiscent in mood and material, recalls the "Gershwin" theme of the second dance and the theme of the introduction and its characteristic accompaniment. The ballet ends with the flute, clarinet, and trumpet softly flutter-tonguing as they approach the blues cadence.

Arthur Honegger (1892–1955)

Although Arthur Honegger was a member of "Les Six," he never held much in common with their objectives. His parents were Swiss; his early musical training was Germanic. In fact, it was not until he was twenty-one that he entered the Paris Conservatory. Though he readily admitted that he owed to France his intellectual awakening and his musical affinity, his debt to German musical tradition was apparent in his preference for the large Germanic architectural forms that he combined with a rich chromatic style and polyphonic texture. International fame came to him early through the sensational success of his dramatic oratorio *King David* (1921) and through his glorification of the locomotive in the tone poem, *Pacific 231* (1923). Among his dramatic works, two others, *Judith* (1926) and *Jeanne d'Arc au bûcher* (*Joan of Arc at the Stake;* 1935), have been particularly successful. Three among his instrumental works—the *Pastorale d'été* (*Summer Pastorale;* 1920), the *Concertino* for piano and orchestra (1924), and the last of his five symphonies—are still performed with some frequency. While Honegger was in sympathy with many of the ideals and the musical vocabulary of the nineteenth century, he did not hesitate to use contemporary developments when they were well-suited to his purposes. His characteristic lyricism is given a new dimension through infusions of polytonality, quartal harmony, dissonant counterpoint, and driving, complex rhythms.

Francis Poulenc (1899–1963)

Francis Poulenc remained faithful to the original principles of "Les Six" longer than any of the others. His early works in particular are witty, gay, and often outrageous in their use of comic songs and popular music-hall instrumental combinations and tunes. Some of this flippancy can also be found in a number of his later works, but this is not necessarily the dominant side of Poulenc. A contrasting style is exemplified in *Le Bestiaire* (*The Zoo;* 1919), an early song cycle for mezzo-soprano, string quartet, flute, clarinet, and bassoon, which possesses a melodic freshness and sensitivity that we regularly come to expect in the mature Poulenc. Among his instrumental works, the Concerto for two pianos (1932) and the Concerto for organ, strings, and percussion (1938) are particularly attractive. Much of his more serious nature, however, is revealed in his vocal works. Supple lyricism and sensitive phrase structures permeate his more than one hundred and fifty songs, numerous choral works, and operas. His major religious works for chorus include the *Litanies à la Vièrge Noire de Rocomadour (Litanies to the Black Virgin of Rocomadour;* 1936); Mass in G (1937); *Stabat Mater* (1951); and the *Gloria* (1961). In 1957, his serious opera *Les Dialogues des Carmélites (Dialogues of the Carmelites;* 1953–55) was produced at La Scala in Milan. This superb opera is probably his most important work.

Olivier Messiaen (b. 1908)

While Messiaen's importance to twentieth-century music is widely recognized through his exploration of new serialization parameters and as a teacher; his considerable contribution as a composer has been relatively ignored.

It has been through his innovative concepts of rhythm, inspired in part by Hindu rhythmic structures, that Messiaen has made his most original contribution to Western musical language. He carefully avoids the occurrence of a background meter; constructing instead, a rhythmic organization based on irregular multiples of small basic units of duration such as the sixteenth note. He frequently sets up such patterns as a rhythmic ostinato, at times in emulation of the medieval isorhythmic motet, by having a melodic *color* and a rhythmic *talea* each with a different number of units, thereby creating a constantly shifting alignment of the two when they are repeated.

In addition, he has utilized a number of synthetic scales (modes) of varied repetitive conjunct patterns of whole and half steps (e.g., 1, ½, ½; 1, 1, ½, ½; ½, 1) providing him with a varied melodic and harmonic alternative to the traditional scales. The harmonic implications, both polytonal and diatonic, of these scales are explored in his works largely for their coloristic value, frequently as repeated chords or as parallel chords to accompany his expressive melodies.

The major impetus in Messiaen's career has been his religious faith. "The first idea that I wished to express, the most important because it is placed above all else, is the existence of the truths of the Catholic faith. . . . This is the main aspect of my work, the most noble, without doubt the most useful, the most valid . . . the only one perhaps that I will not regret at the hour of my death." Nearly everything that he has written is directly associated with this belief. *Trois Petites Liturgies de la Présence Divine (Three Short Liturgies of the Divine Presence;* 1944) for orchestra; *Et exspecto resurrectionem mortuorum (And I expect the Resurrection of the Dead;* 1964) for brass, woodwinds, and percussion; and *La Trans-figuration de Notre Seigneur Jésus-Christ (The Transfiguration of Our Father Jesus Christ;* 1965–69) for piano, cello, flute, clarinet, xylorimba, vibraphone, marimba, chorus, and orchestra are representative works illustrative of the unique musical language he has utilized to symbolize these dogmas. Even the ten movement *Turangalîla-symphonie* (1948) represents one of the three aspects of divine love (love of God, nature, and human love) as defined by Messiaen in its subject matter, the love of Tristan and Isolda.

Regarding love of nature, Messiaen has said, "the home of music . . . the true forgotten face of music . . . is somewhere in the woods, in the fields, in the mountains, by the sea, among the birds. . . . I doubt that one can find in any human music, however inspired, melodies and rhythms that have the sovereign freedom of bird song." *Oiseaux exotiques (Exotic Birds;* 1956) for piano, winds, and percussion; and *Catalogue d'oiseaux (Catalogue of Birds;* 1956–58) for piano intimately reflect his philosophy.

His contributions to the literature for keyboard, particularly the organ, have been extensive and of unique importance in twentieth-century music. Like his other works, nearly all have a religious basis. His *Vingt Regards sur l'Enfant Jésus (Twenty Gazes on the Infant Jesus;* 1944) for piano; and *Apparition de l'Eglise éternelle (Apparition of the Eternal Church;* 1931), *L'Ascension (The Ascension;* 1934), and *La Nativité du Seigneur (The Nativity of the Lord,* 1935) for organ are among the best known. His role of influence in stimulating the new generation of composers following World War II is discussed in Chapter 23.

chapter 13

Other Countries

ITALY

Italian composers had almost completely neglected instrumental writing during the nineteenth century—opera reigned supreme, and the heritage of the Italian seventeenth- and eighteenth-century masters lay dormant. Ottorino Respighi, already discussed in the chapter on impressionism, was the first twentieth-century Italian to reexplore the possibilities of instrumental music; however, he was too steeped in the traditions of Richard Strauss and Debussy to create a truly contemporary expression. Alfredo Casella (1883–1947), Ildebrando Pizzetti (1880–1968), and Gian Francesco Malipiero (1882–1973), on the other hand, were more successful in establishing a base upon which other twentieth-century Italian composers could build.

Luigi Dallapiccola (1904–75)

Luigi Dallapiccola combined the twelve-tone style of the Viennese expressionists with the gentle Mediterranean elegance of his native Italy to create a personal style that is both dramatic and lyric, atonal but with tonal implications, and possessed of genuine emotional feeling but without the angularity and depressing sentiments of the Viennese. His early works are tonal, and many recall the seventeenth-century Italian instru-

202

Luigi Dallapiccola

mental forms. His assimilation of serialism as a part of his personal expression was a long process that began when he was first introduced to the works of Berg and Webern while he was a student. A turning point in the development of Dallapiccola's mature style is evident in his opera *Volo di notte* (*Night Flight;* 1940), based on the story by Antoine de Saint-Exupéry. Twelve-tone and diatonic passages intermingle as varied means in depicting the ideas expressed in the story. The *Canti di prigionia* (*Songs of Imprisonment;* 1938–41) for chorus and percussion orchestra, with texts by three famous prisoners—Mary Stuart, Boethius, and Savonarola—is a highly sensitive work of great power that utilizes the twelve-tone system more consistently than *Volo di notte*. His opera *Il prigioniero* (*The Prisoner;* 1944–48) is totally committed to strict dodecaphonic procedure, and yet the contrapuntal texture and the fluid expressive vocal line reveal a musical language closer to the old Italian polyphonic style than to that of the Viennese expressionists. His other important works include the *Liriche greche* (*Greek Lyrics;* 1942–45) for soprano and orchestra; the ballet *Marsia* (1942–43), one of his few purely orchestral works; *Job* (1950), a mystery play; the *Canti di liberazione* (*Songs of Liberation;* 1955) for chorus and orchestra; and *Preghiere* (*Prayers;* 1962), three songs for bass-baritone and chamber orchestra.

Dallapiccola: *CINQUE FRAMMENTI DI SAFFO (FIVE
FRAGMENTS OF SAPPHO)*

Five Fragments of Sappho (1942) was written as the first of three song
cycles known later as the *Liriche greche*. In the words of the composer,
they "not only constitute my first step on the way to dodecaphony, but—
having been written during the period in which I completed the libretto
for *Il prigioniero* and began to write the music for it—they demonstrate
that, if one side of my personality demanded tragedy, the other attempted
an escape toward serenity." *Fragments* is scored for soprano and a chamber orchestra consisting of flute, piccolo, oboe, E-flat clarinet, B-flat
clarinet, bass clarinet, bassoon, horn, trumpet, harp, celesta, and piano,
and one each of the four string instruments. The luminous, sunlit world
of ancient Greece is cleverly depicted through Dallapiccola's quasi-
impressionistic use of the twelve-tone technique and his imaginative use
of the instrumental ensemble. The vocal line is completely singable and
expressive without the jagged, neurotic leaps found in the vocal writing
of the Viennese expressionists Schoenberg and Webern. The orchestral
background is quietly moving, never obtrusive, and makes much use of
parallel fifths and constantly shifting rhythms.

I. Translation: Evensong, you bring back all that the bright dawn scatters:
You bring back the sheep, you bring back the goat,
You bring back the child to its mother.

The first fragment is based on a single row that the voice sings in all
four versions, first with the original row (O), then in retrograde (R), next
in retrograde inversion (RI), and finally in the inversion of the row (I):

Example 134.

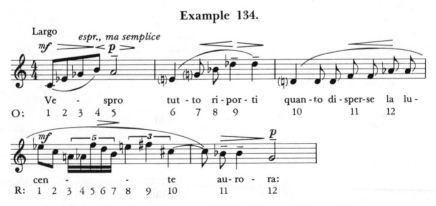

Examples 134–136: Used by permission of Edizioni Suvini Zerboni, Milan.

204

The flute begins an imitation of the voice at the distance of half a measure and the imitation is continued throughout by various woodwind instruments while the rest of the instruments provide a constantly shifting background based on motives from the tone row. The interval of a fifth assumes considerable importance throughout this entire fragment. The final chord, as an example, is made up of five superimposed fifths.

II. Translation: O my Gongyla, I pray you:
Put on your whitest tunic and come before me:
I wish you always to be beautiful in your clothes.
Thus adorned, you make those who look at you tremble;
And I am happy this is so, because your beauty
reproaches Aphrodite.

Dallapiccola has crowded an astonishingly large number of twelve-tone combinations into this delightful, quiet song. Three rows are identified with the voice part, and at least seventeen more appear in the quasi-canonic instrumental accompaniment:

III. Translation: Gentle Adonis is dead, O Cytherea:
And what shall we do?
Beat your breasts for a long time, maidens, and
rend your clothes.

In keeping with the words of the text, this song is very slow and mournful. The woodwinds quietly introduce the first tone row as the strings provide a background in harmonics. The voice enters with a new tone-row, and then continues with the opening row. The two rows then appear in retrograde, and a climax occurs on the last three words of the poem. The song ends as it began, with the woodwinds quietly repeating the opening row. The opening phrases of this song illustrate the expressive lyric quality so closely associated with Dallapiccola's distinctive use of the twelve-tone system:

Example 135.

Example 135. Continued

re - a: e no - i, e no - i che fa - re - mo? "

IV. Translation: The moon shone full when they stopped close to the altar:
And the Cretan women in harmony, began on light feet,
To circle around on the tender, newly-risen grass.

The mood remains tranquil, but the pace is faster than in the previous song. The voice part intones the text in a calm recitative style while
the instruments play an accompaniment, utilizing at least twenty different
twelve-tone combinations.

V. Translation: For a long time I spoke with Aphrodite in a dream.

The final song is the most highly organized in the cycle. It opens with
the strings and harp playing a tone row that they immediately repeat in
retrograde. The voice enters with a new row, which it too immediately
reverses as the strings repeat their row in its original form. The strings'
tone row is now shared by the harp, celesta, and piccolo, while the other
row is performed first by the horn and voice and then by the oboe. The
opening tone row is now played by the strings and then by the harp in
retrograde as the sound fades into silence. The opening phrase of the
voice part, heard each time this row appears, is typically Italianate in its
expressive lyricism:

Example 136.

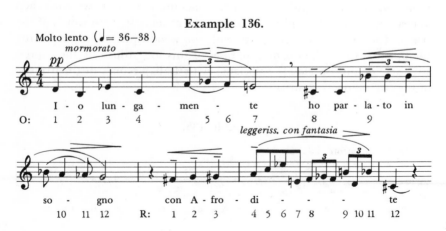

Molto lento ($\quad= 36–38$)
mormorato
pp

I - o lun - ga - men - te ho par - la - to in
O: 1 2 3 4 5 6 7 8 9

leggeriss. con fantasia

so - gno con A - fro - di - - - te
10 11 12 R: 1 2 3 4 5 6 7 8 9 10 11 12

SPAIN

Manuel de Falla (1876–1946)

The nationalist musical awakening in Spain at the turn of the century first manifested itself in a recognition of the importance of authentic folk music based on the modes and traditional Spanish rhythms, and in a renewal of interest in the sixteenth-century Spanish composers, Cabezón, Morales, and Victoria. Principal credit for this movement goes to Felipe Pedrell (1841–1922), who as a professor at the Conservatory in Madrid influenced a large number of composers, including Manuel de Falla, Spain's foremost composer of this century. Falla's first recognition as a composer came as a result of his winning first prize in a national competition with his opera *La Vida breve* (*Life is Short;* 1905). He spent the next seven years in Paris, where he became friendly with Debussy, Dukas, Ravel, Fauré, Satie, and Roussel. Dukas promoted a production of the as yet unperformed opera, *La Vida breve,* and in 1913 it was successfully produced in Nice and Paris. These performances and the subsequent introduction of the opera to Madrid audiences soon established Falla as an important twentieth-century composer. With the outbreak of war in 1914, Falla returned to Spain, where he wrote the two ballets that es-

Manuel de Falla

Music Division, The New York Public Library at Lincoln Center. Astor, Lenox and Tilden Foundations.

tablished his worldwide reputation, *El Amor brujo (Love, the Magician;* 1915) and *El Sombrero de tres picos (The Three-Cornered Hat;* 1919). Both ballets exploit Andalusian folk idioms: the first contains a vocal part filled with the ardor and rhythm of the gypsies, and the second depicts the life and humor of the peasants. Orchestral suites extracted from these ballets have become part of the standard orchestral repertoire. The "Ritual Fire Dance," in particular, from *El Amor brujo* has become one of the most popular pieces of twentieth-century music. Although Falla lived to be seventy years old, his output was very small, a consequence of the very high standards he set for himself.

Falla: *EL SOMBRERO DE TRES PICOS (THE THREE-CORNERED HAT)*

Music for the *Three-Cornered Hat* was first performed in Madrid in 1917 as background music to a pantomime based on a novel by Pedro Antonio de Alarcón. When Serge Diaghilev, the impresario of the Ballet Russe, heard it, he commissioned Falla to extend the work and enlarge the score for a full-scale ballet. Falla willingly obliged, and the first performance of the ballet took place in London in 1919. The brilliance and remarkable originality of the music, imaginative décor (scenery and costumes by Picasso), and choreography by Léonide Massine combined to make this a memorable première. The music is filled with wild passion, exotic beauty, and propulsive rhythms inspired by traditional folk dances including the *farruca, fandango, zapateado,* and *jota.*

The ballet is based on a centuries-old story made familiar through its many versions since the time of Chaucer. Alarcón's version of the tale, previously used by Hugo Wolf in his opera *Der Corregidor,* concerns a miller, his pretty wife, and the Corregidor, the governor of the province, whose symbol of office is his gold-laced, three-cornered hat. The Corregidor, fascinated by the miller's flirtatious wife, orders the miller arrested so that the way might be clear for a little affair. Now pursued by the amorous Corregidor, the miller's wife nimbly avoids his advances, and in the process the clumsy man tumbles into the millstream. Becoming a little frightened at what she has done, she runs off, and the Corregidor philosophically removes his clothes, and while waiting for them to dry, goes to sleep in the miller's bed. The miller returns unexpectedly and finds the Corregidor in this compromising situation. He dons the Corregidor's clothes and then scratches a message on the wall stating that the Corregidor's wife is no less desirable than his own. When the Corregidor awakens, he has no alternative other than to put on the miller's clothes if he is to rescue his own wife. Obviously outwitted by the miller, the

Corregidor is unmercifully ridiculed by the villagers. Finally he escapes, and there is a general dance to celebrate the miller's triumph.

Three dances from Part II of the ballet are often heard in concert version: the "Neighbor's Dance," the "Miller's Dance," and the "Final Dance."

"The Neighbor's Dance." The main theme is heard immediately, quietly played by the violins:

Example 137.

Examples 137–140: Used by permission of the copyright holders J & W Chester, Ltd.

An interesting shift in rhythm is effected as Falla changes the meter from $\frac{3}{4}$ to $\frac{3}{8}$. Between various appearances of the theme, the orchestra simulates the strumming of a guitar. The orchestral texture, reminiscent of Ravel, is remarkable for its exotic color and nationalistic elements.

"The Miller's Dance." The second dance is a *farruca*, introduced with a horn call followed by a cadenza played by the English horn. There are two principal ideas in this piece, the Andalusian rhythm of the farruca, and a Moorish melody. The rhythmic idea, heard immediately following the cadenza, suggests vigorous foot stamping:

Example 138.

A hauntingly beautiful melody, played by the oboe accompanied by *sostenuto* strings and harp, follows immediately:

Example 139.

Example 139. Continued

cresc. - ***f***

The rhythmic idea returns, a guitarlike passage is added to it, and a significant climax is reached before the sound subsides. A gradual *accelerando* and *crescendo* then build to a whirlwind finish.

"*Final Dance.*" A short introduction leads directly to a rousing *jota*, played by the violins and woodwinds, accompanied by a steady eighth-note rhythm from the brass, timpani, and low strings:

Example 140.

Interludes descriptive of the Spanish countryside separate the numerous appearances of the jota with splashes of brilliant colors and throbbing rhythms that at times seem to approach the primitivism of Bartók and Stravinsky. There is a profusion of short melodic phrases and rhythmic ideas that appear momentarily and then vanish. One interlude, featuring a lyric phrase in the violins imitated canonically by the horns, reaches a passionate climax before giving way to a more playful idea that leads back to the original jota. After the last appearance of the jota, the meter changes to $\frac{2}{4}$ as the music becomes wilder in its abandonment, bringing the ballet to a brilliant, exhilarating close.

SWITZERLAND

Adjacent to France and Germany, both in the forefront of contemporary music, Switzerland has remained largely conservative, only modestly affected by the trends of the past decades. Two Swiss composers,

Ernest Bloch and Frank Martin, reached beyond the inhibitive musical influences of their country and found their own identities in relation to the larger contemporary scene of Europe.

Ernest Bloch (1880–1959)

Bloch first came to the attention of the general public through a performance of his opera *Macbeth* in Paris in 1910. The work won him many ardent champions, including a number of critics who consider it one of the great operas of this century. It was about this time that he began to give conscious recognition to his Hebraic spiritual inheritance by composing music that reflected the spirit of the melismatic cantillation of the synagogue. The rhapsodic, intense "Hebraic" expression of this music is unique with Bloch, and constitutes its most outstanding characteristic. This spirit is directly reflected in a number of impressive works, including *Trois Poèmes Juifs* (1913); *Schelomo,* a Hebrew rhapsody for cello and orchestra (1915–16); the *Israel Symphony* (1912–16); *Baal Shem: Three Pictures of Chassidic Life* (1923) for violin and piano; the *Sacred Service* (1933) for baritone, chorus, and orchestra; and *Pièces hebraïques* (1951). His other principal works retain elements of this rhapsodic quality, but within the discipline of neoclassic formal construction. Several must be counted among the significant works of the first quarter of

Ernest Bloch

Music Division, The New York Public Library at Lincoln
Center. Astor, Lenox and Tilden Foundations.

this century: the Sonata for Violin and Piano No. 1 (1920); the Quintet for Piano and Strings (1923); and the Concerto Grosso No. 1 (1925). Toward the end of his life, Bloch experimented successfully with twelve-tone technique in his Concerto Grosso No. 2 (1952) and the *Sinfonia Breve* (1954). From 1916 on, Ernest Bloch spent most of his life in the United States. As a gifted teacher in his adopted country, he taught a number of significant American composers, including Douglas Moore, Roger Sessions, Randall Thompson, George Antheil, and Quincy Porter.

Bloch: *SCHELOMO (SOLOMON)*

The subject for Bloch's "Hebraic Rhapsody," written for the cellist Alexander Barjansky, was initially inspired by a figurine of Solomon created by the cellist's wife. Solomon is shown in the figurine as "weary of life, weary of riches, weary of power." Bloch re-creates the king with music that is in turn dramatic, rhapsodic, declamatory, and reverent. Many of the stylistic elements in this work show a strong impressionistic influence, particularly in the brooding, introspective passages.

Many of the melodic motives that appear throughout the three sections of the rhapsody are first introduced in the cantillation of the introduction. Bloch further unifies the work by closing each of the three sections with the opening phrases of the cadenza that ends the introduction:

Example 141.

Examples 141–145: Copyright © 1918, 1945 by G. Schirmer, Inc. Used by permission.

The first section opens with a dotted-note theme, played by the violas, which is punctuated by the harps and celesta:

Example 142.

The cello comments, and then the theme is repeated quietly by the brass and oboes. The cello now enters with a long monologue that features a sharply rhythmic phrase. The brass and oboes again repeat the theme, this time more insistently, before diminishing for the next entrance of the solo cello. The mood is rhapsodic as the dotted-note figure is developed. The second principal theme of the first section is passionately intense, characterized in part by the Hebraic sound of the augmented second:

Example 143.

The cello continues this theme, the brass again repeat the first theme, and then the entire orchestra sweeps to an excited climax as the violins sing out the second theme. There is a *decrescendo,* and soon the first section closes with the solo cello playing the cadenza of the introduction.

The second section opens with a theme based on a traditional Hebrew melody that is imitative of the sound of the *shofar* (ram's horn). The bassoon announces the characteristic rhythmic figure, and then the entire melody is played by the oboe:

Example 144.

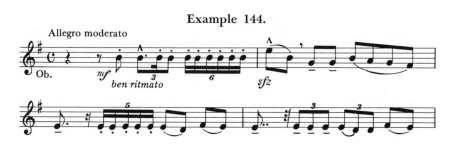

213

Example 144. Continued

The solo cello repeats this theme and then reflects upon a number of motives from the introduction while the opening rhythmic figure of this section is repeated as an orchestral background. Gradually, a climax is reached as the brass declaim the theme of this section against the dotted-note figure from the first section. At the height of the climax, the orchestra sounds the opening notes of the cello cadenza, and the sound fades.

The third section opens very quietly with the timpani playing the opening of the shofar theme while the solo cello enters with a new, meditative melody:

Example 145.

The cello reintroduces the second theme of the first section as a gentle soliloquy. The orchestra then plays the new theme, very quietly and in a very high register as the cello continues. The various themes and motives of the first section return, and the section slowly builds in intensity. An emotional climax is reached when the strings dramatically play the second theme of the first section. A short coda ends the work with the cello playing the theme of the opening cadenza, now sadly and disillusioned, as if saying, "Vanity, vanity, all is vanity."

Frank Martin (1890–1974)

Unlike Ernest Bloch, Frank Martin spent most of his life in his native country. Beginning in 1928, he was for many years director of the Jaques-Dalcroze Institute, and he was also the founder and director of the Technicum Moderne de Musique. Recognition, other than in his own country, came late for him; it was, in fact, 1945 when his *Petite Symphonie Concertante* for harp, harpsichord, piano, and double string orchestra focused international attention on his works.

Martin's style underwent frequent changes during his long creative career. His early works were traditional, strongly influenced by Fauré and by impressionism. His later interest in ancient and Eastern rhythms during the 1920s is reflected in a number of works, including *Rhythmes* (1926) for orchestra. In 1932 he began to experiment with twelve-tone techniques and for a short period of time composed in strict style. Searching for a personalized expression within the Schoenberg influence, he began to combine twelve-tone techniques with tonal harmonic and melodic elements. It is principally this means that we associate with his mature style, a style that makes use of harmonically related progressions, sequential sections, pedal bass, and diatonic elements. The oratorios *Golgotha* (1945–48) and *La Mystère de la nativité* (1960), the Violin Concerto (1951), and the Concerto for harpsichord and small orchestra (1952) are among his more important mature works.

ENGLAND

The nationalist movement, led by Vaughan Williams, effectively severed the inhibitive bonds of German and Italian musical dominance in England. The way was now open for the next generation of English composers to pursue their individual paths with freedom and assurance. The most important among them, in addition to Benjamin Britten, are William Walton and Michael Tippett, both of whom have produced music of major international importance.

William Walton (b. 1902)

William Walton first came to prominence when he was just twenty with his *Façade,* a delightfully fascinating setting of a series of poems by his friend Edith Sitwell. Walton set her poetry as a rhythmic recitation accompanied by a jazzlike chamber ensemble, perfectly complementing the varied moods of the verses. After a rather brief period of experimentation with the classicism of the twenties, he became an important advocate of neoromanticism. His most successful works are the Viola Concerto

(1929), the oratorio *Belshazzar's Feast* (1931), the First Symphony (1934), the Violin Concerto (1939), and the music he wrote for the films *Major Barbara* (1941), *Henry V* (1944), and *Hamlet* (1947). The success of his opera *Troilus and Cressida* (1954) is centered principally in England. His harmonic style, based upon twelve tones around a center, owes much to the influence of Hindemith. His style is further characterized by fluent lyricism, rhythmic vitality, and great sensitivity in the use of larger forms.

Michael Tippett (b. 1905)

Michael Tippett's importance in the contemporary scene must be measured in terms of both his distinguished compositions and his influential role as an educator. The present generation of young composers and the English public in general owe much to him. His earlier works, including the *Fantasy Sonata* for piano (1938), the Concerto for double string orchestra (1939), and the oratorio *A Child of Our Time* (1941) are all readily accessible from the listener's standpoint. This oratorio is a telling indictment of war, poignantly underlined in the choral sections through the use of spirituals. His mature output, centered largely in the abstract forms, is meticulously structured, rhythmically and contrapuntally complex, and may be generally characterized as having a penetrating, sincere inner expressiveness; outward emotional display generally finds little place in his later compositions. Typical works of this period include

Michael Tippett

four symphonies (1945, 1958, 1972, 1977), the Piano Concerto (1956), the Concerto for Orchestra (1963), and the operas *King Priam* (1962), *The Knot Garden* (1970), and *The Ice Break* (1977).

Other British Composers

A number of composers younger than Britten recently have achieved considerable importance. Wilfrid Mellers (b. 1914), Anthony Milner (b. 1925), and Kenneth Leighton (b. 1929) are among those who have made significant contributions by following established twentieth-century traditions. Others, including Alexander Goehr (b. 1932), Peter Maxwell Davies (b. 1934), and John Tavener (b. 1944), are representative of a vigorous new progressive element in English composition.

GREECE

Nikos Skalkottas (1904–49)

The significance of the Greek composer Nikos Skalkottas to the development of twentieth-century music went largely unnoticed during his lifetime. Schoenberg, his teacher, thought very highly of his work and publicly declared Skalkottas to be his most gifted pupil after Berg and Webern. Following an extended period of study in Germany, Skalkottas returned to Greece and remained there for the rest of his life, playing violin in both the State and Opera orchestras. There he led a lonely, withdrawn life, isolated from contemporary musical trends, and yet he composed continuously. His output was prodigious—he wrote twelve symphonies, fifteen concertos, over fifty chamber works, and a large body of choral and vocal music. At his death, none of these had been published, and only a few had been performed.

Because of his relative isolation, Skalkottas's style developed in a highly personal and original manner. In his constant attempts to synthesize the old and the new, he integrated the Schoenberg method with a number of his own modifications. For instance, when writing in a strictly contrapuntal style, he used as many as four tone rows simultaneously. Furthermore, he always used the row in its original form and pitch, never in retrograde, inversion, or transpositions of the row. As a consequence, the row and its development are quite easily followed throughout a composition. Like Dallapiccola, his melodies are drawn out, singable, and yet remain serial music. His individual modifications of the serial technique also greatly facilitated his use of traditional classic forms. During recent years, his music has begun to be published, and performances of his works have been more frequent. As a consequence, he is gradually becoming recognized as one of the powerful musical voices of this century.

CZECHOSLOVAKIA

Bohuslav Martinu (1890–1959)

Janáček's successor, Bohuslav Martinu, is the most frequently performed Czech composer of this century. He lived most of his adult life outside his native country, and though the years he spent in Paris and the United States surely left their imprint upon his works, he never lost his musical affinity for the Czech national folk heritage. The neoclassic tendencies of his romantic-tinged expressive idiom were formed largely as a consequence of his studies with Roussel. Martinu's harmonic practice, while complex at times, is basically traditional and his formal structures are classic. His large output includes ten operas, ten ballets, six symphonies, and a considerable amount of choral and chamber music.

HOLLAND

Willem Pijper (1894–1947)

Holland's most significant twentieth-century composer, Willem Pijper, developed a theory of composition that he called the *Keimzelle* (germ cell) theory. According to this theory, which he ultimately applied to all of his writing, an entire composition could be derived from a small melodic-harmonic unit. Complex contrapuntal structures, polytonal and polyrhythmic techniques, and a substantial classical orientation also characterize his works. As editor of *De Muziek*, Holland's leading musical journal, he exerted a strong influence on Dutch musical thought, and as the head of the Rotterdam Conservatory, he trained a generation of Dutch composers. His Third Symphony (1926) is among his most successful works. Two large a cappella choral works based on old Dutch ballads, *Heer Halewijn* (1920) and *Heer Danielken* (1925), are favorites in Holland.

HUNGARY

Zoltán Kodály (1882–1967)

In addition to Béla Bartók, Hungary produced one other composer of international renown during the twentieth century—Zoltán Kodály. He and Bartók were classmates at the Royal Academy of Music in Budapest, and they later collaborated in research on folk music. While Bartók left Hungary and integrated the Hungarian folk idiom with advanced European musical thought, Kodály remained in Hungary and pursued a

Zoltán Kodály

basically conservative stylistic path. He continued his folk music research, and joined the faculty of the Academy of Music, where he continued to teach during most of his career. Because of his preoccupation with nationalistic folk elements, his style is more tonally oriented than Bartók's, and it possesses a far greater melodic orientation. Choral works and songs dominate an output in which his greatest success was the *Psalmus Hungaricus* (1923) for tenor solo, chorus, and orchestra. An orchestral suite extracted from his opera *Háry János* (1926), the *Galanta Dances* (1934), *Budavári Te Deum* (1936), and the *Missa Brevis* (1945), along with his enlightened pedagogical method for teaching music to children, have further enhanced his reputation.

SOVIET RUSSIA

Aram Khatchaturian (1903–78)

In addition to Shostakovich and Prokofiev, one other Soviet composer, Aram Khatchaturian, has achieved significant international prominence. Khatchaturian derived much of his melodic inspiration from the folk music of his native Armenia and from the various other cultures of the Georgian Republic. His music is a development of the exoticism of Rimsky-Korsakov, characterized by a rhapsodic quality, by highly colorful, lavish orchestration, and by powerful, driving rhythms. His international reputation was gained through his Piano Concerto (1936), the Violin Concerto (1940), the ballet *Gayane* (1942)—which includes the ever-popular *Saber Dance*—and the Cello Concerto (1950).

GERMANY

Carl Orff (b. 1895)

During the thirties, when Hindemith's music was banned in Germany, a number of composers whose music was acceptable to the Nazi regime came into some degree of prominence. Among them, Carl Orff is the best known. His reputation is based entirely upon his works for the stage, of which his first large work, *Carmina Burana* (1936), is the most celebrated. It is a setting of medieval student *Goliard* songs written in a mixture of Latin, German, and French, scored for chorus, solo singers, two pianos, five timpani, and a large percussion section, in addition to the regular orchestra. Its attractiveness may be attributed to its simplicity of melodic line, uncomplicated by counterpoint and thematic development, and its incisive, vigorous rhythms. Orff later added two sequels: the extremely erotic *Catulli Carmina,* based on Latin poetry by Catullus, and *Trionfo di Afrodite* based on Latin and Greek texts by Catullus, Sappho, and Euripides. Orff has also been involved in music education. His method for teaching music in the elementary school is in wide use today, and his *Gebrauchsmusik* for children, including the *Schulwerk (Schoolwork),* contains a large amount of ensemble music for beginners and amateurs.

part IV

PRINCIPAL
AMERICAN
COMPOSERS

INTRODUCTION

European artists and conductors performing European music continued to dominate the American musical scene well into the opening decades of the twentieth century. Even the American composers of the New England school were largely under the old-world influence. Having studied with European-trained John Knowles Paine and George Chadwick, they then continued their studies in Germany. Others, however, particularly those who had studied with Edward MacDowell at Columbia or Dvořák at the New York Conservatory, attempted to break away from this tradition by taking advantage of American folk idioms. Briefly popular, their efforts gradually disappeared from the concert hall largely because, in their attempts to create an American nationalism, they had merely grafted Indian and Negro folk elements onto late-nineteenth-century German romanticism.

Professional musical activity and the public's interest in music in the United States during these years, however, was growing at a remarkable rate. New orchestras were formed, large auditoriums and opera houses were built, and there was a growing realization of the importance of teaching music in the public schools. Following the appointment of the great German conductor Artur Nikisch as its director in 1891, the Boston Symphony began to develop as one of the leading orchestras of the world.

The Chicago Symphony was organized in 1891 by Theodore Thomas; the New York Philharmonic, established in 1842, began to grow in stature during the opening decade of the century; the Philadelphia Orchestra was formed in 1900, and the Minneapolis Orchestra was begun in 1903. During that same decade, the "Golden Years" at the Metropolitan Opera House began with the arrival of such singers as Enrico Caruso and Geraldine Farrar. This was also the period in which the world-famous virtuoso violinists Fritz Kreisler and Mischa Elman, pianists Ignaz Paderewski, Josef Hoffman, and Sergei Rachmaninoff, and a number of great operatic stars undertook extensive tours throughout the country. All were recorded by the newly developed recording industry, and regular broadcasts of music had become a fact by the 1920s.

Having emerged from World War I as one of the world's most important powers, the United States began to take chauvinistic pride in its home-grown culture. Commissions, fellowships, and prizes were offered to American composers, festivals of American music were created, conductors such as Leopold Stokowski, Serge Koussevitsky, and Dimitri Mitropoulos frequently programmed American music, and American composers began to seek ways of uniting for their mutual benefit. As a consequence of this kind of support and interest, a highly gifted and articulate group of composers developed and was soon recognized internationally. Together with the great influx of European composers during the late thirties and the forties, they made the United States the musical center of the world.

chapter 14

Charles Ives
(1874-1954)

Charles E. Ives, perhaps the most original creative genius in the history of American music, was so far ahead of his time that it took nearly fifty years for the importance of his works to be fully recognized and evaluated; in fact, Ives's music anticipated the innovations of nearly every composer of the twentieth century. The following tribute to Ives was found among Arnold Schoenberg's papers after his death:

> There is a great man living in this country—a composer.
> He has solved the problem how to preserve one's self and to learn.
> He responds to negligence by contempt.
> He is not forced to accept praise or blame.
> His name is Ives.

Much of Ives's originality can be directly attributed to his first and most influential teacher—his father. George Ives was a musical jack-of-all-trades. In addition to teaching a variety of instruments, he was a church organist, a band and choir director, and an accomplished arranger. Intrigued by his exposure to accidental juxtapositions of sounds such as those created by two bands playing in different keys at the same time and by students playing different pieces in adjacent rooms, he attempted to stretch the ears and strengthen the musical minds of his students by having them sing in one key while he accompanied them in a different

Charles Ives

key. He gave his son a training so thorough that by the time he was fourteen, Charles was the regular organist at the First Baptist Church in Danbury, Connecticut, and had been honored by having a composition of his played by the Danbury band. Charles's father also exposed him to the popular music of the time—dance tunes, revival hymns, patriotic marches, and sentimental ballads. Many of these tunes later found their way into his compositions.

After receiving his degree in music from Yale University, where he studied with Horatio Parker, Ives, with considerable insight for one so young, decided that the music he wanted to write was not likely to provide him with a respectable income. He therefore decided upon a dual career as composer and businessman, and in 1907, he helped form the firm of Ives and Myrick, which ultimately became the largest insurance agency in the United States. It was at this time, during the years 1908 to 1916, that he was most active as a composer. After a long work day, he would come home and compose frantically almost every night. He turned out page after page of manuscript, tossing them over his shoulder in a heap on the floor. When the piles became too high he packed them in boxes and stored them away. Frustrated in his attempts at recognition, and overworked as a result of trying to lead two lives, he suffered a severe heart attack in 1918 and subsequently wrote very little.

Ives translated everything he saw about him, everything he experienced and felt, into sound. He was profoundly influenced by the Concord transcendentalists, who believed "that man, nature, and God are one, and that truth and integrity are attainable by man only to the degree that he perceives his own identity with the creative forces of the universe. . . ." In translating the sights and sounds of his native New England into music, he used indigenous minstrel songs, patriotic tunes, and hymns, and depicted many aspects of his environment with delightful but telling accuracy. The amateur town band, the off-pitch church organ, and the confused sounds of a parade all appear in his music. He, like Walt Whitman, asserted his right to be himself, unfettered by European dogma. Each felt that art could encompass the rugged pioneer virtues, and that strong masculinity and a preoccupation with art were not mutually exclusive.

Charles Ives explored a whole new world of sound in almost complete isolation from the rest of the world; in fact, he never heard any of his orchestral works performed until decades after their composition. Among his innovations, perhaps the most striking, from the standpoint of the listener, is his use of simultaneous musical occurrences such as the description in *Three Places in New England* of two bands marching toward one another, each playing its separate tune, each in a key different from the other. Similarly, he delighted in the juxtapositions of sound created through the use of as many as five different meters at the same time, and the simultaneous use of contrasting tempos, necessitating the use of more than one conductor. It is remarkable that before the end of the nineteenth century, he had already begun to use atonality, polytonality, tone clusters, quartal harmony, and nearly every rhythmic device later associated with the twentieth century, long before these innovations were explored by Schoenberg, Stravinsky, and Bartók. He even experimented with a rhythmic tone row in his *Chamber Music Set* (1906–11), a rhythmic procedure forty years ahead of its time in Western music.

His works include four numbered symphonies, and a fifth titled *A Symphony: Holidays* (1904–13); two orchestral sets, the first of which is better known as *Three Places in New England* (1903–11); a number of pieces for chamber and theatre orchestra including *The Unanswered Question* (1908), *Central Park in the Dark* (1898–1907), and two *Tone Roads* (1911, 1915). He also wrote two string quartets, six violin and piano sonatas, three piano sonatas—the second of which is the monumental *Concord Sonata* (1909–15)—nearly two hundred songs, and a number of organ and choral works. In 1919, while recuperating from his heart attack, he resolved that despite the indifference shown his music, it deserved to be published. He therefore printed and published, at his own expense, three volumes—the *Concord Sonata* in 1919, *Essays before a Sonata* (designed to accompany the sonata as a form of program notes, but finally printed separately because of its length) in 1920, and *114 Songs* in 1922. They were sent to libraries, music critics, musicians, and anyone who asked for them. Many of them, according to Ives's biographer, Henry Cowell, were "used to adjust the height of a piano bench in the studios of more than one of the best-known musicians of the day." The extraordinary diversity found in this song collection is typical of Ives. Aaron Copland wrote of them:

> Almost every kind of song imaginable can be found—delicate lyrics, dramatic poems, sentimental ballads, German, French, and Italian songs, war songs, songs of religious sentiment, street songs, humorous songs, hymn tunes, folk tunes, encore songs; songs adapted from orchestral scores, piano works, and violin sonatas; intimate songs, cowboy songs, and mass songs. Songs of every character and description, songs bristling with dissonances, tone clusters, and "elbow chords" next to songs of the most elementary harmonic simplicity.

The scope and importance of Ives's imaginative experimentation first came to be recognized in 1939 with a critically acclaimed performance of his *Concord Sonata*. The American pianist John Kirkpatrick devoted years of study to preparing this incredibly difficult work for performance, and finally, in January of 1939, he performed it at Town Hall in New York. It was received so enthusiastically that one movement had to be repeated and the entire sonata was performed again at a second Town Hall recital the following month. Each movement of this piano sonata, whose full title is Sonata No. 2 for Piano—"Concord, Mass., 1840–1860," is a musical portrait of a famous Concord writer. Its four movements depict Emerson, Hawthorne, the Alcotts, and Thoreau. This astonishing work, without question, contains the most advanced compositional techniques of its time. Tone clusters, chords in seconds and fourths, the extended absence of a tonal center, sections without bar lines or even a meter are juxtaposed with references to the ordinary in a mélange of styles and precipitous moods. Ives makes frequent reference to the opening theme of Beethoven's Fifth Symphony throughout the sonata, a theme which signifies, Ives says, "the spiritual message of Emerson's revelations—the Soul of humanity knocking at the door of divine mysteries radiant in the faith that it *will* be opened—and that the human will become the Divine."

In 1947, when his Symphony No. 3 (1911) was belatedly honored by being awarded the Pulitzer Prize, Ives told the Pulitzer committee who made the award, "Prizes are for boys, I'm grown up," and gave the five hundred dollars away. Ives's Symphony No. 4 is one of the most unusual works in the entire symphonic literature. In addition to requiring the usual symphony orchestra, it is further scored for chorus, a small brass band, three pianos, and a pipe organ, and requires three conductors for performance. Its movements are "Prelude," "Scherzo," "Fugue in C Major," and a very slow "Finale." The symphony makes use of quarter tones, every conceivable type of chord structure, and highly complex rhythmic structures. At one point in the second movement, in fact, twenty different rhythmic ideas occur simultaneously. The symphony also makes use of quotations from at least twenty other compositions ranging from "Yankee Doodle" to material from the *Concord Sonata*. At the end of the "Scherzo," for instance, he uses the "Country Band March" (also used in *Three Places in New England*) and adds to it "Yankee Doodle," "Marching through Georgia," "Turkey in the Straw," "Long, Long Ago," "Reveille," and "The Irish Washerwoman."

Ives frequently depicts various aspects of a musical idea simultaneously, resulting in a kind of heterophony in which the melody is at times surrounded by clusters of adjacent tones. His counterpoint often consists of setting different melodies against each other with complete independence of harmony and rhythm—the more familiar the tune, the more independent the lines. The second movement of the Fourth Symphony presents a particularly good example of this Ivesian characteristic. He did much the same thing with harmonies by setting them as independent lines of counterpoint. It seems that every possible harmonic combination can be found in his music, each created and used to fit a particular need. As early as 1890 Ives used irregular meters such as $\frac{5}{4}$, $\frac{7}{4}$, $\frac{9}{2}$, $\frac{11}{8}$, and even $\frac{6\frac{1}{2}}{2}$. More characteristically, however, Ives employed a complex rhythmic counterpoint in which three or more rhythms and meters are used simultaneously. The story is told that when Nicholas Slonimsky conducted Ives's "Washington's Birthday" (the first movement of the *Holiday Symphony*), he gave at the same time, seven beats with a baton, three beats which his left hand, and two beats by nodding his head.

Ives is the United States' great musical primitive. His music, while highly original, is frequently rough hewn. He seldom went to concerts or associated with other composers, and as a result knew nothing of the music being written by such composers as Schoenberg and Stravinsky. He did not realize that other composers were also having their troubles in creating new music. The knowledge might have encouraged him and might also have led him to a more systematic investigation of his many harmonic and rhythmic innovations.

Aaron Copland's often quoted statement about Ives characterizes the man and his music with telling insight: "He lacked neither the talent nor the ability nor the metier nor the integrity of the true artist—but what he most shamefully and tragically lacked was an audience. 'Why do you write so much—which no one ever sees?' his friends asked. And we can only echo, 'Why indeed?' and admire the courage and perseverance of the man and the artist."

Ives: *THREE PLACES IN NEW ENGLAND*

Ives's *First Orchestral Set,* subtitled *A New England Symphony:* "Three Places in New England," was written between the years 1903–14. Heartily booed and hissed at its first performances, it has in recent years become one of Ives's most popular works.

First Movement: *The "St. Gaudens" in Boston Common: Col. Shaw and his Colored Regiment.* Inspired by the emotional impact of the Augustus St. Gaudens monument depicting Colonel Shaw and a group of marching soldiers from the Negro regiment he commanded during the Civil War, Ives wrote a prefatory poem to this movement which begins:

> Moving,—Marching—Faces of Souls!
> Marked with generations of pain,
> Part-freers of a Destiny,
> Slowly, restlessly—swaying us on with you
> Towards other Freedom! . . .

Hushed, solemn, it opens with a three-note motive, played by the piano and flute, which becomes the generating melodic cell of the movement:

Example 146.

Examples 146–150: Copyright 1935, Mercury Music, Inc. Used by permission.

This motive is developed by the strings in a quiet, almost impressionistic manner, before it unfolds quite naturally into a reminiscence of the phrase "I'm comin' " from Stephen Foster's "Old Black Joe":

Example 147.

Although the rhythmic and harmonic structures themselves are quite complex, the texture itself is predominantly homophonic. The basic tonality is A minor, and although there are many keys superimposed upon it throughout the movement, the A minor foundation remains unshaken except for the climax, where C major is asserted in a triumphant *fortississimo*. Immediately following this brilliant climax, the A minor foundation quietly returns. The basic motive now leads into two other Civil War songs, Root's "Battle Cry of Freedom" and Work's "Marching through Georgia," the first played by the flute and the other by the violins underscored by a traditional military beat from the drums:

Example 148.

The movement ends quietly as the motive is played successively by the strings, trumpet, and finally the viola, quadruple *piano* (*pppp*).

Second Movement: *Putnam's Camp, Redding, Connecticut*. In the preface to this movement, Ives wrote, "Near Redding Center, Connecticut, is a small park preserved as a Revolutionary Memorial; for here General Israel Putnam's soldiers had their winter quarters in 1778–79. Long rows of stone camp fire-places still remain to stir up a child's imagination. The hardships which the soldiers endured and the agitation of a few hot-heads to break camp and march to the Hartford Assembly for relief,

231

is part of Redding history." At a Fourth of July picnic some time ago, a child wanders from the other children, looking for old soldiers in the woods. He dreams of the old camp and seems to see the Goddess of Liberty pleading with the soldiers not to forget their "cause," but unheeding they march out to a popular tune of the day. When Putnam returns to lead them, the cheering soldiers turn back. The child awakens and runs back to the picnic to "listen to the band" and join in the fun.

In this movement Ives combines the village band music of a nineteenth-century Fourth of July picnic with visionary music of the Revolutionary War. All of the confusion and frantic gaiety of a village picnic with two bands simultaneously playing in competition with each other and quotations of various patriotic tunes combine in a burst of pyrotechnical virtuosity that has no equal in orchestral literature. The music begins loud and brassy in march rhythm. After five measures of the main theme, a lively band tune ("Country Band March," also used in the second movement of Ives's Symphony No. 4) is played by the strings:

Example 149.

Rhythmic complexity descriptive of the milling crowd increases, and snatches of popular tunes are heard as if some of the band members are warming up. The music gradually dissipates and finally stops as the child drifts off into his dreams. A quiet march rhythm begins in the strings and woodwinds, and then the brass, piano, and drums join in with a faster march to produce a fascinating polymetric situation in which four measures in the faster tempo equal three of the other. The pace quickens, and the volume and dissonance increase until, in a state of musical pandemonium, the movement ends with a drunken reference to "The Star-Spangled Banner."

Third Movement: *The Housatonic at Stockbridge.* The title is from a poem by Robert Underwood Johnson that Ives quotes at the beginning of the movement. It begins:

> Contented river! in thy dreamy realm—
> The cloudy willow and the plumy elm . . .
> Thou hast grown human laboring with men
> At wheel and spindle; sorrow thou dost ken; . . .

The strings begin with a tranquil murmuring background depicting the calmly flowing river as the horn and English horn present a serene hymnlike melody:

Example 150.

The descriptive "current" of sound gradually increases in volume, rhythmic complexity, and dissonant structure until a striking *fortississimo* climax is reached. The rush of sound suddenly stops, and a quiet reminiscence of the opening motive brings the movement to a *pianissimo* close.

chapter 15

Edgard Varèse
(1883-1965)
and
Elliott Carter
(b. 1908)

EDGARD VARÈSE

Varèse was born in Paris and received his musical training there, first at the Schola Cantorum under d'Indy and Roussel, and then at the Conservatory under Charles-Marie Widor. Although his early works were influenced to a certain extent by Debussy and Richard Strauss, it was a statement by Ferrucio Busoni in his "Sketch of a New Esthetic of Music" that had the greatest influence on the youthful Varèse: "Music was born free; and to win freedom is its destiny." Varèse spent the rest of his life following this credo through his attempts to free sound from any control except that of its designer.

In 1915, he left Europe after being discharged from the French army because of ill health. All of the music he had written up to this time was lost, some in a Berlin fire, the rest abandoned in Paris. He settled in New York and soon became an active propagandist for the new music by organizing concerts devoted to contemporary works. Together with Carlos Salzedo he founded the International Composers Guild in 1921 and was responsible for the premières of works by Bartók, Berg, Chávez, Cowell, Hindemith, Schoenberg, Stravinsky, and Webern, among many others. While Varèse's contemporaries experimented within the framework of the traditional elements of music, he explored completely new directions for rhythm structures and sound materials in his attempt to recreate the sounds of the machine age. The first to accept all audible resources as material for music, the thoroughly unconventional Varèse inevitably focused his experimentation with sound on the percussion section, whose almost limitless potential for varied sounds and rhythmic effects offered him the widest latitude for his expression. He transcended melody and harmony in an idiom that throbbed, shrieked, clanged, and hissed with the sounds of machines and the city.

Limited in number, many of Varèse's compositions written in the twenties and thirties reflect his early interest in science. His works of the twenties include *Offrandes* (1921), a setting of two surrealistic poems for voice and chamber orchestra; *Amériques* (1918–22) for large orchestra, his first work begun in this country—a "symbol of discovery"; *Hyperprism* (1923) for two woodwinds, seven brass, and sixteen percussion instruments; *Octandre* (1924) for seven wind instruments and double bass; and *Intégrales* (1925) for wind instruments and percussion. During the next decade he wrote just four works: *Ionisation* (1931), for an "orchestra" of thirty-five percussion instruments, probably his best-known work; *Equatorial* (1934) for voice, brass, organ, percussion, and two theremins (an electrophonic instrument invented in 1924); *Density 21.5* (1936) for un-

Edgard Varèse

Music Division, The New York Public Library at Lincoln Center. Astor, Lenox and Tilden Foundations.

accompanied flute, written for his friend Barrère to perform on his new platinum flute (21.5 is the specific gravity of platinum); and *Metal* (1936). It was nearly sixteen years later that Varèse began to compose again. He had, in his own words, "been waiting a long time for electronics to free music from the tempered scale and the limitations of musical instruments." In a lecture at the University of Southern California in 1939, Varèse said:

> Personally, for my conception, I need an entirely new medium of expression: a sound producing machine . . . here are the advantages I anticipate from such a machine: liberation from the arbitrary, paralyzing tempered system; the possibility of obtaining any number of cycles, or, if still desired, subdivisions of the octave, and consequently, the formation of any desired scale; unsuspected range in low and high registers; . . . the possibility of obtaining any differentiation of timbre, of sound-combinations; . . . cross-rhythms unrelated to each other, treated simultaneously, or to use the old word, "contrapuntally," since the machine would be able to beat any number of desired notes, any subdivision of them, omission or fraction of them—all these in a given unit of measure or time that is humanly impossible to obtain.

This was spoken seven years before the first primitive tape recorder became commercially available and fourteen years before electronic sound production. The development of the tape recorder offered him the means he had sought to enter an entirely new world of sound resources. In 1954 he wrote *Déserts*. Scored for woodwinds, brass, percussion, piano, and prepared tape interpolated in the score at three points, it is a large ABACABA form in which A is played by instruments, B is a processed tape of sounds Varèse had collected from a foundry, a sawmill, and factories, and C is a processed taping of the sounds of percussion instruments. In 1958, at the age of seventy-five, he was commissioned to write a work for the Brussels World's Fair to be used in the Phillips Pavilion designed by Le Corbusier. This work, *Poème Électronique,* will be discussed in a later chapter.

Varèse: *IONISATION*

Ionisation is scored for a percussion ensemble of thirty-five instruments to be played by thirteen performers. The instruments are divided into three classifications: those of definite pitch, including tubular chimes, keyboard glockenspiel with resonators, and piano; those of indefinite pitch, including gong, tam-tam, six different sized drums, cymbals, triangle, sleigh bells, anvils, Chinese blocks, claves, maracas, slapstick, tambourine, bongos, and a hybrid instrument known as a string-drum or lion's-roar; and a variable pitch instrument, the siren. The entire work is based upon the contrasts and emotional impact that are achievable through rhythm and sonority used without the constructive principles of melody and harmony. Despite this fact, form is present—a variant of sonata-form—in which there are two subjects, a development section, a recapitulation, and a coda.

The eight-measure introduction that opens the work begins quietly but in its last measure comes to a sudden *fortissimo* with the entrance of the metal instruments. The first subject then enters quietly, played by the *Tambour militaire* (field drum) accompanied by two bongos playing a rhythmic figure that can be considered a countersubject:

Example 151.

Examples 151–152: Permission to reprint granted by Colfranc Music Publishing Corp., Copyright Owners.

Following a few measures derived from the introduction, the *Tambour militaire* repeats the first subject, this time with the countersubject played by the bass drums. The bongos enter after two measures in strict imitation of the theme. The first subject is then developed in various instruments, ending with a *crescendo* to a *fortississimo* from the side drums and cymbals.

The second subject is played by the bongos, *Tambour militaire*, Chinese blocks, maracas, and *Tarole* (flat military drum), rhythmically punctuated by the bass drums:

Example 152.

During about twenty measures of development, rhythmic motives from the two subjects appear in various instruments. The metal instruments then build to a *fortissimo* crash prolonged by a *fermata,* after which a few measures of introductory material lead to the recapitulation. The first subject is played once more by the *Tambour militaire,* but the bongos now play a new counterpoint. The second subject is shortened to two measures that, in a rapid *crescendo,* lead to the coda. Here the instruments of definite pitch enter for the first time, and in blocklike harmony. Fragments of the first theme played by the *Tambour militaire* are heard, and then the work ends with a long *fermata.*

ELLIOTT CARTER

As an undergraduate at Harvard, Carter majored in philosophy and English literature; it was not until his senior year that he decided upon music as a career. As a graduate student there, he studied with Walter Piston. In 1932, he went on to study with Nadia Boulanger in Paris for three years. After his return, he spent some time in New York as a critic and director of the American Ballet Caravan, the group that first performed his imaginative ballet *Pocahontas* (1939). In 1940, he joined the faculty of St. John's College, Annapolis, where he taught "music as a liberal art" in addition to teaching Greek, mathematics, physics, and philosophy. Subsequently, Carter held teaching positions at the Peabody Conservatory of Music, Columbia University, M.I.T., and the Juilliard School of Music. Most recently, he has been Professor of Musical Composition at Yale University. As an articulate proponent of contemporary composition, he has served on the Board of Directors of the League of Composers, the International Society for Contemporary Music, and the American Composers Alliance. He has twice been the recipient of Guggenheim Fellowships and has received a number of awards, including the Pulitzer Prize in 1960.

Elliott Carter

For Carter, the process of development has always been unhurried and painstakingly meticulous; in fact, it was not until he was forty that he had developed a truly personal compositional style. His earlier compositions in particular show the influence of Debussy and Stravinsky. Carter's close friend, Charles Ives, has had a more direct and lasting influence on his works. The most important among the characteristics of Carter's musical style that can be said to have been derived directly from the music of Ives—the "simultaneous contrasting levels of musical activity"—is his tendency to have each instrument in a work do "its own thing" at times rather than collaborate in a unified texture. His music written before the mid-forties—including the ballet *Pocahontas* (1939), the *Pastoral* (1940) for viola and piano, *The Holiday Overture* (1944), and *The Harmony of Morning* (1944)—has a strong American and a basic neoclassic orientation. Beginning with the Sonata for Cello and Piano in 1948, his works have increased in textural density and rhythmic complexity as principal characteristics in the evolution of an experimental style of striking originality and expressiveness. By the middle of the 1950s, Elliott Carter had become one of the most admired composers of his generation.

239

The melodic ideas of his mature style are long-breathed, fluent, and expressive, surrounded by a dense, dark texture of sonorous dissonant elements. The resulting effect for the listener is frequently one of seemingly unrelieved tension. There is a monumentality about these works that reflects the largeness of his musical conception and intense seriousness.

Carter once said, "One technical fad after another has swept over twentieth-century music as the music of each of its leading composers has come to be intimately known. Each fad lasted a few years, only to be discarded by the succeeding generation of composers, then by the music profession, and finally by certain parts of the interested public." Carter's accomplishments are not marked by what he called "fads"; his works are instead devoid of formula. One of the few technical features of his music that in itself can be considered an innovation is his use of the principle of "metrical modulation." He developed this system in his attempt to extend the rhythmic range of his music and to maintain a greater control over changing meters and tempos. Richard Franko Goldman, who first used the term "metrical modulation" in describing this aspect of Carter's music, defines the technique as "a means of going smoothly, but with complete accuracy, from one absolute metronomic speed to another, by lengthening or shortening the value of the basic note unit." This reflects an American tendency, according to Roy Harris, to think of rhythm in its smallest units rather than in its largest units, as European musicians are trained to do. For instance, Carter, when using quintuples in a duple meter, as in the example below, thinks of each of the five notes as a new unit in its own right that then becomes the basis of a new meter. Note how the music accelerates from a tempo of ♩ = 80 to ♩ = 100 through metric modulation:

Example 153.

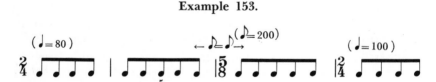

The following examples taken from Carter's Second String Quartet depict the care with which he notates rhythmic changes. The notes immediately before and after the tempo changes have the same time value, facilitating the tempo change from ♩ = 140 to ♩ = 175 in the first example and from ♩ = 175 to ♩ = 105 in the second example:

Example 154.

His major works written since 1948 include three string quartets (1951, 1959, 1972) that are among the finest of this century, *Eight Etudes and a Fantasy* (1950) for woodwind quartet, *Pieces for Four Kettledrums* (1950), the Sonata for Flute, Oboe, Cello, and Harpsichord (1952), Variations for Orchestra (1955), Double Concerto for Harpsichord and Piano (1961), Piano Concerto (1965), the Concerto for Orchestra (1970), and most recently, *A Symphony of Three Orchestras.*

Carter: STRING QUARTET NO. 2

Commissioned by the Stanley Quartet in 1959, Carter's Second Quartet was first performed by the Juilliard Quartet in 1960. Six weeks later it was awarded the Pulitzer Prize in music, and subsequently won the New York Music Critics Circle Award for 1960 and the UNESCO First Prize in 1961. Carter once described his scores as being dramatic scenarios with each performer acting out a part with his instrument, both as an individual and as a participant in the ensemble. The characterization and interplay of the four "personalities" involved is the basis of the work. Each instrument has its own sphere of musical activity, expressed by its gravitation around certain intervals. There is no literal repetition, no recapitulation, and no strict imitation—the result is a kind of purposeful improvisation. In order to dramatize the individuality of the participants, Carter suggests that "the performers be more widely spaced than usual on the stage so that each is definitely separated from the others in space as well as in character. . . ."

The quartet has the customary four movements; however, they are linked by solo cadenzas. Carter has also provided the work with an Introduction and Conclusion. All of the sections are played without pause and are unified rhythmically by metric modulation.

Introduction. The four participants are introduced in this section. Each instrumental part has an individual character and its own characteristic intervals. The first violin displays a mercurial bravura style; its characteristic intervals are the minor third and perfect fifth. The second violin is strongly rhythmic and uses the percussive effects of various kinds of pizzicato; its intervals are the major third and major seventh. The viola is predominantly expressive, partly because of its use of glissandos and portamentos; its characteristic intervals, in keeping with its temperament, are the augmented fourth and minor seventh. The cello's lyric and rhapsodic qualities approach the first violin in temperament; the perfect fourth and minor sixth are its characteristic intervals. Following the introduction of all four instruments, the first movement begins without pause.

I. Allegro fantastico. The first movement is dominated by the "fantastic, ornate, mercurial" first violin, which presents all of the thematic material of the movement. The opening eight measures, shown in the following example, include most of the movement's thematic material. The first four notes shown are particularly important in the expansion of the movement's musical ideas:

Example 155.

Note the almost exclusive use of the intervals of the minor third and perfect fifth.

The other instruments enter individually, each displaying its particular characteristics. The three gradually gain in importance and by the end of the movement, each has attained an equality with the first violin. In the final two measures of the movement, each instrument is given at least one of its characteristic intervals:

Example 156.

The first two movements are linked by a viola cadenza. Characteristically, it has a long, expressive, singing melodic line, while the first violin and cello flicker an accompanying figuration.

II. Presto scherzando. The second movement is dominated by the second violin, whose steady pizzicato rhythm, while repeated throughout most of the movement, is constantly at variance with the other instruments. When they play in $\frac{5}{4}$ meter, the second violin is in $\frac{4}{4}$; when they are in $\frac{3}{4}$, it is in $\frac{2}{4}$. It is not until the final measures that all four instruments finally play in the same meter $\left(\frac{4}{4}\right)$. The opening measures of the movement show how carefully Carter notates this characteristic conflict of meters:

Example 157.

The line in the middle of the score presents a simplified alternate rhythmic notation for the second violin, indicating how its independent part should sound. The other three instruments play quietly throughout the movement, each retaining its respective character. The first violin moves in murmuring triplets while the viola plays *espressivo* in longer note values. The cello moves in a duple rhythm, sometimes quickly with the first violin and then in longer notes with the viola. The cello ends the movement rhapsodically with a *crescendo* leading into its cadenza.

The second cadenza roams impetuously over the entire cello range, dynamically as well as technically. It begins loud, intense, and very expressive, descending through almost four octaves before relaxing on the lowest string. Halfway through the cadenza, the note values gradually lengthen, and the mood becomes tranquil. The first violin is used to accompany the cadenza with persistent thirds and fifths while the viola sighs, and the second violin's strings are plucked insistently.

III. Andante espressivo. The viola dominates the third movement. Beginning in slow broad lines, it grows increasingly expressive as the dynamics fluctuate constantly from *piano* to *forte* and back, until near the end of the movement, a climax is reached. Throughout the movement, the other instruments weave a slow contrapuntal web around the viola line, imitating it in augmentation, in diminution, and occasionally in inversion:

Example 158.

At the end of the movement all of the instruments gradually play in slow uneven note values as the rhythmic pulse becomes more and more vague—almost nonexistent. Animation finally returns with the expressive unaccompanied cadenza of the first violin using a free recapitulation of thematic material from the first movement. The other instruments join in quietly and unobtrusively at the end of the cadenza to introduce the final movement.

IV. Allegro. The four participants cooperate fully for the first time in this movement. Melodic motives are divided among various instruments, not in a pointillistic manner, but through the emphasis of various notes in the score:

Example 159.

The top line of the example is the melodic resultant of the bracketed notes. An interchange of characteristic intervals also suggests collaboration among the instruments as they drive relentlessly to a climax, arrived at after a long series of metric modulations. At that point, Carter initiates an extraordinary polyrhythmic passage that ends the movement:

Example 160.

The accented notes (*ff*) bring out a series of harmonic intervals that have been featured throughout the movement; however, the intervals are now produced cooperatively rather than individually as before.

The Conclusion is similar to the Introduction, but with the participants stressing ensemble rather than diversity. The characteristic intervals are gradually isolated and fade away, and the quartet ends on a single pizzicato note by the second violin.

chapter 16

Aaron Copland
(b. 1900)

Aaron Copland was born in Brooklyn of immigrant Russian-Jewish parents. "I was born," he writes, "on a street in Brooklyn that can only be described as drab. . . . Music was the last thing anyone would have connected with that street. In fact, no one had ever connected music with my family or with my street. The idea was entirely original with me." At his own insistence, he began studying piano. Later, he worked with Rubin Goldmark, a conservative but very thorough composition teacher, and then in 1921 he went to France to continue his musical studies at the American School of Music at Fontainebleau. While there, he accidentally discovered the pedagogical genius of a young harmony teacher, Nadia Boulanger (1887–1979), and the following year he left the school to study privately with her for two years in Paris. While studying with Mlle. Boulanger, he wrote a number of piano pieces, some songs, a ballet (later arranged as the *Dance Symphony*), music for string quartet, and four a cappella motets.

On his return to the United States in 1925, Copland was commissioned by Mlle. Boulanger to write an organ concerto for her coming tour of the States as an organist. The concerto was performed with the New York and Boston symphonies to mixed reviews. Copland later rewrote the concerto as his First Symphony. Two successive Guggenheim Fellowships enabled Copland to begin devoting all of his energies to composition. It was at the second performance of the Organ Concerto

Aaron Copland

in Boston that Copland became reacquainted with the conductor Serge Koussevitsky (Mlle. Boulanger had arranged for Copland to play some of his works for Koussevitsky in Paris in 1924). This was the beginning of a long and profitable relationship for both men, well attested to by the long list of first performances of Copland's works by the Boston Symphony Orchestra conducted by Koussevitsky.

Copland composes slowly and methodically; in fact, works written during a given period of his life may have been sketched many years earlier. It is still possible, however, to define several periods in his development. Following his French student days, his first period after returning to the States was brief; it lasted just four years, from 1925 to 1929. Searching for an idiom that "would immediately be recognized as American in character," he briefly adopted the popular jazz expression of the time for the compositional style he used in writing *Music for the Theater* (1925) and the Piano Concerto (1926). Following his *Symphonic Ode* (1929), which marks the end of his first period, he turned to a style strongly influenced by the objective, constructivist works of Stravinsky current at the time. During this rather short period he wrote the Piano Variations (1930), the *Short Symphony* (1933; appears in 1937 in a reduced version as the Sextet), and the *Statements for Orchestra* (1935). The *Piano Variations* is for many a landmark in twentieth-century piano music. He stated recently, "I can see now that the Piano Variations of 1930, because of the concentration there on a few notes, was the real beginning of my interest in serial writing." The entire work is derived from a four-note motto heard at the very beginning: E–C–D♯–C♯. The theme in its entirety consists of a row of ten notes used both melodically and harmonically:

Example 161.

The ten-minute work contains nineteen variations and a finale—a miracle of concise structure. Elements of Stravinsky, Schoenberg, and Bartók can be heard, but they are all assimilated into a very personal Copland idiom.

Soon, for reasons that he explained in his book *The New Music,* Copland broke with his musical past. Realizing that by using a musical idiom that was largely incomprehensible to the average listener, a composer could run the risk of completely alienating his public, he simplified his means, and created the communicative style by which he is now best known. This style incorporates many American folk elements including Shaker hymns, cowboy tunes, Mexican folk songs, and Latin American rhythms. Three American ballets—*Billy the Kid* (1938), *Rodeo* (1942), and *Appalachian Spring* (1944)—all now best known as concert pieces; the *Outdoor Overture* (1938) and the opera *The Second Hurricane* (1935), both written for high school performance; *El Salón Mexico* (1936); and the music for the films *Of Mice and Men, Our Town, North Star, The Red Pony,* and *The Heiress* are particularly important works written during this period in his development. He continued to compose abstract works, but they too were written in a more accessible style. The Piano Sonata (1941), the Symphony No. 3 (1946), and the Quartet for Piano and Strings (1950) are particularly notable among these works. During this period, he also wrote *A Lincoln Portrait* (1942), an opera *The Tender Land* (1954), and *Twelve Poems of Emily Dickinson* (1950).

Of his latest period Copland writes, "At the end of the Second World War, younger men, like Pierre Boulez, effectively demonstrated that the twelve-tone method could be retained without the German esthetic, and by 1950, I was involved. I was interested in the simple outlines of the theory and in adopting them to my own purposes. As a result, I began to hear chords I wouldn't have heard otherwise! Here was a new way of moving tones about that had a freshening effect on one's technique and approach. This, to me, was and remains the principal attraction of serial

Aaron Copland

Music Division, The New York Public Library at Lincoln Center. Astor, Lenox and Tilden Foundations.

writing." The Piano Quintet, written immediately after the Dickinson songs, was his first conscious attempt at serial music. The Piano Fantasy (1957) and the Nonet (1960) both present a successful rapprochement between serialism and his more traditional style. The Fantasy is in many ways reminiscent of the Piano Variations. All of the material in the thirty-minute work is derived from the opening phrase; there is a ten-note row (the remaining two notes are used as a cadence formula); and there is a preoccupation with the sonorous possibilities of the piano.

Example 162.

The *Connotations* (1962) for orchestra, on the other hand, is a more conscious effort on Copland's part to make the serial technique central in his thinking. It was commissioned by the New York Philharmonic as part of the opening celebration festivities of the Lincoln Center for the Performing Arts. He said that he "decided to compose a work that would bring to the opening exercise a contemporary note, expressing something of the tensions, aspirations, and drama inherent in the world of today." Tension is immediately evident as the brass, backed by the percussion, declaim the opening in a tone row that appears in three four-note chords. "The subsequent treatment," he writes, "seeks out other implications—connotations that the composer himself may only gradually uncover. The listener, on the other hand, is free to discover his or her own connotative meanings, including perhaps some not suspected by the author." *Connotations* is, according to Copland, "a free treatment of the baroque form of the chaconne. A succession of variations, based on the opening chords and their implied melodic intervals, supplies the basic framework." Although the row is heard most often simultaneously in a chord series, it does also appear melodically. The example below shows it in chord form, and melodically in original and transposed inversion:

Example 163.

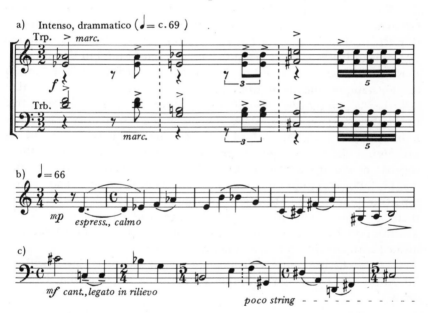

Copland's use of serial technique, like that of Stravinsky, who also turned to serialism in the 1950s, is extremely personal, and adds to rather than detracts from his style.

Copland is essentially a lyricist who, except for his latest period, has expressed himself in a tonal idiom based on a pandiatonic harmonic structure. His melodies, uncomplicated and direct in their appeal, frequently possess a pronounced modal flavor, particularly when derived from folk material. He is fond of the tonal ambiguities made possible both through the immediate juxtaposing of major and minor relationships and through the use of polytonality. Copland often contrasts his lyric writing with movements filled with propulsive rhythmic excitement punctuated with displaced accents and multimetric sections.

As a teacher, lecturer, writer, pianist, conductor, and composer, he has influenced a generation of composers, and in his unremitting efforts to further American music, he has sought to protect and champion the interests of American composers. He has indeed become the elder statesman of American music.

Copland: *APPALACHIAN SPRING* ("BALLET FOR MARTHA")

Appalachian Spring was composed in 1943–44 on a commission from the Elizabeth Sprague Coolidge Foundation as a ballet for Martha Graham. The score, originally orchestrated for a chamber ensemble of thirteen instruments, was arranged as a concert suite for full orchestra by Copland in 1945. In its present form, it received the Pulitzer Prize for music in 1945 and the award of the Music Critics Circle of New York as the outstanding theatrical work of the season of 1944–45. The ballet describes "a pioneer celebration in spring around a newly-built farmhouse in the Pennsylvania hills in the early part of the last century. The bride-to-be and the young farmer-husband enact the emotions, joyful and apprehensive, their new domestic partnership invites. An older neighbor suggests now and then the rocky confidence of experience. A revivalist and his followers remind the new householders of the strange and terrible aspects of human fate. At the end the couple are left quiet and strong in their new house." One feels that Copland genuinely knows these people, so sincere and compassionate are his musical portrayals in a score permeated with the spirit of early American music.

The orchestral suite is divided into eight sections, played without interruption. Copland's description of the program is included in the analysis:

I. Very slowly. "Introduction of the characters, one by one, in a suffused light." The first section is in the form of an introduction. There is a hushed feeling of expectancy as each of the characters—bride, husband, neighbor, revivalist—comes forward and bows to the audience. A hymnlike melody is presented with a characteristic Copland emphasis on the intervals of the fourth and fifth.

Appalachian Spring

Martha Swope, New York City.

Appalachian Spring

Martha Swope, New York City.

II. Fast. "A sudden burst of unison strings in A major arpeggios starts the action. A sentiment both elated and religious gives the keynote to this scene." The theme, heard first in fragments, is then given a complete statement. Once more the intervals of the fourth and fifth are emphasized:

Example 164.

Examples 164–167: Copyright 1945 by Aaron Copland; Renewed 1972. Reprinted by permission of Aaron Copland, Copyright Owner, and Boosey & Hawkes, Inc., Sole Publishers and Licensees.

III. Moderate. "Duo for the bride and her intended—scene of tenderness and passion." The music takes on a more expressive and passionate quality through an extension of a thematic motive from the introduction, now enhanced with a fuller, richer harmony. The intensity subsides, and the section ends very quietly.

IV. Quite fast. "The Revivalist and his flock. Folksy feeling—suggestions of square dances and country fiddlers." Segments of the tune are tossed from oboe to flute to clarinet before being played completely through by the violins:

Example 165.

At the end of this section it appears that some members of the flock may have imbibed too freely—the meter continuously alternates between $\frac{2}{4}$ and $\frac{5}{8}$.

V. Still faster. "Solo dance of the bride—presentiment of motherhood. Extremes of joy and fear and wonder." The opening notes of the introduction to this section are accentuated by sharp chords cast in meter shifts from $\frac{3}{8}$ to $\frac{3}{4}$ to $\frac{5}{8}$ to $\frac{4}{4}$. A sudden *accelerando* introduces the theme of the solo dance:

Example 166.

This, the longest section of the suite, ends as it began, with sharp chords in changing meters accentuating the opening three notes of the dance.

VI. Very slowly (as at first). "Transition scene to music reminiscent of the introduction." This short scene opens with a theme from the third section, and then the hymnlike theme of the introduction is stated. All is very tranquil and hushed.

VII. Calm and flowing. "Scenes of daily activity for the bride and her farmer-husband. There are five variations on a Shaker theme. The theme—sung by a solo clarinet—was taken from a collection of Shaker melodies compiled by Edward D. Andrews and published under the title *The Gift to be Simple*. The melody I borrowed and used almost literally is called *Simple Gifts*." The theme is a simple sixteen-measure binary melody:

Example 167.

For the first variation, the theme is presented simultaneously by the bassoon in E-flat minor and oboe in G-flat major. The second variation introduces the theme played half as fast (augmentation) by the trombone, joined later by the horn while the strings and woodwinds play a light dancing accompaniment. The third variation features the trumpet and trombone playing the theme at its original speed, accompanied by scale passages from the violins and violas. The next variation simultaneously presents the two sections of the theme. The final variation states the theme as a triumphant chorale played majestically by the entire orchestra.

VIII. Moderato—Coda. "The bride takes her place among her neighbors. At the end the couple are left quiet and strong in their new house. Muted strings intone a hushed prayer-like passage. The close is reminiscent of the opening music."

chapter 17

Walter Piston (1894-1976) and William Schuman (b. 1910)

Both Walter Piston and William Schuman established their principal musical expression through classical abstract forms, and in that sense are considered classicists among American composers of this century. Schuman also found considerable identification with nationalist traits. Piston, on the other hand, carefully avoided what he considered the self-conscious "Americanism" of some of his contemporaries, preferring to think that "If . . . composers will increasingly strive to perfect themselves in the art of music and will follow only those paths of expression that would seem to take them the true way, the matter of a national school will take care of itself . . . the composer cannot afford the wild-goose chase of trying to be more American than he is."

WALTER PISTON

Walter Piston was born in Maine and remained a New Englander throughout his life. As a boy he studied the violin and taught himself to play the piano. He worked his way through the Massachusetts School of Art by playing in dance and theatre orchestras and then enlisted in the Navy as a musician during World War I. His formal training as a composer began in 1920 when he entered Harvard University (Virgil Thomson was a fellow student). After graduation, he won a John Knowles Paine

Walter Piston

Fellowship, which enabled him to go to Paris to study with Nadia Boulanger for two years; on his return to the United States, he joined the Harvard music faculty, became chairman, and remained there until his retirement in 1960. Leonard Bernstein, Arthur Berger, and Elliott Carter are among the many significant composers who have studied with him. His recognition of the impact of twentieth-century compositional techniques on traditional concepts led him to write his three widely used theory textbooks—*Principles of Harmonic Analysis* (1933), *Harmony* (1941, rev. 1948), and *Counterpoint* (1943). He later published another important text, *Orchestration* (1955).

Most of Piston's compositions are absolute works cast in large rounded forms. In describing an aspect of his objective, neoclassic outlook, he said of one of his abstract works, "I could wish that my music be first heard without the distraction of preliminary explanation. . . . The symphony was composed with no intent other than to make music to be played and listened to." He wrote very little vocal music and just one stage work. His compositional output includes eight symphonies, four concertos (one for two pianos, two for violin, and one for viola), *Tunbridge Fair* (1950) for band, five string quartets, a large number of other chamber works, and a considerable amount of piano music. His most popular work is an orchestral suite that he extracted from his ballet *The Incredible Flutist* (1938). Piston received many awards and honors during his lifetime. Among them are two Pulitzer Prizes (for the Symphony No. 2 and Symphony No. 7), a Guggenheim Fellowship, and the New York Music Critics Circle Award.

Within an essentially tonal framework, Piston frequently employs polytonality and some serialist techniques. His expression is objective, restrained, and well-suited to his preference for the clarity of classical forms. He is a consummate craftsman, possessed of a remarkable ability to handle his musical materials and ideas. Driving rhythms and sharp dissonance frequently punctuate his texturally varied expressions. Piston's music is also eminently playable. In contrast to much of the music written during this period that stretched the capabilities of the instruments and extended the techniques of the performers, his music is always kind to the performer and stays well within the ready capabilities of the instrument. "I must say I've always composed music from the point of view of the performers. I love instruments, and I value the cooperation of the performers. I believe in the contribution of the player to the music as written. I am very old-fashioned that way."

Piston: SYMPHONY NO. 4

Piston's Fourth Symphony was written in 1950 on commission for the 1951 centennial celebration of the University of Minnesota. Lyric expressiveness and classic design meet amiably with the positive tonal idiom of this readily accessible work.

First Movement: *Piacevole* (pleasant). In Piston's words, this is "an easy-going moderately fast movement in large two-part form." The first of its two themes is a long, graceful melody played by the violins against a simple harmonic and rhythmic background:

Example 168.

Examples 168–173: Used by permission of Associated Music Publishers.

Note the prominence of the interval of a fourth in its structure. Although sharp dissonances do appear unexpectedly and significantly in the working out of this idea, the tonality is unashamedly G major. Other instruments gradually enter, creating a contrapuntal texture of great warmth. The motion quickens as the eighth-note figure from the theme is developed. A climax is reached, and then subsides as the clarinet introduces the second theme, a halting idea in a new key that contrasts sharply with the opening theme:

Example 169.

Other woodwinds enter with variants of the theme, and then the strings make their own comment as the section slows for the bassoon's quiet repetition of the theme. The A section returns in the dominant followed by the B section in the tonic. A short coda, in which the first theme is again presented, ends the movement quietly.

Second Movement: *Ballando* (dancing). For reasons of contrast, Piston placed this, the scherzo movement, between the gently moving opening movement and the slow movement. The form is a classical rondo (ABACAB). The principal theme is a vigorous idea characterized by its irregular meters and form:

Example 170.

The B theme, in $\frac{6}{8}$ meter, is a waltz whose melody is played by the low strings and woodwinds to an "oom-pah-pah" accompaniment by the violins and harp. After a return of the main theme, the C theme enters, in $\frac{2}{4}$ meter, with the violins playing an old-fashioned country dance, one of Piston's few uses of an outright Americanism. The remainder of the movement continues as indicated in the letter-diagram of the form.

Third Movement: *Contemplativo.* The slow movement, in $\frac{12}{8}$, is a continuous expansion of a melodic idea, recalling the *fortspinnung* practice of eighteenth-century composers. The clarinet introduces the melody unaccompanied:

Example 171.

The English horn and viola take over the melody and extend it; then it is developed by the strings and woodwinds. A contrasting middle section begins with a flute solo; soon, imitative entries build to a climax in which the horns play a variant of the original theme *fortissimo* with octave displacements. Variants of the theme are then played by the woodwinds and strings, gradually diminishing in volume as the original mood of the movement returns.

Fourth Movement: *Energico.* The finale, in the tonality of B-flat, is in sonata-form. A strongly syncopated first subject recalls the vigorous brilliance of the second movement:

Example 172.

The movement's rhythmic energy gathers even more momentum when the brass enter, offering a striking contrast to the subsequent statement by the oboe of the lyric, smoothly flowing, second subject:

Example 173.

Example 173. Continued

Following a statement of this subject by the violins, the development section begins quietly, with the first subject in the woodwinds. The intensity gradually increases, and at the height of the climax, there is a return to the tonality of B-flat to introduce the formally conventional recapitulation. The restatement of the second subject, however, is vested with new interest as the bass clarinet and bassoons play it in canon with the unison strings. The movement ends with a short but stirring coda.

WILLIAM SCHUMAN

William Schuman's early contact with music was entirely within the jazz idiom. While still in high school in New York, he formed a jazz band and later worked as a song plugger for a Tin Pan Alley music publisher. Together with his boyhood friend, Frank Loesser, he wrote over forty popular songs, one of which was published. In 1933, however, he completely abandoned the popular field and entered Columbia University, where, two years later, he received a degree in music. After a short period in Leipzig, where he studied conducting, he returned to the States and began his teaching career at Sarah Lawrence College. He remained there until 1945, when he accepted an appointment as president of Juilliard School of Music. In 1962, he left Juilliard to become the first president of the Lincoln Center for the Performing Arts.

Success as a composer came to Schuman quickly, including an impressive number of significant first performances, citations, and awards while he was still in his thirties. He received two Guggenheim Fellowships (1939, 1940), the first Town Hall–League of Composers Award in 1942, the first annual New York Music Critics Circle Award (1942), the first Pulitzer Prize for music (1943), and the first Brandeis University Creative Arts Award.

Much of Schuman's musical productivity has been expressed through classical abstract forms—notably the symphony—and through classic polyphonic textures, contemporized through the use of dissonant contrapuntal techniques. These neoclassic tendencies also manifest themselves

William Schuman

through his use of such forms as the fugue, toccata, and passacaglia. Broad, sweeping melodies and dramatic exuberance further characterize his works. For him, melody and rhythm, rather than harmony, are important motivating forces: "I write by singing, not by sitting at the piano." His continued adherence to tonality is probable due to the influence of Roy Harris, with whom he studied for two years and who has since remained his close friend.

The best-known among Schuman's eight symphonies is his Third, written in 1941; however, his Fifth (*The Symphony for Strings;* 1943), Seventh (1960), and Eighth (1962) are undoubtedly his strongest works in this form. Other outstanding large-scale works are the Concerto for Piano (1942), the Concerto for Violin (1947), the Fourth String Quartet (1950), *Credendum* (1955)—a three-movement symphonic work commissioned by the United States State Department for UNESCO—and the *Song of Orpheus* (1961) for cello and orchestra, commissioned by the Ford Foundation for Leonard Rose. He has also written three ballets— the exciting *Undertow* (1945), and two written for Martha Graham, *Night Journey* (1947), and *Judith* (1948)—a number of fine choral works, including *Pioneers* (1937), *Holiday Song* (1942), and two cantatas: *This is Our Time* (1940) and a *Free Song* (1942), which received the Pulitzer Prize. His most popular compositions are two of his shorter works, the *American Festival Overture* (1939), and the *New England Triptych* (1956), based on three tunes by the early New England composer William Billings.

Schuman: SYMPHONY NO. 3

The New York Music Critics Circle of New York selected Schuman's Symphony No. 3 as the best new American orchestral work performed in New York during the 1941–42 season. Since that time, audiences throughout the United States and Europe have consistently received this symphony with great enthusiasm. It is an extremely complex work, written for a very large orchestra, and is divided into two parts each of which consists of two seventeenth-century contrapuntal forms expressed within the twentieth-century idiom.

Part One: Passacaglia and Fugue. This part presents a considerable departure from the traditional passacaglia-and-fugue format used by Bach. Rather than use a comparatively simple four- or eight-measure theme as a repetitive figure, Schuman begins this passacaglia with a seven-voice canon that continues for forty-eight measures. Each voice in the canon enters at the space of seven measures a semitone higher than the previous voice. All the principal themes of the symphony are derived from this opening seven-measure theme:

Example 174.

a) Passacaglia (♩= 60–66)

The interweaving of the seven voices in the slow tempo of the movement results in a very rich lyric sound intensified by the woodwinds and horns in the last three entries. In the fiftieth measure, the strings begin a triplet figure accompaniment for the trumpets and trombones as they play a variant of the theme. The woodwinds enter with another variation and then the cellos initiate a sixteenth-note passage of ascending and descending scales while the violins play a new variation. The passage gradually intensifies until a climax is finally reached with all of the brass. In the final variation, the strings play a dotted rhythm while four trombones blare out a slow, *fortississimo* variant of the passacaglia theme. The fugue section actually consists of three fugues, each based on a different motive taken from the opening passacaglia theme. The first four-measure subject, based on the characteristic interval of a fourth, heard in the second and sixth measures of the passacaglia theme, is played by the horns:

Example 175.

There are seven entrances in the fugue's exposition, and as in the passacaglia, each is a semitone higher than the previous one. The last entrance, played by four trumpets together with the entire orchestra, reaches a *fortissimo* climax, which is followed by a stretto based on an inversion of the opening three notes of the fugue. There is a brief interlude in which the clarinet and flute quietly play a variant of the passacaglia theme as a connecting link with the second fugue. The English horn introduces this fugue with a variant of the theme just heard, at twice the tempo. The second fugal exposition consists of four successive entrances by the various woodwind sections, at the intervals of a fourth, second, and seventh, of a five-measure theme:

Example 176.

The woodwinds continue the eighth-note motion and the muted string section enters with a choralelike section. The eighth-note motion becomes more agitated and the strings more intense, as a climax is reached with the string section returning to the subject of the second fugue. At the height of the climax, the timpani enters alone, playing a savage rhythmic section that serves as a link with the third fugal subject. The strings enter *fortissimo* playing a dotted rhythmic accompaniment to a brassy declaration of the subject by the horns. The subject is eight measures long, again featuring the octave leap of the passacaglia theme. Its tonality centers around B-flat, the tonality of the passacaglia. The strings continue the insistent dotted rhythm as the exposition unfolds. Four entrances, played by various brass and woodwind combinations, culminate in a brilliant fourth-entry climax played by two trumpets and two trombones. The strings and woodwinds continue the rhythm antiphonally as the trombones and horns develop this fugal subject, *fortissimo*. A short coda opens with the entire brass section playing a choralelike theme based on the original passacaglia. Note again the characteristic leap of the octave. A massive climax ends the first part of the symphony.

Part Two: Chorale and Toccata. The Chorale opens with a slow contrapuntal introduction played by *divisi* (divided) violas and cellos. The chorale theme, derived from the passacaglia, is played by the solo trumpet as the violins join the other strings in a blocklike harmonic accompaniment:

Example 177.

The flute continues the chorale and then the strings, in a slightly faster tempo, play a contrapuntal variation beginning *pianississimo* followed by a gradual *crescendo*. The high register woodwinds and strings now play the chorale theme in harmony, *fortissimo*, while the low woodwinds and strings accompany with a contrapuntal line played in octaves. The sound abates, and four horns enter quietly playing a two-part contrapuntal variation. The chorale ends gently as the bassoons and contrabassoon sustain a B-flat into the beginning of the Toccata.

The Toccata is a brilliant virtuoso display piece dominated by a driving triplet rhythm. It opens with a tapped-out rhythm by the snare drum against the sustained B-flat of the chorale ending. The bass clarinet enters with the theme. It is treated imitatively by the other woodwinds as the snare drum continues. An interlude follows with the woodwinds playing the theme, at one-fourth its original speed, against a rhythmic background played by the timpani. The triplet rhythm returns now, in the woodwinds and snare drum, with the xylophone doubling the piccolo. The next section features a cadenza by the entire string section. It opens with the cellos playing motives from Part One. They are joined by the violas and then by the violins in a very free virtuoso section that leads back to the original driving tempo. The strings now play the theme of the chorale very quietly in a repeated sixteenth-note rhythm that is continued while the brass and low woodwinds play a choralelike variant of the toccata theme. The triplet rhythm returns and continues through a brilliant coda.

chapter 18

Samuel Barber
(b. 1910)

Samuel Barber has never been part of the American nationalist movement; he preferred instead a more eclectic, international idiom. His continued popularity is due for the most part to the fact that he writes in an accessible, consistently lyric style. He finds the traditional forms and structures still viable, and although he does at times make unexpected forays into atonality and shifting modality, his music is basically tonal. His writing is characterized by charm, restraint, and craftsmanship.

Barber was born in West Chester, Pennsylvania. At the age of thirteen he joined the first class of students who entered the Curtis Institute of Music when it was founded in 1924. While there, he studied piano, voice, and composition. His early works, written while he was still a student at Curtis, display a conservative lyricism and easily accessible harmonic idiom. Expressiveness, refined craftsmanship, confident use of the larger forms, and a lyric sensitivity that reflects his training as a singer were hallmarks of his creativity even during those early years. *Dover Beach* (1931) for voice and string quartet, the Cello Sonata (1932), and the Overture to *The School for Scandal* (1932) were all written before he graduated.

He won the Prix de Rome in 1935 and Pulitzer Fellowships in 1935 and 1936. While in Rome he wrote the Symphony No. 1 (1936), the String Quartet in B minor (1936), the *Adagio for Strings* (1936; an arrangement of the slow movement of the quartet), and the *Essay for Orchestra No. 1* (1937). In Italy, Barber met the conductor Arturo Toscanini, who was so impressed with Barber's talent that he chose the *Adagio for Strings* and the *Essay for Orchestra* to conduct with the NBC Symphony and with other orchestras throughout Europe, giving Barber the distinction of being the first American composer whose works were performed by the NBC Symphony under Toscanini's direction.

During the forties, Barber began to assimilate a number of progressive procedures into his style. His basically romantic expression became enriched by polytonal and other dissonance elements, serial techniques, and polyphonic and rhythmic complexities. It was as if he had suddenly become aware of the music of Stravinsky and Schoenberg. This period includes a number of particularly important works. His first departure from conventionality was in *A Stopwatch and an Ordnance Map* (1940), a setting of Stephen Spender's poem about the death of a soldier in the Spanish Civil War, scored for men's voices and three timpani (with optional brass). This was followed by the *Essay for Orchestra No. 2* (1942), which employs polytonality; the *Symphony Dedicated to the Air Forces* (1944), with its dissonant harmonies and angular melodies; the *Capricorn Concerto* (1944), a neoclassic concerto grosso for flute, oboe, trumpet, and strings; a very attractive and effective Concerto for Cello and Orchestra (1945); and the highly dramatic ballet written for Martha Graham, *The Cave of the Heart* (1946), which he later rescored for full orchestra as a tone poem and retitled *Medea's Meditation and Dance of Vengeance* (1955).

Samuel Barber

Some of Barber's finest works are those in which he employs the voice. *Knoxville: Summer of 1915* (1947; on a text by James Agee) for soprano and orchestra; the mystical *Prayers of Kierkegaard* (1945) for soprano solo, chorus, and orchestra; and the dramatic scena, *Andromache's Farewell* (1962) for soprano and orchestra are particularly important large works for voice. Two collections of songs for voice and piano, *Mélodies Passagères* (1952) and the *Hermit Songs,* settings of translations of medieval Irish poems by monks and scholars, are important additions to contemporary art song literature.

Barber decided to extend the scope of his writing for the voice by composing an opera. His search for an appropriate librettist, however, took years. Ultimately, he turned to his friend Gian Carlo Menotti for a libretto. The result, *Vanessa,* was premièred at the Metropolitan Opera House in 1958 and received the Pulitzer Prize in music later the same year. Barber, using a rather thin plot, constructed a grand opera in four acts that contains a remarkable dramatic power and that effectively projects the moody, brooding atmosphere of the text. In concept, the opera is a belated echo of the late-nineteenth-century French grand opera style; unfortunately, Barber's harmonic idiom for *Vanessa* never enters the twentieth century.

In 1966 Barber was commissioned by the Metropolitan Opera Company to write an opera for the opening of its new home in the Lincoln Center for the Performing Arts. For the occasion, he wrote another grand opera, *Anthony and Cleopatra,* to a libretto adapted for him by the talented Italian stage director, Franco Zeffirelli. It had a rather limited success, probably because of its conservative idiom and retrospective style and format.

Barber: OVERTURE TO *THE SCHOOL FOR SCANDAL*

The Overture to *The School for Scandal* (1932) was first performed by the Philadelphia Orchestra in 1933 after winning the Bearns Prize from Columbia University. This highly attractive work, written for large orchestra, was inspired by Sheridan's Restoration comedy.

The Overture is in classical sonata-form and opens with a six-measure fanfarelike introduction featuring the woodwinds. The first subject, played lightly by the violins, suggests the gossiping of the ladies in the play:

Example 178.

The theme stretches out, and then after a *crescendo*, is repeated *fortissimo* by all the strings against a staccato background in the horns and wood-winds. A connecting passage leads to a few measures of the opening fanfare, which now introduces the second subject, a long-breathed lyric melody in the relative major, played by the oboe:

Example 179.

Slightly slower than original tempo

The theme is repeated by the violins and then during the statement of a closing theme, the original tempo returns, leading to the opening fanfare, which now introduces a short development section. This section is de-voted entirely to the development of material from the first subject. A *fortissimo* climax is reached, and the recapitulation begins. A short coda states the first subject *pianissimo* in the strings, and after a brief climax, the opening fanfare is heard again, ending the overture in the same gay, lighthearted mood with which it began.

Barber: CONCERTO FOR PIANO AND ORCHESTRA

Samuel Barber's piano concerto was commissioned by the publisher G. Schirmer as a part of the firm's one hundredth anniversary celebration. It was first performed in 1962 by the Boston Symphony and the following year received the Pulitzer Prize for music. In writing this concerto, Barber returned to the romanticism of his early works by reaffirming his allegiance to the principles of tonality, and by writing thoroughly vocal, expressive melodic lines. The result is a readily accessible work, demanding virtuoso skill, which has already found an important place for itself in the concerto repertory.

First Movement: Allegro appassionato.   Barber based this movement, in E minor, on the principles of sonata-form. The piano cadenza that opens the movement presents two motives, the first melodic, the second rhythmic:

Example 180.

Examples 180–184: Copyright © 1962 by G. Schirmer, Inc. Used by permission.

Both of these motives are used prominently in the various connecting passages and development of material throughout the movement. The first subject, announced by the violins, flutes, and oboes, is presented in combination with a contrapuntal line played by the violas and English horn. It is an extremely expressive musical idea whose inner structure outlines a descending chromatic line:

Example 181.

The subject is repeated, and then after being begun by the piano, it is continued by the English horn and violas while the piano plays a cascade of chromatic sixths. After a slight development of this idea, the opening motive of the movement returns. The excitement gradually subsides, and the second subject, in a tempo less than a third of that of the first subject, is played intensely by the oboe against a soft harmonic background by the strings:

Example 182.

The descending seventh at the end of each of the first two measures of this subject and at the end of each of the two phrases of the first subject relates these subjects both to one another and to the opening motive of the concerto. The second subject, repeated by the violins, reaches a high peak of intensity and then gradually subsides as a closing subject, based on the two opening motives of the concerto, begins a scherzo-like section. A short cadenza then leads to the development section.

This section is concerned almost exclusively with the melodic, rhythmic, and contrapuntal development of the two opening motives of the concerto. A highly chromatic virtuoso cadenza for the piano, based on the first subject, ends with a long chromatic run leading directly to the recapitulation. Following the reappearance of the scherzo-like section, the tempo changes to an *Allegro misterioso* for the coda. The movement ends with a flourish by the entire orchestra and soloist as the brass and high woodwinds triumphantly reassert the opening notes of the movement.

Second Movement: Moderato. This "canzone," the most consistently tonal among the three movements, opens with a theme played alternately by the flute and oboe against a whispering string tremolo accompaniment derived from the theme's lovely poetic melody:

Example 183.

Example 183. Continued

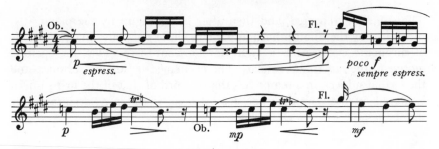

The piano then states the theme and extends it, developing the final phrase first with the woodwinds and then with the strings. The entire theme is played again by the piano with its own triplet thirty-second-note accompaniment. The thirty-second-note pattern by the piano continues as the violins take up the theme and bring it to an intense climax. The mood of the beginning returns as the piano ends the movement playing a few notes from the theme.

Third Movement: Allegro molto. The finale is a brilliant show piece in rondo form. The meter is $\frac{5}{8}$ throughout; the main theme is rhythmic, strong, and vibrant:

Example 184.

The tempo slows considerably for the second theme, a chromatic oriental-sounding tune played by the oboe accompanied by the xylophone. Following a series of chromatic runs by the piano, the main theme returns, played first by the bassoon and then by all the woodwinds accompanied by the piano. After an impressive *fortissimo* climax, the piano plays a chromatic run that moves, within a few measures, from *fortissimo* to *pianissimo* for the entrance of the third theme, presented in a slower tempo by three flutes and a bass clarinet, accompanied by three trombones and harp. This graceful theme is repeated by the piano and then the movement reaches a stormy moment as the brass play the theme against chromatically altered scales in the strings and woodwinds. The clamor subsides and the timpani begins a connecting *accelerando* passage to introduce a return of the main rondo theme. Following instrumentally varied statements of this idea, the second theme enters *fortissimo* played by the full orchestra. A restatement of the opening notes of the movement, first by the piano, and then in combination with the entire orchestra, brings this impressive concerto to a conclusion.

chapter 19

Latin America

During the opening decades of the twentieth century, Latin American musicians, encouraged by state support of the arts, made a concerted effort to achieve independence from European musical domination. Composers continued to remain receptive to the latest directions of European composition; however, they now sought out their own unique expression of national identity by infusing their music with both native Indian and Negro elements.

Heitor Villa-Lobos (1887–1959)

Brazilian music in particular achieved international recognition during these years, through the works of a highly gifted group of composers. Foremost among them was Heitor Villa-Lobos. While still a young boy, he studied theory and cello with his father in Rio de Janeiro; when he was eighteen, he made the first of three major excursions into the remote regions of Brazil, composing and collecting folk material as he traveled. There was a brief interlude at the National Institute of Music and two more trips to the interior, and then he began composing seriously. A grant from the Brazilian government in 1923 enabled him to study in Paris, where he came under the influence of Ravel, and also became well acquainted with the works of J. S. Bach. In addition to composing, he spent much of his mature career in the dual roles of educator and conductor.

Heitor Villa-Lobos

The remarkably prolific Villa-Lobos produced over two thousand works, representative of nearly every form and medium. In his creative enthusiasm, however, he exercised very little self-criticism or restraint, and as a consequence, the most profound and original among his works are freely mixed with the trivial and derivative. He was generally a neo-romantic by nature, and his typical lyric, tonally oriented, and harmonically derived idiom is well seasoned with striking dissonance, polytonality, and vigorous rhythmic propulsion. A series of sixteen *Chôros* are among his most representative compositions. They range in medium from a guitar solo (*Chôro No. 1*) to *Chôro No. 13,* scored for two orchestras and military band. Villa-Lobos appropriated the name *chôros* from the music played by bands of young improvisational entertainers. To him, the *chôros* became "a new form in which are synthesized the different modalities of Brazilian, Indian, and popular music, having for principal elements, rhythm and any typical melody of popular character. . . ." *Chôro No. 10* (1925), for chorus and orchestra, is the best known of the series, and has been presented as a ballet under the title *Jurupary*.

In the series of nine suites for various instrumental combinations that he entitled *Bachianas Brasileiras* (1930–45), Villa-Lobos attempted to combine the harmonic and melodic atmosphere of rural and urban

278

Brazil with the musical style of Bach. The final movement of the second suite ("The Little Train of Caipira"), and the *Bachianas Brasileiras No. 5* are among his best-known works.

Villa-Lobos: *BACHIANAS BRASILEIRAS NO. 5*

The *Aria* movement of this celebrated work was written in 1938. Seven years later, he added the *Dansa*. It is scored for soprano and an orchestra of eight cellos. Villa-Lobos purports to evoke the spirit of Bach in Brazilian costume through these suites. The principal resemblance to Bach in this work centers in the long, flowing *cantilena* line of the opening *Aria*, which recalls Bach's familiar "Air" from the Suite No. 3.

I. Aria (Cantilena). The cellos open the movement with a running pizzicato figure, simulating a guitar accompaniment for the vocal line that enters three measures later. The enchantingly beautiful long melodic line for the soprano is intoned as a vocalise on the neutral vowel sound "Ah," doubled by a solo cello:

Example 185.

Examples 185–187: Used by permission of Associated Music Publishers.

The solo cello then repeats the long melody. The tempo increases slightly for the middle section of this ABA movement, and the voice passionately extols the beauties of the night in the words of a poem by Ruth Corrêa. The repeated notes of the vocal line are given poignancy through the intensity of the highly chromatic, dissonant cello accompaniment:

Example 186.

Translation: At midnight, when luminous clouds slowly move across
the expansive sky, the moon rises, glorifying all nature.

The melody of the first section returns, hummed by the soprano.

II. Dansa (Martelo). This movement, also in ABA form, is a spirited dance song whose subtitle, *Martelo* (hammered), suggests the persistent rhythmic dance character of the Brazilian *emboladas*. The text,
by the poet Manoel Bandeira, is addressed to the love-bird of the Cariri
wilderness. After a four-measure introduction, the voice enters, continuing
the running figure of the first cellos in the manner of a Brazilian patter
song:

Example 187.

Translation: Irerê, my little bird from the wilderness of Cariri,
Irerê, my companion, where are you going? Where my
dear, where is Maria? . . . (Sing once more my Irerê like
the birds which awaken Maria at dawn. Birds of the
wilderness, sing your songs! La! lia! lia! lia!)

The section ends with a tone sustained by the singer for seven
measures as the tempo slows for the B section. It opens with the
lower cellos in $\frac{3}{8}$ meter against the $\frac{2}{4}$ of the melody played initially by
the first cellos and then imitated by the soprano. Following a sudden
return to the original tempo, the cellos play a strong martellato figure
in 3–3–2 rhythm. The martellato character changes to pizzicato, and the
voice enters with a new theme. After a short connecting passage, the A
section returns, ended this time with a shout.

Carlos Chávez (1899–1978)

Carlos Chávez is Mexico's counterpart to Brazil's Villa-Lobos. Vir-
tually self-taught in music, he showed great promise even during his teens.
Searching for his own musical identity within the spirit of the Mexican
Revolution, he immersed himself in the native music of the outlying

Carlos Chávez

regions of Mexico. His first important work in the Mexican style was the ballet *El fuego nuevo* (*The New Fire;* 1921). After a period of extensive travel throughout Europe and the United States, he returned to Mexico and founded and was appointed conductor of the Orquestra Sinfónica de México. He was later appointed director of the National Conservatory of Music. In his varied roles as composer, conductor, lecturer, and administrator, he was able through the years to exert a considerable influence on the development of contemporary nationalist music in Mexico.

Chávez successfully combined native national characteristics with contemporary compositional methods. Austere in its tonal economy, his style possesses great rhythmic motor drive, is largely contrapuntal, and is filled with colorful dissonance. He seldom actually quoted folk material, but rather interpreted what he had heard in his own enlightened terms.

The "Indian" ballet, *Los cuatro soles* (*The Four Suns;* 1926), and his "machine age" ballet-symphony *H. P.* (*Horsepower;* 1927) are both based on folk material and utilize native percussion instruments in their instrumentation. With his first two symphonies, *Sinfonía de Antígona* (1933)—based on incidental music he wrote for Cocteau's version of Sophocles' Antigone—and the *Sinfonía India* (1936), the two pieces by which he is best known, Chávez reached the culmination of his primitive, nationalistic period. His works from this point are more nearly neoclassic in their orientation. The Concerto for Four Horns (1939), the Concerto for Piano (1940), and the Violin Concerto (1950) of this period are among his finest works. His ballet *Hija de Colguide* (1944), known as *Dark*

Meadow in Martha Graham's production, is quite familiar to audiences in the United States. His final works display a more dissonant character. *Il Invention* (1963), for instance, is an atonal work. In 1969 he wrote the Suite *Fuego Olimpico* for the Olympic Games in Mexico City.

Alberto Ginastera (b. 1916)

The Argentinean composer Alberto Ginastera has achieved a position of international importance in the contemporary musical scene. A year before graduating from the National Conservatory, he wrote the ballet *Panambí* (1937), his first major work to receive significant recognition. He came to the United States on a Guggenheim Fellowship during 1945–46, and then on his return to Buenos Aires, he founded the Conservatory of Music and Art and served as its director for a number of years. During the past two decades, his works have been widely performed by leading orchestras throughout the world. His early works, all inspired by folklore, are filled with passionate chants and the rhythms of Argentine *gaucho* folk dances. They have a dynamic primitivism likely derived from Stravinsky's early compositions. *Panambí, the Argentine Dances* (1937) for piano, the ballet *Estancia* (1941), the *Concierto Argentino* (1941) for orchestra, and the *Sinfonia Porteña* (1942) are all from this period. As his harmonic language became more advanced, his nationalism lessened and he adopted a more neoclassic approach that ultimately led him toward serialism. Representative compositions of this phase of his development include the Overture to Goethe's *Faust* (1944), the Sonata for Piano (1952), the *Variaciones Concertantes* (1953), and *Pampeana No. 3: Pastoral Symphony* (1954). His setting of six Aztec, Mayan, and Indian sources, scored for soprano and an orchestra of fifty-three percussion instruments, was an outstanding success at the Inter-American Music Festival of 1961.

He fully committed himself to serialism with his Violin Concerto (1963) and the opera *Don Rodrigo* (1964). *Don Rodrigo,* compared to Berg's *Wozzeck* because of its use of *Sprechstimme* and instrumental forms for each of its scenes, won unanimous critical acclaim when it was presented by the New York City Opera in 1966. *Bomarzo* (1963) and *Beatrix Cenci* (1971) are his most recent works in the operatic idiom.

part V

OTHER
AMERICAN
COMPOSERS

chapter 20

Nationalists

After the frantic, experimental decade following World War I many American composers turned to musical Americana for inspiration. Folk songs, dances, legends, cowboy songs, as well as the quickening pace of urban life, provided rich material to be exploited. By the 1930s, American nationalism in music had come of age, recognized at home and abroad through performances at all of the major musical centers. Basically, it was a conservative trend that sought to reach a large audience through more direct communication. This conservative, nationalistic movement coincided with a similar movement in painting exemplified in the works of such artists as Charles Burchfield, Edward Hopper, Thomas Hart Benton, and Grant Wood.

Virgil Thomson (b. 1896)

Virgil Thomson was born in Kansas City. Although he studied at Harvard and then lived in Paris for fifteen years, he never lost the simplicity and naïveté of his Midwestern heritage and never forgot his years as a church organist among Southern Baptists. He describes himself as a romantic, but his Americanism is almost always in evidence, particularly in his works written after 1926. He went to Paris for the first time in 1921 with the Harvard Glee Club and remained there to study with Nadia Boulanger. The following year he returned to Harvard, graduated, and

Virgil Thomson

taught there for a few years. However, the lure of Paris was too strong; he went back in 1925 and remained there until the Germans invaded France at the beginning of World War II. During these years, Paris was the cultural center of Europe. Its salons were the gathering places for many fine young writers, poets, and artists as well as musicians. While in Paris, Thomson came in contact with many of the proponents of the then current avant-garde. Among them were Cocteau, Picasso, Gertrude Stein, Satie, and Milhaud. It was Satie's satiric surrealism and childlike gravity that struck a responsive chord in Thomson's American pseudo-innocence; in fact, Thomson has often been called the American Satie. His irreverence, eclecticism, spontaneity, and juxtaposition of totally unrelated ideas all reflect this influence. The amusing *Sonata da Chiesa* (1926) and the Baptist-oriented *Symphony on a Hymn Tune* (1926–28) are representative works of these years.

At this time in Paris, Gertrude Stein was mothering many expatriate poets, painters, and assorted eccentrics who looked to her for the guidance and friendship that she gave so freely. Thomson became a member of her circle and, to her great delight, set many of her poems to music. Although she had little interest in music (she did, however, admire Satie's *Socrate*), she agreed to collaborate with Thomson on an opera. The opera, *Four Saints in Three Acts* (1928) was premièred in Hartford under the auspices of the Society of Friends and Enemies of Modern Music in 1934. Reflecting on the collaboration, Virgil Thomson wrote:

> It was early in 1927 that Gertrude Stein and I conceived the idea of writing an opera together. . . . For me the cooperation had been a happy one

288

from the beginning and its memory is still sweet. Miss Stein had said when she gave me the completed play, 'Do anything with this you like; cut, repeat, as composers have always done; make it work on a stage.' Actually, I made no cuts or repeats in my first version. I put everything to music, even the stage directions, because they made such lovely lines for singing. . . .

Putting to music poetry so musically conceived as Gertrude Stein's has long been a pleasure to me. The spontaneity of it, its easy flow, and its deep sincerity have always seemed to me just right for music.

Twenty years later, they collaborated on a second opera, *The Mother of Us All* (1947). This unjustly neglected opera is a witty, charming, yet deeply moving account of the life and career of America's feminist leader Susan B. Anthony.

After returning to the United States in 1940, Thomson became the music editor of the *New York Herald Tribune,* a position he held until 1954, when he decided to devote more of his time to composition. Four volumes of Thomson's critiques have been published.

A large part of the widespread reputation he has achieved as a composer is based on the music he wrote for a series of documentary films: *The Plow that Broke the Plains* (1936); *The River* (1937); *Tuesday in November* (1945); and *The Louisiana Story* (1948). Thomson leans heavily

Four Saints in Three Acts
The Bettmann Archive.

on indigenous American music in all these films: cowboy tunes for *The Plow,* white spirituals for *The River,* waltzes and hymns for *Tuesday in November,* and Acadian songs and dances of the bayou country in *The Louisiana Story.*

Roy Harris (1898–1979)

Roy Harris early identified himself musically with the American scene—its people and the Western plains of his birth. To many, he became the very personification of what they felt an American composer should be. His music has a basic simplicity that carries with it an aura of sincerity and an epic quality reminiscent of the wide open spaces of America rather than its crowded fast-paced cities. His training in harmony and composition, begun when he was in his twenties, produced rapid and impressive results. By 1926, one of his first works, the Andante for Orchestra, was chosen to be performed at the Festival of American Music in Rochester. It was an immediate success. At the suggestion of Aaron Copland, Harris went to Paris to further his studies with Nadia Boulanger. His return to the United States was a triumph—American music had found a new voice.

Harris reached the peak of his inspiration during the thirties, a period highlighted particularly by his Third Symphony (1938), the Piano

Roy Harris

Quintet (1936), and the String Quartet No. 3 (1937). Paradoxically, as his technique improved and his music took on more sophistication, his inspiration seemed to wane, and by the fifties he had drifted out of the mainstream of American music. His compositions include twelve symphonies, two concertos, a considerable amount of chamber music, four sonatas, and two major choral works, *The Song for Occupations* (1934) and the *Symphony for Voices* (1935), both for a cappella chorus on texts by Walt Whitman.

Harris's music is characterized by his use of long-flowing melodies, asymmetrical rhythms, and sharp differentiations among the various orchestral choirs. He was a dedicated contrapuntalist—canonic devices, passacaglias, and fugues are all prominent features of his compositional technique. His harmonic idiom is essentially diatonic, although, particularly during the thirties, he used the more remote, archaic sounds of modal scales and harmonies. Open fifths, strings of parallel chords, and bitonal combinations of seemingly unrelated triads further characterize his harmonizations.

Harris: SYMPHONY NO. 3

The Third Symphony, Harris's most often performed work, was completed in the fall of 1938, and was first introduced on February 24, 1939, by the Boston Symphony conducted by Serge Koussevitsky. Although Harris does not quote folk-song material directly in this work, his melodic material is readily identified as a kind of idealized expression of the American hymnal and folk tradition. An outline of the extraordinarily well-balanced expressive content and formal means of the five contrasting sections in this one-movement symphony has been provided by the composer:

> Section I. *Tragic*—low string sonorities. Section II. *Lyric*—strings, horns, woodwinds. Section III. *Pastoral*—woodwinds with a polytonal string background. Section IV. *Fugue*—dramatic. A. Brass and percussion predominating. B. Canonic development of materials from Section II constituting background for further development of fugue. C. Brass climax, rhythmic motif derived from fugue subject. Section V. *Dramatic*—tragic. A. Restatement of violin theme of Section I; tutti strings in canon with tutti woodwinds against brass and percussion developing rhythmic motif from Section IV. B. Coda—development of materials from Sections I and II over pedal timpani.

The cellos open the symphony with an extended melody whose modal flavor and asymmetrical groupings within a steady quarter-note movement give it a quality reminiscent of our psalm-tune heritage.

Example 188.

Examples 188–190: Copyright © 1939, 1966 by G. Schirmer, Inc. Used by permission.

The melodic intervals subsequently increase in size, and as other instruments are added, the texture takes on a parallel organumlike quality. The orchestral color changes for the beginning of the lyric Section II. The melodic material, long and extremely fluid in its phrase lengths, metrical groupings, and tempo, is played antiphonally between the strings and woodwinds. For the pastoral, the strings have a polytonal arpeggio figuration as an impressionistic background for a pastoral theme played by the English horn:

Example 189.

The strings continue the figuration as various woodwinds, brass, and combinations of winds are heard playing both variants of this theme and answering phrases. Toward the end of the section the phrases are shortened, and a climax is reached as the dramatic fugue theme enters, angular and rhythmic, with a sense of urgency:

Example 190.

The development of the fugue builds to a brass climax, and then the violins restate their theme from the lyric section to begin the last section. The violins and woodwinds then play the theme canonically as the brass and percussion continue to interject the rhythmic motif of the fugue. The tempo broadens, and the coda begins with a steady beat by the timpani, as themes from the first and second sections appear and are developed. The dramatic-tragic mood is omnipresent as this epic symphony draws to an impressive close.

William Grant Still (1895–1978)

William Grant Still was born in Mississippi and grew up in Little Rock, Arkansas. Still's parents, both of whom were secondary school teachers, exposed him to a wide variety of musical experiences during his formative years. After graduating from high school, he enrolled in Wilberforce University. His mother wanted him to be a doctor, knowing that although he was obviously talented in music, a career in music for a black

William Grant Still
Cleveland Public Library.

could be both socially and financially unrewarding. Nevertheless, he spent most of his time at the university directing the band, organizing musical ensembles, and writing music for performance by these ensembles. After graduation, he played odd jobs in dance bands and for vaudeville acts and then in 1916 enrolled at Oberlin College in Ohio.

Still moved to New York after serving in the Navy during the war. While there he immersed himself in commercial music, playing in musicals and arranging music for W. C. Handy, Paul Whiteman, Donald Vorhees, and Earl Carroll. He studied for a while at the New England Conservatory with George Chadwick, who acquainted him with American music and impressed upon him the importance of nationalism in music. He then worked for two years as a scholarship student with Edgar Varèse, who introduced him into new paths of musical expression.

In the twenties, Still began to concentrate on larger, serious works. He had been composing and arranging music for about ten years and now felt that he was ready to express himself in the larger orchestral forms. *From the Land of Dreams* (1924), for three voices and chamber orchestra in the avant-garde style of Varèse, was performed by the International Composers' Guild in New York in 1925. In 1926 *Darker America* (1924), a tone poem for chamber orchestra, was also performed by the Guild. However, it was the performance of his *Afro-American Symphony* in 1931 by Howard Hanson and the Rochester Symphony that first brought him widespread recognition. The *Afro-American Symphony* is generally considered his greatest work.

After writing *From the Land of Dreams,* Still turned to a more nationalistic style based on the development of the black idiom and the treatment of black subjects. In his words, "Although my compositions in Mr. Varèse's dissonant idiom brought me to the attention of metropolitan critics, I soon decided that this was not representative of my own musical individuality, and adopted a racial form of expression." Proud of his black heritage, he used Afro-American titles for many of his works. His inspiration was drawn from all forms of black music: work songs, spirituals, blues, ragtime, and dances. Some of his works written during this period, roughly between 1925 and 1940, include *From the Black Belt* (1926), an orchestral suite; *La Guiablesse* (1927), a ballet based on a Martinique legend; *Kaintuck* (1935), for piano and orchestra; *Lenox Avenue* (1937), ballet suite for orchestra, chorus, and narrator; *Three Visions* (1935), a piano suite; and a trilogy of larger works—*Africa* (1928), the *Afro-American Symphony* (1930), and the Symphony in G minor (1927). The G minor Symphony was written for the Philadelphia Orchestra at the request of Leopold Stokowski.

In the mid-thirties, Still moved to California and began composing in the form he loved most: opera. His first opera, *Blue Steel* (1934), based on the conflict between the old voodoo beliefs and modern materialistic life, embraced both the jazz idiom and the spiritual. His second opera, *Troubled Island* (1941), was presented in 1949 by the New York City Opera Company. It is based on a libretto by Langston Hughes about the life of the Haitian liberator Jean Jacques Desselines. His most recent opera, *Highway 1, U.S.A.* (1962), was premièred in 1963 at the Festival of American Music in Miami.

As he grew older, Still's musical style became more traditional, and he drew on all American folk idioms for inspiration, not only those of the black, but also those of the Indian, Spanish-American, and Anglo-American. *Plainchant for America* (1941), *Festive Overture* (1944), *Danzas de Panama* (1948), *The Peaceful Land* (1960), *The Path of Glory* (1962), and many chamber music works for various combinations entitled *Folk Suites* are from this period. Still's total of more than one hundred works includes seven operas, four ballets, over thirty large orchestral compositions, many piano pieces, and a large number of songs and choral works. Among his vocal compositions, the most celebrated is the cantata *And They Lynched Him on a Tree* for two choruses, contralto, narrator, and orchestra. Based on a text by Katherine Chapin, it received its first performance in 1940 by the New York Philharmonic. He also wrote the music for the film *Pennies from Heaven* and for such TV shows as the *Perry Mason Show* and *Gunsmoke*. William Grant Still received many honors, commissions, and honorary degrees during his lifetime and has been justly called the "Dean of Afro-American composers."

Still: *AFRO-AMERICAN SYMPHONY*

"Long before writing this symphony I had recognized the musical value of the *Blues* and had decided to use a theme in the *Blues* idiom as the basis for a major symphonic composition." Still devised his own blues theme, which, in its various guises, is the unifying thread of this symphony. The *Afro-American Symphony* has the special distinction of being the first symphony written by a black to be played before an American audience.

First Movement: Moderato assai. The first movement is in sonata-form, modified through the use of variation development techniques as a replacement for motivic development. This technique is used in all of the movements and is well-suited to the songlike themes used by Still throughout the symphony.

After an introduction in which the main theme is alluded to by the English horn, the blues theme is played by a muted trumpet. It is in a standard twelve-measure blues pattern:

Example 191.

Examples 191–194: © 1935 by J. Fischer & Bro. © renewed 1962 and assigned to Novello & Co. Ltd. 1970. Used by permission.

After being repeated by the clarinet, a rhythmic variation follows in the violins. The second subject, played by the oboe, is in the style of a spiritual and is in three-part song form.

After a short development of material from the principal theme, the recapitulation begins with the violins playing the second subject. The blues rhythm is then heard for the last time. A short coda, in a more relaxed tempo, ends the movement.

Second Movement: Adagio. The slow movement, in F (major and minor), reflects a mood of pathos in keeping both with the movement's subtitle, "Sorrow," and with the following prefatory excerpt from a poem of Paul Laurence Dunbar:

> It's moughty tiahsome layin' 'roun'
> Dis sorrer-laden earfly groun'
> An' oftentimes I thinks, thinks I
> 'Twould be a sweet t'ing des to die
> An' go 'long home.

An introduction derived from the blues theme opens the movement. The oboe then plays the expressive principal theme:

Example 192.

After a repetition of the theme by the violas, a transition section featuring the English horn leads to a second subject derived from the blues theme. The second subject, begun by the flute and continued by the violins, is also in F, but alternates between major and minor, in the blues tradition. Following its repetition, the principal theme is developed at some length. There is a final statement of the principal theme shared by the flute and bassoon and then a coda, similar to the introduction, ends the movement "as quiet as possible."

Third Movement: Animato. The scherzo is the most popular movement of the symphony and has often been played as a separate entity. It is carefree and witty, and uses a tenor banjo to accentuate the dancelike rhythms. The underlying mood is one of humor illustrating the verses of Dunbar that preface the movement:

> An' we'll shout ouah halleluyahs,
> On dat mighty reck'nin' day.

The form of the movement, like that of the second movement, is a variant of sonata-form, with both subjects in the same key—in this case A-flat.

The movement opens with a short introduction based on the principal subject. The main theme of the subject, marked by a distinctive syncopated figure, is then announced by the violins:

Example 193.

The second subject is actually a variation of the main theme. A development of the rhythm and motivic structure of the principal subject follows, and then toward the end of the movement, the main idea returns in the flute. A coda featuring a more *legato* version of the main theme by the violins ends the scherzo.

Fourth Movement: Lento, con risoluzione. In describing this movement, Still said, "The Fourth Movement is largely a retrospective viewing of the earlier movements with the exception of its principal theme. It is intended to give musical expression to the lines from Paul Laurence Dunbar which appear on the score: 'Be proud, my race, in mind and soul. . . .'"

The principal theme sets the appropriate mood of somber nobility, played slowly and with dignity by the strings:

Example 194.

The theme is repeated and extended and then followed by a subordinate theme at a slightly quicker tempo. This theme, played by the flute and oboe, is also derived from the blues theme. After it is developed at great length, the original tempo returns as the cellos play the principal theme. The tempo abruptly quickens to a *Vivace* in $\frac{6}{8}$ meter and the principal theme is heard in a series of rhythmic variations. The tempo then slows to a *Maestoso* as the main theme is stated proudly by the brass while the strings play an obbligato ostinato variant of the scherzo theme as a final note of affirmation.

chapter 21

Experimentalists and Progressives

EXPERIMENTALISTS

Two American composers, Henry Cowell and Carl Ruggles, both ardent admirers of Charles Ives, were largely responsible for carrying the impetus of Ives's experimentation into the second quarter of the twentieth century. In their forward-looking works, both anticipated many trends to come, but while Henry Cowell achieved considerable fame both in the United States and abroad, Carl Ruggles has remained relatively unknown.

Henry Cowell (1897–1965)

Henry Cowell began his career as a daring experimentalist, and by the time he was twenty, according to his own records, he had written nearly two hundred works of all descriptions, including a symphony and an opera. His extraordinarily large output—about a thousand compositions—includes twenty symphonies, fifteen concertos, many choral and chamber works, and hundreds of piano pieces and songs.

Henry Cowell was born in Menlo Park, California, of intellectually eccentric parents whose educational philosophy allowed him to grow up without any formal schooling; in fact, the only formal education of any kind he received as a child was through his violin lessons. His early musi-

Henry Cowell

BMI Archives.

cal "training" consisted of learning ecclesiastic modes from a neighboring organist, Oriental music from Chinese neighbors in San Francisco, and Irish folklore and folk songs from his fiddling and ballad-singing relatives on farms in Kansas, Iowa, and Oklahoma. By the age of twelve he was supporting himself and his mother through raising and selling desert plants. He managed to buy an old upright piano and soon began to produce music at an astonishing rate. His first public concert, given in 1912 (at the age of fifteen), consisted of his own piano music, including the first of his published works, *The Tides of Manaunaun* (1911). The theorist and teacher Charles Seeger convinced Cowell that a more systematic study of composition was necessary for his development and so he enrolled in the University of California at Berkeley, where he finally acquired a conventional training in harmony and counterpoint. He later studied composition in New York with Percy Goetschius and musicology in Berlin as a recipient of a Guggenheim Grant. From 1923 to 1928 he concertized throughout Europe in a series of concerts sponsored by, among others, Bartók and Janáček. He was the first American composer to be invited to play in Russia; in fact, some of his piano music was first published in Russia.

300

Cowell explored many new resources of the piano in his early piano works, including his innovative playing of groups of notes with the fist or forearm (he named these sounds "tone clusters") and his unconventional methods of producing sounds by plucking, brushing, muting, and striking the open piano strings. *Antimony* (1914) requires that both arms be used simultaneously on the keyboard, *fffff* (*fortississississimo*). For the *Aeolian Harp* (1923) he provided the following instructions: "All of the notes . . . should be pressed down on the keys, without sounding, at the same time being played on the open strings of the piano with the other hand"; for *The Banshee* (1925) he instructs the player to scrape his fingers along the bass strings to produce a wailing sound. In using the fist (which is not clenched tightly) or the forearm, he says, "The keys should be pressed down rather than struck, in order to obtain a smooth tone quality and a unified sound." He adds that in most cases the weight of the forearm is sufficient without any added muscular effort. The following example from *Tiger* (1928) illustrates Cowell's use of the tone cluster:

Example 195

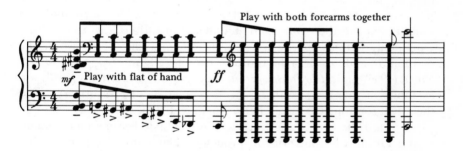

Used by permission of Associated Music Publishers.

A flat or sharp below the cluster symbol is used to indicate that only black keys are used; a natural indicates white keys. No accidental, as in the example, indicates that all notes are to be played between the upper and lower notes indicated.

Cowell also experimented with rhythmic patterns, particularly poly-rhythms in which groups of five, seven, nine, and eleven notes are played in combination and in juxtaposition with regular eight-note patterns. In his book *New Musical Resources,* he proposed a new notation that introduced various shaped notes to express various divisions of the beat: a triangular shape for groups of three and its multiples, square notes for groups of five and multiples, a diamond shape for groups of seven, etc.

The following example from *Fabric* (1917) illustrates this new notation:

Example 196.

Used by permission of Associated Music Publishers.

In the 1930s, long before indeterminacy became a serious issue in music, Cowell discovered in writing for Martha Graham and other dancers that his pieces were insufficiently adaptable to their specialized needs. As a consequence, he invented "elastic form," by which a composition could be expanded or contracted and altered in various ways so that "the individual rhythms, phrases, sentences, sections, the whole work, the rhythmical and tonal orchestration" become elastic. *The Sound-Form No. 1* (1936) and *Hilarious Curtain Opener and Ritournelle* (1939) are examples of this "form." In his *Mosaic Quartet,* the performers create their own continuity from a series of composed "blocks."

Toward the end of the thirties, Cowell's style became more conservative. This first became evident through his affinity for Gaelic and Celtic traditions that influenced works such as *Shoonthree (Sleep Music,* 1940), *Tales of the Countryside* (1941), a *Celtic Set* (1943), and a *Gaelic Symphony* (1943). At the same time, he became interested in native American folk music and wrote the *Old American Country Set* (1937), *Fiddler's Delight* (1940), *Back Country Set* (1945), and a series of eighteen *Hymn and Fuguing Tunes* (1944–64) based on the fuguing tunes of William Billings (1746–1800), an early New England composer and tune-book compiler. Cowell had always regarded Oriental music as a valid source for a modern composer's inspiration. After a visit to the East in 1956–57, he combined Oriental scales, sonorities, and rhythms with traditional Western elements, in works such as the *Persian Set* (1957), *Ongaku* (1957), and the Symphony No. 13 (*Madras Symphony,* 1958). In his late works, Cowell combined the fuguing style with dissonant counterpoint, Irish folk song, Oriental devices, and tone clusters in a synthesis of disparate elements that in its uniqueness is unmatched by any other composer.

Contemporary composers owe him a debt as a pioneer, and many have reason to be grateful for his personal encouragement and help. He has consistently been the champion of new music. He founded organizations that published and performed new works, and edited magazines that propagandized for them. He wrote over four hundred articles and reviews on every aspect of music from the psychology of music to ethnomusicology, and he provided a cohesive influence that went far towards reconciling progressive and traditional elements in the second quarter of this century. According to the music critic Peter Yates, "He has been one in a succession of great teachers, among them Horatio Parker, Ernest Bloch, Nadia Boulanger, Arnold Schoenberg, Walter Piston, Paul Hindemith, and Roger Sessions, who have decisively influenced the growth of American musical thought." Cowell is also the author of three books: *New Musical Resources* (1930), *American Composers on American Music* (1933), and, with his wife, Sidney Cowell, *Charles Ives and His Music* (1955), the definitive work on that composer.

Cowell: *THE BANSHEE*

The Banshee, written in 1925 when Cowell was in Europe concertizing, is one of the first of his works to require direct manipulation of the piano strings. It requires two performers, one standing at the crook of the piano and the other seated while holding down the damper pedal throughout the composition. Haunting, exotic effects are created by glissandos along the open strings in imitation of Irish mythology's banshee, a mysterious female spirit who flies over the house of one who is about to die, shrieking and moaning. Cowell intended through *The Banshee* to recreate the spirit of his Irish ancestors.

Example 197.

The Banshee

Explanation of Symbols

"The Banshee" is played on the open strings of the piano, the player standing at the crook. Another person must sit at the keyboard and hold down the damper pedal throughout the composition. The whole work should be played an octave lower than written.

R. H. stands for "right hand." L. H. stands for "left hand." Different
ways of playing the strings are indicated by a letter over each tone,
as follows:

(A) indicates a sweep with the flesh of the finger from the lowest string
     up to the note given.

(B) sweep lengthwise along the string of the note given with flesh of
     finger.

(C) sweep up and back from lowest A to highest B-flat given in this
     composition.

(D) pluck string with flesh of finger, where written, instead of octave
     lower.

(E) sweep along three notes together, in the same manner as (B).

(F) sweep in the maner of (B) but with the back of finger-nail instead
     of flesh.

(G) when the finger is half way along the string in the manner of (F),

     start a sweep along the same string with the flesh of the other
     finger, thus partly damping the sound.

(H) sweep back and forth in the manner of (C), but start at the same

     time from both above and below, crossing the sweep in the
     middle.

(I) sweep along five notes, in the manner of (B).

(J) same as (I) but with back of finger-nails instead of flesh of finger.

(K) sweep along in manner of (J) with nails of both hands together,

     taking in all notes between the two outer limits given.

(L) sweep in manner of (C) with flat of hand instead of single finger.

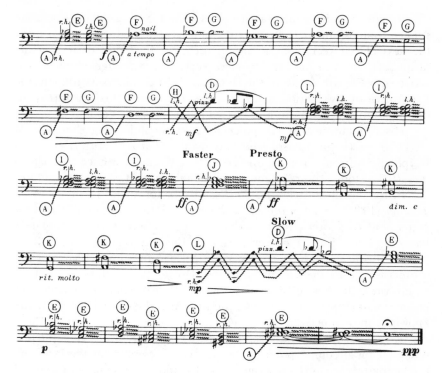

Carl Ruggles (1875–1971)

Carl Ruggles was an admirer and lifelong friend of Charles Ives. Where Ives's music is far-ranging, however, accepting "the tawdry and the trivial as well as the sublime," Ruggles's music is generally consistent, and embodies only one aspect of Ives's music: free, dissonant polyphony without tonal implications. Ives did not rely on a "system" in composing; by contrast, Ruggles spent many years perfecting a system, which he then used in all of his music. His entire musical output, that which he has allowed to survive, was written between 1919 and 1945, and comprises an even smaller output than that of his musical contemporary Webern. Like Webern, he constantly sought perfection, polishing and reworking his handful of works until he was completely satisfied with their final sound and shape. He never theorized or propagandized, preferring to let his admirers do it for him. Charles Seeger, Henry Cowell, John Kirkpatrick, and Lou Harrison are all eloquent, enthusiastic, and articulate champions of his music.

305

Ruggles was born in Massachusetts of old New England stock. He studied composition at Harvard with John Knowles Paine and then spent the next eleven years conducting an orchestra he founded in Winona, Minnesota. In 1923 he went to New York, where for ten years he was active with Edgard Varèse in the International Composers' Guild and the Pan-American Association of Composers. The rest of his life was spent in comparative isolation in a converted schoolhouse in Vermont.

His reputation as a composer rests on the following short list of works: *Toys* (1919), for soprano and piano; *Men and Angels* (1922), a symphonic suite for five trumpets and bass trumpet, revised in 1938 as *Angels,* for four trumpets and three trombones; *Men and Mountains* (1924), for chamber orchestra; *Portals* (1926), for string orchestra; *Sun-Treader* (1932), for large orchestra; *Evocations* (1937–45), four chants for piano; and *Organum* (1945), for large orchestra. *Sun-Treader,* Ruggles's largest and most important work, was performed for the first time in Paris in 1932. It did not receive an American performance until 1966, when it was performed by the Boston Symphony Orchestra at a three-day festival of his works in Maine. Few of his works have been recorded and his music is seldom performed in this country. As a result, he is virtually unknown to most American concert-goers.

Ruggles's "system" has been called by Virgil Thomson "non-differentiated secundal counterpoint." The intervals presented on the beats are predominantly seconds, sevenths, or ninths, and the various contrapuntal voices are similar in character and contour—"non-differentiated." The result is polyphonic with regard to voice-writing but homophonic in its basic sound. He also exploits the chromatic element of the twelve tones of the scale to a remarkable degree by not repeating a tone or its octave in a melodic line until nine or ten of the others have intervened. The total result is atonal in concept, with levels of dissonance differentiated in preference to the traditional dissonance-consonance relationship. In spite of the music's textural complexity and intellectual conception, it is rhapsodic in its emotional impact, and, according to Charles Seeger, "pure intuition." The following passage from the opening measures of *Portals* typifies Ruggles's melodic style:

Example 198.

non dim.

Ruggles has often been compared to Arnold Schoenberg. They were both mystics and were both driven by an inner compulsion and conviction to follow a lonely path without regard for public acceptance or rejection. Wilfred Mellers, in his book on American music, says, "Both were amateur painters who, in their visual work, sought the expressionistic moment of vision. Both, in their music still more than in their painting, found that the disintegrated fragments of the psyche could be reintegrated only by a mystical act. Schoenberg, a Viennese Jew, had an ancient religion and the spirit of Beethoven to help him; Ruggles had only the American wilderness and the austerities of Puritan New England. For this reason he sought freedom—from tonal bondage, from the harmonic straitjacket, from conventional repetitions, from anything that sullied the immediacy and purity of experience—even more remorselessly than Schoenberg. . . . In Schoenberg's 'free' atonal music and in Ruggles's chromatic polyphony there is a minimum of repetition, for each piece is a new birth."

PROGRESSIVES

Many American composers preferred to remain basically within the mainstream, but in order to satisfy their need for greater and more varied means of expression, they explored and exploited new paths already opened by the neoclassic followers of Stravinsky and the dodecaphonic school of Schoenberg and Webern. This group, the Progressives, wrote music using serialism, atonality, and dissonant counterpoint, and some even incorporated controlled aleatoric techniques. Many continued to write music in the closed forms of the past. Elliott Carter, Roger Sessions, William Schuman, Wallingford Riegger, George Rochberg, and Lukas Foss are all representative of this group.

Roger Sessions (b. 1896)

Roger Sessions was born in Brooklyn, but he is a New Englander by ancestry and residence. His intellectual precocity was evident at an early age: he wrote an opera at the age of twelve and entered Harvard Uni-

307

Roger Sessions

versity at the age of fourteen. After graduating, he went to Yale for two years of study with Horatio Parker; then, at the age of twenty-one, he joined the faculty of Smith College and taught there for four years. Feeling the need for further training, he continued his composition studies with Ernest Bloch. When Bloch came to Cleveland as Director of the Cleveland Institute of Music, Sessions came with him as his assistant. He left Cleveland in 1925, and spent the next eight years in Florence, Rome, and Berlin, sustained in part by a Guggenheim Fellowship and the Prix de Rome. During these years, he assiduously avoided Paris and the Boulanger circle. Since his return to the United States in 1933, he has exerted a profound influence on many young composers both through his teaching at the University of California (1945–53) and Princeton (1935–45; 1953–59), and through his active promotion of contemporary music. Together with Aaron Copland, he organized the Copland-Sessions concerts of contemporary music in New York (1928–31), was a member of the League of Composers, and for many years was president of the United States' section of the International Society for Contemporary Music. He has written three books: *The Musical Experience of Composer, Performer, and Listener* (1950), *Harmonic Practice* (1951), and *Reflections on the Musical Life in the United States* (1956).

In addition to favoring abstract forms in his compositions, Sessions is a meticulous craftsman, much like Piston in a number of ways. He has always stressed the intellectual manipulation and the "coherent and living

308

expression" of his musical ideas. "I reject any kind of dogma or platform. I am not trying to write 'modern,' 'American,' or 'neo-classic' music." His later works in particular display the use of an "over-all continuity pattern" that the contemporary American composer Elliott Carter characterizes as music in which "ideas come to the surface, gain clarity and definition, and then sink back into the general flow." Sharp dissonance, complex rhythmic structures, and a tenuous tonal organization influenced by, but not committed to, Schoenbergian chromaticism and polyphonic techniques make his music written after 1930 increasingly difficult for the relatively inexperienced listener to assimilate. With the Quintet for Strings (1958), Sessions adapted serialist techniques to his highly personal style. He believes, however, that while the series may provide a practical tool for the composer, he must define the tonal areas implicit in the row. "Two tones a fifth apart will still produce the effect of a fifth, and . . . will convey a sensation similar to that of a root and its fifth, or of a tonic and its dominant." This acceptance of serialism as an important technique in his musical thought released a renewed flood of creative energy. Most of his works were in fact written after he was fifty. By contrast, Sessions's early music, written while he was under the influence of Bloch and others, is filled with both a number of neoclassic traits and a rich romantic expressiveness. The brilliant incidental music he wrote for Andreyev's play *The Black Maskers* (1923), for instance, provides one with a readily accessible introduction to his works.

Self-critical by nature, Sessions has written comparatively few compositions; one should note, however, that there are very few "little" works among them. In addition to his eight symphonies (1927–68), his larger works include two concertos (1935, 1956), three string quartets (1936, 1951, 1957), one quintet (1958), three piano sonatas (1930, 1946, 1965), a Mass (1958), the *Idyll of Theocritus* (1956), for solo soprano and orchestra, and two operas, *The Trial of Lucullus* (1947) and the monumental *Montezuma* (1964).

Lukas Foss (b. 1922)

Lukas Foss is one of the most gifted among the younger generation of American composers. He is an outstanding pianist and conductor as well as a virtuoso composer. A true eclectic, he has written music that embraces neoclassic, neobaroque, and American nationalist elements, all combined with the romanticism of his German heritage.

Foss was born in Berlin and began composing at the age of seven. By the time he was fifteen he had completed two operas. His father, a professor of philosophy, and his mother, a painter, realizing the implications of what was happening in Germany in the thirties, left for Paris in

Lukas Foss

1933 and then came to the United States in 1937. He entered the Curtis
Institute of Music at the age of fifteen and graduated at eighteen, remarkably accomplished as a pianist, conductor, and composer. He then
joined the first class to enter the newly established Berkshire Music Center
in Tanglewood, Massachusetts, founded by Serge Koussevitsky. Other
members of that class included Leonard Bernstein, Eleazer de Carvalho,
and Lorin Maazel. While there, he studied composition with Hindemith
and conducting with Koussevitsky. He also came under the influence of
another of the Center's composition teachers, Aaron Copland. In 1942 he
won a Pulitzer Traveling Scholarship and three years later received a
Guggenheim Award, the youngest musician to receive either honor.

The first of Foss's works to attract immediate attention was a cantata,
The Prairie (1943), on a text by Carl Sandburg. It is an American work
that displays the strong influence of Copland on every page. The technical
mastery of his materials in this work for soloists, full chorus, and orchestra
is remarkable for one so young (he was only twenty-one when he completed it). *The Prairie* was followed by two more vocal works: *Song of
Anguish* (1945) from the Book of Isaiah, for baritone and orchestra, and
Song of Songs (1946), for soprano and orchestra. In these works, his
Copland-inspired Americanism is combined with the Jewish cantillation
of the Bible. By contrast, Foss's instrumental music of this same period
is characterized by Hindemith's neoclassic contrapuntal influences. These
works include the Symphony in G (1944), the String Quartet in G (1944),

the Oboe Concerto (1947–48), and the brilliant virtuoso Piano Concerto No. 2 (1951–52).

One of the most impressive works of Foss's pre-1960 period, *A Parable of Death* (1952), is scored for tenor, narrator, mixed chorus, and orchestra. According to Wilfred Mellers, "The narrating voice—usually a dangerous device in a large-scale work—is handled with uncannily theatrical flair: in which respect Foss is . . . comparable with Britten. Both men are remarkable for sheer musical ability combined with dramatic instinct; both are fine conductors and pianists of acute sensitivity. Both use their theatrical instinct to objectify their twentieth-century awareness of neurosis." In 1958 Foss wrote the *Symphony of Chorales,* one of his finest instrumental works. Its four movements are each based on a Bach chorale tune. Commissioned by the Koussevitsky Foundation, it was written in homage to Dr. Albert Schweitzer. Foss has also written three operas, all brilliantly whimsical, and all eminently popular with opera workshops around the country: *The Jumping Frog of Calaveras County* (1950), based on a short story by Mark Twain; *Griffelkin* (1955), a fantasy commissioned by the NBC Opera Theater; and the "nine-minute" opera, *Introductions and Goodbyes* (1960).

In 1953 Foss became Schoenberg's successor as professor of composition at the University of California at Los Angeles. While there he organized the Improvisation Chamber Players (piano, clarinet, cello, and percussion), for whom he was pianist and conductor. The improvisations of the group are in the spirit of the "jam sessions" of early jazz, although the advanced planning used makes it more akin to modern jazz. His works after 1960 reflect his growing preoccupation with chance music and, inevitably, electronic music, both discussed in a later chapter. Foss became the conductor and musical director of the Buffalo Philharmonic in 1963, a position that has provided him with an excellent opportunity to champion the cause of contemporary music.

Foss: *A PARABLE OF DEATH*

Foss has created a moving work of great lyricism and moving power in *A Parable of Death* for narrator, chorus, tenor solo, and orchestra. It was commissioned by the Louisville Philharmonic Society. Foss based the work on a poignant story by the Austrian poet Rainer Maria Rilke (1875–1926), and it is given added depth through the interpolation of Rilke's poetry. Its seven sections tell a tale of two lovers who turned from the world to enjoy their love in solitude. They realize that Death will come to them as he does to all, but they attempt to shut him out. Finally, they welcome him into their house. The Narrator tells the story while the tenor and chorus add a commentary, using Rilke poems dealing with Death.

Foss derived the contrapuntal texture of this work from baroque practices, whereas the harmonic language reveals the influence of Hindemith and Copland.

I. Prologue. Widely spaced chords in the woodwinds and strings set a mood of austerity and detachment as the Narrator announces the work's title. The chorus then enters with a Gregorian chant-like phrase:

Example 199.

O   God   give un-to ev-'ry man   his Death.

Examples 199–200: Copyright © 1953 by Carl Fischer, Inc., New York. International Copyright Secured. All Rights Reserved. Reprinted by permission of the Publisher.

An imitative treatment of the phrase rises to an impassioned climax at the end of the section.

II. Allegretto. The Narrator begins the tale, soon accompanied by a small group of instruments in which the violin presents the melodic phrase that dominates this section. The tenor continues the melodic line, amplifying it in long melismatic phrases to the words "sing the lovers." After a few words of narration the chorus enters together with the tenor in an impassioned hymn to love, "Sing now in praise of love."

Between the second and third sections, the Narrator continues the tale. "And so the two people turned out of time into solitude. . . . And in the heart of the garden they built a house."

IIIA. After a short woodwind introduction, the chorus enters with a simple unaccompanied choralelike setting of the words "Who built this house where the heart has led?" Note that the dissonant harmony does not disturb the remote, baroque mood:

Example 200.

Who   built   this   house   where the   heart   has   led?

Between each line the orchestra interjects a melodic comment. The Narrator continues between the two parts of Section III.

IIIB. The previous introduction is now amplified and developed under the narration. "To those who have grace of acceptance . . . a landscape enters the house . . . and the light . . . and the wind bearing a fragrance upon its shoulders. . . . One morning there waited at their door . . . the tall and immaculate figure . . . of Death." The chorus repeats the word "Death" as the lovers frantically bolt the two doors of the house.

IVA. The chorus sings an agitated description of their fear and trembling. The Narrator then continues the tale describing their self-imprisonment and the sound of someone attempting to enter. The chorus repeats the agitated section and the Narrator then describes the approaching sound of digging.

IVB. A dramatic chorus, *Maestoso,* comments once more: "Immense is Death. We are his pleasure, laugh as we will."

V. The Tenor sings a moving, Bach-like aria over a contrapuntal, chromatic, three-part accompaniment. The chorus enters, providing a restless, syncopated background to the more rhythmic aria of the tenor. The section ends as "the man and woman receive Death into their house."

VI. The chorus sings "We know him not," alternating polyphonic and homophonic sections in a manner reminiscent of some of Handel's choruses. Death offers the man and woman some seed, and leaves.

VII. Following an introduction similar to that of section III, the Narrator and chorus describe the shrub grown from the seed, which eventually brings forth a pale blue flower—the sprout of Death. The man and woman accept their death with resignation as the work ends serenely.

chapter 22

Dramatists

Interest in the performance of opera in the United States dates from the beginning of the nineteenth century. First in New Orleans and later in Philadelphia, New York, and Chicago, audiences supported performances of European operas given by European musicians and singers. Although a number of attempts were made by American composers during the nineteenth century to express themselves in this idiom, unfortunately, they slavishly imitated their European models. It was not until this century, during the 1930s, that an original "American" expression began to emerge through the use of folk idioms, cowboy tunes, spirituals, hymn tunes, and jazz, and through the use of librettos based on American themes. Motivated by their desire to produce American operas that were "good theatre," composers found in the literary heritage of their country a superb resource of previously untapped material. While most American composers of the pre-1950 period included at least some dramatic works in their compositional output, three among them—Douglas Moore, Marc Blitzstein, and Gian Carlo Menotti—chose to write almost exclusively for the stage.

Douglas Moore (1893–1969)

Working within a basically traditional operatic framework, Douglas Moore adapted his considerable musical capabilities to the taste of a public ready for American opera. He was born in Cutchogue, Long Island, a descendant of John Alden and Miles Standish. Following his graduation from the Yale School of Music in 1917, where he studied with Horatio Parker, he served for a brief time in the navy during the war. He then went to Paris, where he studied with Vincent d'Indy at the Schola Cantorum. His first position was as Curator of Music at the Cleveland Museum of Art. While in Cleveland he studied with Ernest Bloch and had his first major work, *The Pageant of P. T. Barnum*, performed in 1924 by the Cleveland Orchestra. A Pulitzer Traveling Fellowship made possible his return to Paris, this time to study with Nadia Boulanger. In 1926 he joined the music faculty at Columbia University, where he became chairman in 1940 and McDowell Professor in 1943. His years of teaching served as a resource for his two books: *Listening to Music* (1937) and *From Madrigal to Modern Music* (1962).

Almost from the beginning of his career, Moore sought means for identifying himself with Americanisms. He rejected the sophistication of the German and French styles that had been so prominent in his training in favor of a simple, conservative, basically romantic idiom steeped in the literary and musical heritage of his country. *The Pageant of P. T. Barnum* with its country dances, parades, church hymns, and musical sketches of Jenny Lind and General Tom Thumb; his symphonic poem *Moby Dick*

Douglas Moore
Cleveland Public Library.

(1928) based on Melville's novel; and the *Overture on an American Tune* (1931), all give ready evidence of his early commitment to American-based material. His *Village Music* (1942) and *Farm Journal* (1947) and to some extent his Symphony in A (1947) and String Quartet (1933) give further evidence of this commitment among his instrumental works. Moore's natural affinity for vocal writing and love of the theatre were first combined successfully in his setting of Stephen Vincent Benét's story *The Devil and Daniel Webster* as a one-act opera in 1938. Moore used Yankee fiddler tunes and ballads and a characteristic New England background for this opera about a New England farmer who has sold his soul to the Devil for material success. Daniel Webster, acting as his lawyer, successfully sways a jury of traitors and murderers summoned from Hell by the Devil, and wins salvation for his client. Moore's other operas include the 1951 Pulitzer Prize winner, *Giants in the Earth* (1950), based on the book by Ole Edvart Rolvaag; *The Ballad of Baby Doe* (1956), commissioned by the Koussevitsky Foundation to commemorate the bicentennial of Columbia University; *The Wings of the Dove* (1961) based on the Henry James novel; and *Carrie Nation* (1966).

Moore: *THE BALLAD OF BABY DOE*

In 1935 Moore read a newspaper account about an old woman found frozen to death in a miner's shack in Leadville, Colorado. The article recounted the love story of the woman, Elizabeth McCourt (Baby) Doe, and Horace Tabor, as well as Tabor's rise to enormous wealth as owner of the Matchless Silver Mine and his subsequent ruin and death when the United States stopped using silver to back its currency. It was not until 1953 that Moore, in collaboration with the writer John Latouche, finally wrote an opera based on this story. Appropriately enough, it was the Central City Opera that invited him to write the opera, since it was there that Baby Doe had lived before marrying Horace Tabor. The opera was premièred in Central City in 1956 and later was produced by the New York City Center Opera Company in 1958. Since then, it has enjoyed wide popularity. The opera is in two acts and eleven scenes.

Act I. The opening scene takes place in 1880 outside the Tabor Opera House in Leadville, Colorado. A saloon is on one side of the stage and the Clarendon Hotel on the other. Miners and dance-hall girls, in a lively scene that realistically projects the atmosphere of a mining town, tell about the effects of Tabor's affluence in Leadville. Though Moore does not actually use folk tunes, he captures the flavor of the American West through his use of simple melodies and vigorous rhythms:

The Ballad of Baby Doe

Copyright © Beth Bergman.

Example 201.

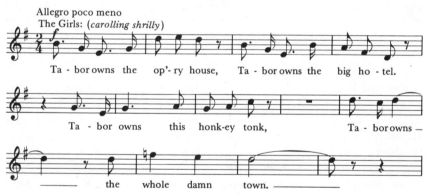

Allegro poco meno

The Girls: (*carolling shrilly*)

Ta - bor owns the op'- ry house, Ta - bor owns the big ho - tel.

Ta - bor owns this honk-ey tonk, Ta - bor owns —

——— the whole damn town. ———

Examples 201–204: Copyright © 1956 & 1958 by Chappell & Co., Inc. International Copyright Secured. All Rights Reserved. Used by permission.

After they leave, Tabor emerges from the opera house followed by four of his cronies. Tabor, in a folk-oriented tune, tells about his rise from humble beginnings to his present eminence. The American folk idiom is suggested through the use of a rousing refrain after each verse of the tune, sung by Tabor's cronies and the chorus of miners and girls who gradually return to the stage:

Example 202.

Allegro con brio

f Tabor:

I came this way from Mas - sa - chu- setts through the Kan - sas

ter - ri - tor - y, Pick and sho - vel in my hand Bel - ly full of

Cronies and Chorus:

gin and glo - ry Dig, you go -phers dig them

holes Dig a - way to save your souls. ——

—— More —— buck- ets of gold than banks can

hold lie deep in Col - o - ra - do.

Tabor and his cronies then dance with the girls. Augusta Tabor, his wife, now enters with four of her friends (wives of the four cronies) and is aghast at the scene. She reproaches Tabor for his lack of dignity and the men's lack of respect for their wives. Everyone leaves except Tabor. As the curtain falls, Baby Doe enters and asks him for directions to the Clarendon Hotel. Throughout the act, the four cronies, the four lady friends, and later the four dandies form a kind of Greek chorus, commenting and occasionally participating in the action.

The second scene begins as Horace, Augusta, and their friends leave the opera, commenting in exaggerated phrases about how much they enjoyed it. Horace remains behind as Augusta enters the hotel; their friends leave. Two girls come out of the saloon commenting about Baby Doe, her background, and the fact that she has apparently set her cap for Horace. He sits unnoticed in the shadows. They leave and Baby Doe is seen in the parlor of the hotel at the piano. She sings the "Willow Song," obviously for Tabor's benefit, although she pretends not to know he is listening. He applauds, and after a brief exchange he sings to her "Warm as the Autumn Light." At its conclusion, Augusta calls down to him to come to bed, and he leaves. The sentimental-dramatic mood and flavor of late-nineteenth-century operetta pervade the entire scene. The following example is from the "Willow Song":

Example 203.

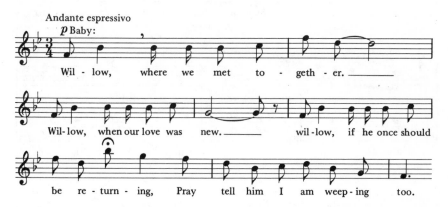

In the third scene, Augusta discovers that Horace has been seeing Baby Doe, and threatens to take action against him even if it means their ruin. Moore carefully delineates their character conflict through his effective use of recitative.

The fourth scene takes place in the hotel lobby. Baby Doe has decided to leave Horace and is writing a letter to her mother explaining why. Augusta enters and threatens Baby Doe, who, while agreeing to leave, pleads with Augusta to understand Horace and allow him to follow his destiny. Augusta is indignant and taunts her as she leaves. Baby Doe, realizing that Augusta's domineering nature will destroy Horace, changes her mind as he enters, and the scene ends with a passionate love duet. It is in waltz rhythm, again in the style of late-nineteenth-century operetta. An emotional climax is reached as they throw off all pretense of concealment and slowly ascend the stairs to her room:

Example 204.

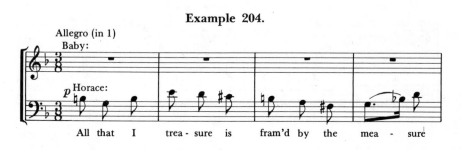

Example 204. Continued

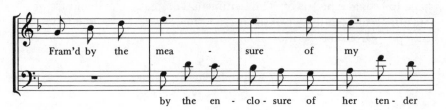

Fram'd by the mea - sure of my

by the en - clo - sure of her ten - der

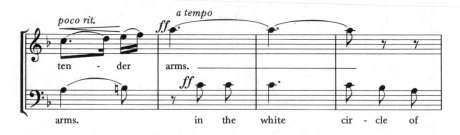

poco rit.   *a tempo*   *ff*

ten - der arms.

arms.   in the white cir - cle of

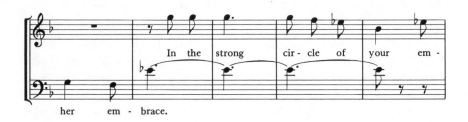

In the strong cir - cle of your em -

her em - brace.

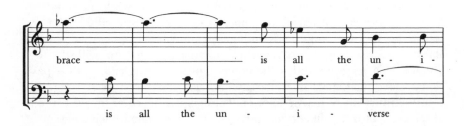

brace   is all the un - i -

is all the un - i - verse

verse   *rit.*   We need to know,

a tempo

I need to know

The fifth scene takes place in Augusta's parlor a year later. Her four lady friends, in Fury-like fashion, tell her about the "indecent" behavior of Horace and Baby Doe and finally reveal the fact that Horace plans to divorce Augusta. In an effective climax, Augusta declares that "he will rue the day" that he attempts to shame her by a divorce.

The final scene of the first act takes place in the Willard Hotel in Washington, D.C., 1883. A reception is being held for Tabor, who is serving a brief interim term as United States Senator, and his new bride, Baby Doe. The four dandies (doubtless from the State Department) act the part of the Greek chorus, foretelling the coming shift to the gold standard. The priest who has just performed the marriage ceremony finds out that he has not been told the truth—that both Tabor and Baby Doe have been divorced. Disgusted, he leaves, and as the guests begin following his example, the President of the United States, Chester A. Arthur, arrives, and the act ends triumphantly as he leads the entire ensemble in toasting the bride.

In Act II, Augusta comes to warn Baby Doe about the impending fall of the silver standard. Tabor refuses to believe it and places his hopes in the election of William Jennings Bryan. When Bryan is defeated, Tabor is ruined. In the final scene Tabor relives moments of his life on the stage of the Tabor Opera House and then dies in Baby Doe's arms. The opera ends with Baby Doe alone, standing before the shaft of the Matchless Silver Mine.

Marc Blitzstein (1905–64)

Marc Blitzstein was born in Philadelphia, studied at the Curtis Institute of Music, and then continued his studies with Nadia Boulanger in Paris and with Arnold Schoenberg in Berlin. His early works are fiercely abstract, percussive, and dissonant. In the thirties, influenced by Kurt Weill (1900–50) and Hanns Eisler (1898–1962), he associated himself with the musical theatre of protest and began to create works of "social significance." His first musical drama, *The Cradle Will Rock* (1937), was written for the WPA Federal Theater. Its opening performance was stopped at the last moment by the Federal Theater because of its left-wing orientation, and Blitzstein hastily moved the production to another theatre, where it was produced without scenery, costumes, or orchestra. It went on to achieve a remarkable success during a Broadway run of 124 consecutive performances. *The Cradle Will Rock* was revived in 1947, and although its content was dated by then, its reception was nonetheless enthusiastic. The drama, which takes place in a night court, focuses on an attempt by a steelworkers' group to form a union despite the devious machinations by management. Blitzstein employs recitatives, patter songs, chorales, blues, and torch songs, blended with contemporary harmonic and contrapuntal techniques, in what Virgil Thomson called "one of the most charming creations of the American musical theater."

In 1949, Blitzstein, with the permission of Lillian Hellman, created a highly impressive opera entitled *Regina* from her play *The Little Foxes*. After a successful run on Broadway, it was revived by Leonard Bernstein in 1953 at the New York City Center with part of its spoken dialogue deleted and the remainder replaced by recitative. Blitzstein included spirituals, ragtime, Handelian recitatives, madrigal-like choruses, arias, and ensembles (notably a quartet by the "good people" who are surrounded by the "little foxes") in this distinguished work.

Blitzstein's final opera, *Sacco and Vanzetti*, commissioned by the Ford Foundation for the Metropolitan Opera Company, was left incomplete at his death in 1964.

Blitzstein's international schooling provided him with a background suitable for combining the best of many worlds in creating his American music dramas. He had a remarkable sense of the theatre and a gift for characterization. He wrote all of his own librettos, complementing his use of colloquial Americanisms with the jazzy musical language of the thirties. His admiration for Kurt Weill, noticeable in his early operas, led him to adapt and translate Weill's *Threepenny Opera* for the American stage in 1952. In 1967 Aaron Copland wrote, "Marc Blitzstein's life exemplifies a truism that bears restatement today: Every artist has the right to make his art out of an emotion that really moves him. Those of our composers who are moved by the immense terrain of new techniques now seemingly within their grasp would do well to remember that humanity's struggle for a fuller life may be equally valid as a moving force in the history of music."

Gian Carlo Menotti (b. 1911)

Menotti was born in Cadegliano, Italy. He is, however, usually considered an American composer because he has spent most of his life in the United States and because his librettos are in English. Following his studies at the Verdi Conservatory in Milan, he came to Philadelphia in 1928 to study composition at the Curtis Institute of Music. He was only twenty-three when he wrote his first successful opera, *Amelia Goes to the Ball* (1934). It was produced at the Curtis Institute in 1937 and the following year by the Metropolitan Opera Company. Because of the success of *Amelia,* the National Broadcasting Company commissioned him to write an opera for radio—*The Old Maid and the Thief* (1938). Like *Amelia,* it is a witty, satiric, charming and successful *opera buffo.* His next opera, *The Island God* (1942), written for the Metropolitan Opera

Gian Carlo Menotti

Company, is his only failure. By contrast, his "musical tragedy," *The Medium* (1946), was an instant success. It had an unprecedented run on Broadway and continued success as a motion picture. It is, in Menotti's words, "the tragedy of a woman caught between two worlds, a world of reality which she cannot wholly comprehend and the supernatural world in which she cannot believe." The plot concerns a spiritualist, who, having faked the appearance of being able to communicate with the dead, is unable to cope with what appears to her to have been a genuine communication. She is so distraught that she gives up her profession and ultimately mistakenly kills her assistant. *The Telephone* (1946), usually programmed with *The Medium,* is a delightful bit of fluff, a perfect foil for the heavy tragedy that follows it.

The Consul (1950) was written for Broadway, where it had a seven-month run at the Ethel Barrymore Theater in 1950. It won the Pulitzer Prize for Music and the New York Drama Critics Circle Award for the best musical play. It has been translated into nineteen languages and performed in over twenty-seven countries. *The Consul* is a political opera—a criticism of the human condition brought about through the totalitarianism that followed World War II. The action takes place in an unspecified European country. John Sorel, patriot and member of a clandestine resistance group, attempts to obtain visas for himself and his

The Consul

San Francisco Opera. Photo by Margaret Norton.

wife, Magda, at the consulate in order to escape to a free country. The Consul, a God-like figure who never appears on stage, has life-and-death power over all the frustrated, frightened people seeking visas. Menotti uses all of his theatrical know-how in this poignant musical drama, combining grand opera effects with a wide variety of contemporary techniques. Menotti's affinity with Puccini and *verismo* is particularly apparent in *The Consul*. The relationship between the villainous police chief and Magda strongly suggests Puccini's *Tosca*, as does the wounded Sorel seeking sanctuary. Both operas, in fact, end with the suicide of the heroine.

The delightful Christmas opera, *Amahl and the Night Visitors* (1951), was created specifically for television on commission by the National Broadcasting Company, and has since become a popular classic. One of Menotti's most ambitious and controversial operas, *The Saint of Bleecker Street* (1954), was premièred on Broadway in December of 1954. It received the Drama Critics Circle Award as the best play of the year, the Music Critics Circle Award as the best opera, and the Pulitzer Prize in music. Here again, he has combined Puccini-like lyricism with contemporary techniques. Unfortunately, its plot of religious hysteria did not find a ready association for many theatre-goers and as a result it did not achieve the success of *The Consul. The Unicorn, the Gorgon, and the*

324

Manticore (1956), a chamber ballet opera described as a "madrigal fable," *Maria Golovin* (1958), and *The Last Savage* (1963) likewise have not completely fulfilled the promise indicated by his earlier works. By contrast, *Help! Help! the Globolinks* (1968), a "children's opera," has been quite successful, particularly among college opera groups. In 1976, his seventeenth and eighteenth operas were produced: *The Hero*, a gently satirical opera of the human condition was premièred in Philadelphia, and a one-act "operatic riddle" called *The Egg* was premièred in Washington D.C. together with a revised version of his one-act opera, *Martin's Lie* (1964).

Menotti's extraordinary success as a musical dramatist is, in part, attributable to the fact that he writes his own librettos. Words and music, as a consequence, intimately reflect the subtleties of the dramatic action. He is an eclectic, not a musical innovator; harmonically and structurally, he is largely a traditionalist who works within the framework of the Puccini *verismo* technique.

part **VI**

NEW DIRECTIONS

INTRODUCTION

At the time of the Second World War, two major directions were well established within the mainstream of music—the tonal, neoclassic style associated with Stravinsky, and the atonal, serial style identified with Schoenberg. A number of other important directions within the mainstream, including conservatism and nationalism, also had a significant number of adherents. Following the war, while most composers continued to follow these established paths, a new group—the experimentalists— began working with a number of entirely new concepts of sound manipulation, sound structure, and sound production. Their experiments produced a number of fascinating new directions in music including *total serialization, electronic music,* and *chance music (aleatoric music).*

chapter 23

Total Serialization

Olivier Messiaen (b. 1908)

In 1946, an International Summer Course for New Music was established at Darmstadt, Germany for the purpose of re-educating German composers to the new music and the compositional and performance techniques that had been created during the years between 1935 and 1945, the years of Nazi domination. Young composers from all over Europe gathered to hear, analyze, and perform contemporary works. The first year was devoted to the neoclassicism of Hindemith and Stravinsky, but during subsequent years, interest centered in serial music, with the techniques of Anton Webern serving as a resource for new serial development. Ultimately, it was the music and experiments of Olivier Messiaen that led to the development of total serialization. As early as 1940 he had written *Quatuor pour la fin du temps (Quartet for the End of Time)*, scored for piano, clarinet, violin, and cello, whose first movement repeats a sequence of twenty-nine chords together with a seventeen-note rhythmic pedal to create a continuous stream of changing combinations. His *Quatre études de rhythme (Four Rhythmic Studies; 1949–50)* contains a piece that serializes pitch, rhythm, intensity, and articulation. In 1952 he wrote a piece called *Timbres-Durées (Timbre-Durations)* in which only noise is used, strictly organized rhythmically and dynamically, while pitch, the

Olivier Messiaen

first parameter to be serialized, is never expressed. Pierre Boulez, Karlheinz Stockhausen, and Iannis Xenakis are prominent among Messiaen's students.

Pierre Boulez (b. 1925)

Pierre Boulez, famed as a conductor as well as composer, has been one of the most outspoken advocates of Webern's pointillism. He argued at Darmstadt for an even greater control of the materials of music in order to extend the principle of serialization to cover all the elements of music. According to him, "if you do not deny, . . . if you do not voice fundamental doubts as to the validity of everything that has gone before, you will never make progress. For us, these doubts developed to the point of total control." He first attempted total serialization in his Second Piano Sonata (1948) and fully realized it in his first set of *Structures* for two pianos (1952). From the following series, which corresponds to the twelve notes of the chromatic scale, Boulez constructed rows of duration, dynamics, and articulation:

Example 205.

duration — ♪ ♪ ♪. ♪ ♪♪ ♪. ♪.. ♩ ♩♪ ♩♪ ♩♪. ♩.

dynamics — *pppp* *ppp* *pp* *p* *meno p* *mp* *mf* *più f* *f* *ff* *fff* *ffff*

articulation —

>	▼	.	⁻	⌒	≥	>	⁻	⋯	∧	sfz ∧	sfz ∧ nomal
1	2	3	4	5	6	7	8	9	10	11	12

332

By applying the serial technique to the above parameters, as well as to pitch, he completely freed himself from all traditional concepts of melody, harmony, and rhythm as well as the tonal concepts of harmony and counterpoint. In 1954 he wrote what many consider his finest work, *Le Marteau sans Maître* (*The Hammer without a Master*), a suite of nine movements based on three surrealistic poems by René Char, scored for alto voice, flute, viola, guitar, vibraphone (a xylophone-like instrument with resonators having electrically operated valves that produce a gentle vibrato), xylorimba (combination xylophone and marimba), and percussion. The vocal and instrumental movements alternate, and in each movement the instruments appear in different combinations, in a manner reminiscent of Schoenberg's *Pierrot Lunaire*. This work marked a departure from the cerebral structures of his earlier works toward a greater expressiveness through the use of sound-color. The pervasive sounds of the vibraphone and xylorimba and the brittle chirping sounds, so characteristic of much of Boulez's music, create an atmosphere of the Far East, while the vocal writing with its melismatic lines and abrupt register changes derives from Webern. There are no conventional themes, only short rhythmic and melodic cells that, while giving the impression of being disjointed and improvisatory, are highly organized serially. After writing this composition, Boulez began to explore the possibilities of less control by using aleatoric techniques.

Pierre Boulez

Representative Italians

The Italians Luigi Nono (b. 1924), Bruno Maderna (1920–73), and Luciano Berio (b. 1925), all of whom had been at Darmstadt, are among those composers who were most strongly influenced by Boulez's concept of total serialization. Maderna's *Serenade for Eleven Instruments* (1954) and Berio's *Nones* (1954) are examples of serialization applied to more than one element of composition. The *Nones* is based on a thirteen-note tone row and rows of seven durations, seven dynamic values, and five articulations. Of all the young Italian composers, Nono is the most definitely committed to the concept of total control and has never deviated from this principle. His finest work is the cantata *Il Canto Sospeso (Song of Suspense;* 1956), a violent work based on letters written by resistance fighters condemned to death during the Second World War.

Karlheinz Stockhausen (b. 1928)

The German composer Karlheinz Stockhausen is probably the most important of those composers influenced by the concept of total serialization during the fifties. He came to Darmstadt in 1951 and there became acquainted with the music of Messiaen and Boulez. Stockhausen went even further than Boulez in discarding all traditional musical concepts. He declared all types of musical forms obsolete, preferring instead that

Karlheinz Stockhausen

each of his works be heard as a series of small time units rather than as a totality. In spite of the fact that each of the small time units is rigorously organized in its various musical elements, his compositions frequently give one the impression of sounding chaotic, lacking in any apparent design. The *Kontra-Punkte* (1953) for chamber orchestra, his first attempt at total serialization, displays the Webern influence in its pointillistic approach to the tone row. The minute differences in duration, dynamics, and articulation that he requires pose considerable difficulties for the performer. The first piece in his *Klavierstücke No. 2* (1954) is so highly organized rhythmically, dynamically, and tonally that an accurate performance becomes nearly impossible. The following example of the opening measures of this piece reveals some of the rhythmic problems. The ratios in brackets compare the number of eighth notes in the grouping to the number expected normally (i.e., 11:10 means that eleven eighth notes should be played in the time span it would normally take to play ten). The five bracketed in the second measure means that the equivalent of five thirty-second notes is to be given the time span of an eighth note; the ratio 5:4 tells the performer to play the equivalent of five eighth notes in the time normally required to play four. The dynamic markings further compound the difficulties:

Example 206.

© Copyright 1954, Universal Edition. Used by permission of the publisher. Theodore Presser Company, sole representative United States, Canada and Mexico.

The *Zeitmasse* (*Tempos;* 1956) for five woodwind instruments is one of Stockhausen's most successful works. In it he combines brilliant instrumental writing with a new approach to rhythm in which five different "levels" of time are used, to be played consecutively or simultaneously. The five "levels" he uses are exact metronomic indications, "as fast as possible," "from very fast to approximately four times slower," "from very slow to approximately four times faster," and "as slow as possible." Instead of using traditional notation for this work, he used a type of proportional notation in which the duration of notes is indicated by the distance between them on the score. Because of its extreme rhythmic complexity, the performers all read from a full score in order to synchronize their parts correctly. Stockhausen's more recent works will be discussed in the next two chapters.

Milton Babbitt (b. 1916)

In America, Milton Babbitt, a trained mathematician as well as a musician, explored the various mathematical possibilities of serialization and developed the concept of total serialization a year before his European contemporaries. His early works, such as *Three Compositions for Piano* (1946), *Composition for Four Instruments* (1948), *Composition for*

Milton Babbitt

BMI Archives.

Viola and Piano (1950), and the song cycle *Du* (1950), are substantially confusing to the ordinary listener because of their intense preoccupation with the mathematical manipulation of the various series. As Babbitt explains it, his works after 1947 "were concerned with embodying the extensions, generalizations, and fusions of certain techniques contained in the music of Schoenberg, Webern, and Berg, and above all with applying the pitch operations of the twelve-tone system to non-pitch elements: durational rhythm, dynamics, phrase rhythm, timbre, and register, in such a manner as to preserve the most significant properties associated with these operations in the pitch domain when they are applied in these other domains." One critic, in writing about one of these works, stated that it was as absorbing "as a new mathematical formulation, and just about as communicative." Because of his insistence that these works be accurately performed in order to be accurately perceived, Babbitt soon turned from writing for instruments to electronic composition. Since 1959, he has been a codirector of the Electronic Music Center operated jointly by Columbia and Princeton Universities.

Total serialization was a short-lived movement; the rapid growth of indeterminism (aleatory) in the 1950s soon provided a strong reaction to the mathematical, quasi-scientific rigor of total control.

chapter 24

Electronic Music

Attempts to bring electronic technology into the field of music date back almost as far as the invention of the vacuum tube, just after the turn of the twentieth century. It was not until the development of the magnetic tape recorder during the mid-1940s, however, that electronic music, as the term is used today, was born. In our present usage, electronic music refers only to music that has been composed from or altered by electronic devices, recorded on magnetic tape, and reproduced electronically through loudspeakers. By definition, then, it does not include music produced by the Theremin, Hammond organ, Solovox, Novachord, electric guitar, or any other electronic instrument.

Experiments with sound manipulation conducted in 1947–48 by the French Radio sound engineer Pierre Schaeffer, first using disks and then the tape recorder, became the basis for the development of electronic music. He found that he was able to record extramusical sounds and modify them electronically, superimpose one tape recording on another, splice tapes, and play his tapes at various speeds, forward or backward. He gave the name *musique concrète* to the new art form he had created.

Soon after Schaeffer's exploration of some of the sound possibilities of musique concrète, experiments began in Germany with electronically generated sound at the Studio for Electronic Music of the West German Radio, founded in Cologne in 1951 by a group of composers and scientists headed by Herbert Eimert and Karlheinz Stockhausen. They found that

338

through the use of electronic sound sources called sound generators, it was possible for a composer to create an entirely new spectrum of timbres. While the Paris School borrowed forms and structures from the past to create programmatic mood pieces, the Cologne School approached electronic music on a more intellectual plane, closely aligning itself with the serialism of the Viennese composers, particularly Webern. It was relatively easy, through electronic means, for them to extend the principle of serialism to all of the parameters of sound. Today, electronic music includes both music that uses, as its basic element, sound produced by electric generators and musique concrète, whose basic sound material is taken from the sounds of nature, industry, traffic, everyday noises, and musical instruments (not necessarily played conventionally).

Electronic music encompasses a multitude of diverse styles, almost as many, in fact, as there are composers using this technique. The concepts of objective and subjective approaches to composition, for instance, are just as valid for electronic music as they are for music written for conventional resources. Works such as *Gesang der Jünglinge* (*Song of the Youths;* 1956) by Stockhausen, *Composition for Synthesizer* (1961) by Milton Babbitt, *Synchronisms No. 1* (1963) by Mario Davidovsky, *I of IV* (1966) by Pauline Oliveras, and Milton Subotnick's *Silver Apples of the Moon* (1967) present a spectrum of contrasts in electronic composition that ranges from extreme expressionism to the most objective and intellectual sound manipulation.

REPRESENTATIVE COMPOSERS

Karlheinz Stockhausen is the leading composer of the electronic music studio in Cologne and has been its artistic director since 1963. He went there in 1953 after working in Paris from 1951 to 1953 with Messiaen and Milhaud and in the Schaeffer laboratory for musique concrète. In 1953 he wrote *Electronische Studie I* using only sine-wave sounds (electronically generated sounds with no overtones); the following year he completed *Studie II* using more complex sound forms. His finest and most convincing electronic work is *Gesang der Jünglinge* (*Song of the Youths;* 1956), which combines synthesized sounds with musique concrète. The text for the work, taken from the Book of Daniel, was first sung and spoken by a boy and placed on tape. It was then dissected and transformed through a wide diversity of techniques and surrounded by a multiplicity of electronic sounds that create a "symphonic" structure. The sound parameters are arranged serially: varying degrees of intelligibility, steps from speech to singing, varying distances of sound (near to far, echo, etc.), dynamics, pitch, speed, etc. In spite of this apparently mechanistic manipulation of its sound elements, the work is highly romantic in its emotional impact. Stockhausen also introduces a spatial concept into the work by directing that it can be heard from five loudspeakers surrounding the audience. In 1960 he wrote *Kontakte,* a combination of electronic and instrumental music scored for electronic sounds, piano, and percussion. He has also written numerous articles on contemporary music and for many years has been coeditor of *Die Reihe,* a German periodical dealing with contemporary music. Since 1960 he has become increasingly concerned with "spatial" music (not a new concept, it is based on the baroque technique of using spatially separated choirs and instrumental groups).

At about the same time as Stockhausen's innovative work in Germany, Milton Babbitt, Otto Luening (b. 1900), and Vladimir Ussachevsky (b. 1913) were experimenting with electronic music in the United States, first with musique concrète and then with generated sound sources (by the end of the 1950s all electronic studios were using both sound sources in combination). They worked at the Columbia-Princeton Center of Electronic Music, where Luening and Ussachevsky served as codirectors. The huge RCA Mark II Electronic Synthesizer was installed at the center in 1959, with the help of a $250,000 grant from the Rockefeller Foundation. Because composing for the synthesizer occurs before sound generation, considerable technical knowledge is required of the composer. Milton Babbitt wrote the first totally synthesized work of any length, *Composition for Synthesizer* (1961). It is a logical extension of his highly serialized instrumental works, except that in this medium, all of the performance problems have been circumvented. It is a virtuoso structure characterized by its remarkable rhythmic intricacy, clearly defined pitches, and a fascinating interplay of semi-orchestral timbres.

Luening and Ussachevsky were among the first in this country to experiment with combining live and prerecorded sound when they collaborated in creating both the *Rhapsodic Variations for Tape Recorder and Orchestra* (1954) and a *Poem in Cycles and Bells* (1954). Among other works of this nature, *Musica su due Dimensioni* (1952), one of Bruno Maderna's most imaginative scores, and Mario Davidovsky's many *Synchronisms* for various instruments and tape (the one for piano and tape won a Pulitzer Prize) are particularly worth noting. Another fine work that features both live and taped music in combination is Luciano Berio's *Différences* (1958–60). Berio, together with Bruno Maderna, cofounded the Studio di Fonologia Musicale at Milan, which has since become an important center of electronic music. *Différences* is a work for multichanneled tape and five instruments—flute, clarinet, harp, viola, and cello. The substance of the accompanying tape is provided by sound materials recorded by the five instrumentalists that then appear both in their original form and in a form altered by electro-acoustical means. In the words of Henri Pousseur, a Belgian composer of the Cologne School, the work forms "an elaboration of the rich possibilities implied by such a complex 'instrument'—brings to life, in its happy alternation of humor and gravity, garrulity and discretion, tenderness and virility, a modern music in the spirit of *'Commedia dell' arte.'* " Milton Babbitt has also contributed significantly to the growing literature for tape and live performers. Attractive as the notion of total control was to him, it was never his intent to circumvent the role of the live musician; he was, in his words, "interested in increasing the resources of music." *Vision and Prayer* (1961), for soprano and synthesized accompaniment; *Philomel* (1964), for soprano and a tape which contains both a synthesized accompaniment and the recorded voice of soprano Bethany Beardslee; *Correspondences* (1966–68) for string orchestra and synthesized accompaniment; and *Reflections* (1975), for piano and tape, are among his works which combine both live and taped elements.

Edgard Varèse's *Poème Électronique* was commissioned for the Philips Pavilion of the 1958 Brussels World Fair. Working with the architect Le Corbusier, Varèse used over four hundred loudspeakers together with pictures and projections throughout the pavilion. This highly important milestone in the development of electronic music was performed almost continuously for six months for over fifteen thousand people daily. According to one critic, "The audience . . . evinced reactions almost as kaleidoscopic as the sounds and images they encountered—terror, anger, stunned awe, amusement, wild enthusiasm."

John Cage (b. 1912) studied with Henry Cowell, Arnold Schoenberg, and Adolph Weiss (a student of Schoenberg). Even Cage's early works reflect his intense preoccupation with experimentation. He was absorbed with all manifestations of sound, even its absence. He learned from Filippo Tommaso Marinetti (the apostle of "futurismo") and Varèse, from Indian and Javanese music, and from the experiments of Cowell. He pioneered in the development of the percussion ensemble (*Construction in Metal,* 1939) and the "prepared" piano (*Sixteen Sonatas and Four Interludes,* 1946–48) . In 1939 he produced his *Imaginary Landscape No. 1,* using two disk recordings of electronically generated sound (made by a telephone company to test its lines), a tam-tam, and a piano. Composed directly on a record disk, it has the distinction of being the first surviving electronic composition. For his *Imaginary Landscape No. 3* (1942), Cage combined percussion with electronic and mechanical devices. *Imaginary Landscape No. 5* (1952) is the first major sound composition composed directly on tape. It is described as "a score for making a recording on tape, using as material any forty-two phonograph records." In 1958, the Studio di Fonologia in Milan produced Cage's *Fontana Mix,* a collage of various noises, instrumental and otherwise. All of Cage's electronic works should be considered in connection with his philosophy of indeterminacy, a compositional factor that is discussed in the next chapter.

THE EQUIPMENT

A transistorized, modular, voltage-controlled electronic music system was developed in the United States in the 1960s that significantly reduced the size and cost of an electronic music studio. Through this system, various types of sound producers and modifiers were interconnected to function cooperatively through the use of patch chords and switches. By 1970, hundreds of these miniaturized synthesizers were in use in universities, conservatories, and private studios throughout the world. The Moog Synthesizer, Buchla Electronic Music System, and ARP Synthesizer are the best known among them. All provide a wide range of sound generation, manipulating equipment, and a keyboard synchronization of the various synthesized sounds. The Putney, the ElectroComp, and the Mini-Moog

Electronic Music Studio

Cleveland Institute of Music.

are small, relatively inexpensive, portable electronic instruments that are particularly appropriate for introductory work at the high school or college level.

Voltage control is the basic element behind the operation of the synthesizer. Through the voltage control system, the composer alters the settings of all modules (sound generators and modifiers) by applying specific voltages to them. Most frequently voltage control is applied to the oscillator, the pitch (frequency)-generating component of the system (on the Moog, for instance, the addition of one volt raises the frequency one octave). Manually operated control devices for voltage control include push buttons, switches, potentiometers, and keyboards. A *sequencer* is an automatic voltage control device.

Studios in which timing, order of events, etc., depend almost entirely on *splicing* (cutting and placing together segments of tape for synchronization) are called *classic electronic studios* to differentiate them from the more sophisticated studios that have been in use since the mid-sixties where voltage-controlled synthesizers are used. Though the equipment varies from studio to studio, certain units are common to all: tape recorders (from mono to eight-channel), amplifiers, speakers, audio generators, white noise generators, filters, mixers, and reverberation units. The sound-generating and modifying modules (independent in the classical studio and interconnected in the voltage-controlled synthesizer) and recording and playback equipment are described in the following pages.

Sound Generators

The basic sound-generating component in an electronic studio is an oscillator. The frequency of its sound output (signal) is controlled by a calibrated dial called a *potentiometer* (pot)—a resistance device similar to a rheostat. The simplest wave shape signal of an oscillator is a sine wave:

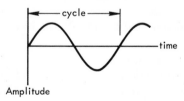

The frequency of the wave is measured by the number of cycles per second. The pure sine wave contains only a single frequency with no overtones, and can only be produced electronically, although the sound of the flute does reasonably approximate its sound character.

Other basic waveforms produced by oscillators are the *sawtooth* wave, which contains the fundamental plus all of its overtones; the *triangle* wave, which contains the fundamental plus all of its odd-numbered overtones; and the *square* wave, which also consists of the fundamental plus all of its odd-numbered overtones, but at a different diminishing amplitude than the triangle wave.

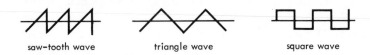

saw-tooth wave   triangle wave   square wave

Another sound type, *white noise,* consists of all audible frequencies at random amplitudes. It can be created directly by a white-noise or random-voltage generator.

Sound Modifiers

Sound modifiers are electronic devices that transform or modify sound by combining, filtering, and distorting sounds. A wide variety of modifiers are possible; in fact, many studios design their own modifiers for specific purposes. Some of the more common sound modifiers found in most electronic music studios are described below.

Modulator: governs the periodic change of any characteristic of sound. To denote the type of modulation, a qualifying term is also required, including the following: *frequency, amplitude,* and *ring* (a form of amplitude modulation). In musical terms, frequency modulation can be described as *vibrato* and amplitude modulation as *tremolo.*

Reverberator: reproduces the same acoustical property in a sound as that produced in an enclosed space in which sound waves bouncing off the walls add a delayed reflection of the sound to the sound. The reverberator can provide this time delay to any audio frequency signal. The term *echo* is used when the repeated sound follows the original sound by twenty milliseconds or more.

Mixer: combines audio signals.

Envelope generator: controls the attack and decay characteristics of sound in varying degrees through the use of a control signal. An *envelope* is the sound contour that makes up the duration of every sound. It consists of an attack, steady state time, and decay.

Amplifier: expands or increases the power of a sound or signal. Together with the envelope generator, a voltage-controlled amplifier can provide a changing envelope to all waveforms.

Filter: transmits and eliminates selected frequencies. A *low-pass* filter cuts out high frequencies, while a *high-pass* filter cuts out low frequencies from the input signal. A *band-pass* filter passes selected bands of frequencies, and a *band-reject* filter rejects selected bands of frequencies. There are dials to select the frequencies or bands of frequencies to be passed.

Recording and Playback Equipment

The final step in the creation of an electronic music composition is the mixing and placing in proper sequence of all the events of the compositional process into a final tape ready for playback. Most electronic studios are equipped with microphones, amplifiers, loudspeakers, and various tape recorders for this purpose. The notational system used for electronic music is not a score in the traditional sense, but is instead a set of working instructions for creating the work on tape.

Computer-generated Sound. The use of digital computers in electronic music generation was first attempted by Lejaren Hiller at the University of Illinois in the late fifties, using the Illiac computer, and was later developed by the Bell Telephone System at their research laboratories in New Jersey. In some of these early attempts, computers were actually used directly to compose music after being programmed with sets of rules for harmony, counterpoint, and composition. *Experimental Music* (1959) by Hiller and Isaacson describes the new technique. Hiller's *Illiac Suite* (1957) was the first large work composed by a programmed computer. Today, computers are being used in an attempt to transcend some of the limitations of the tape studio and synthesizer by serving as control devices for all modules in an electronic music studio and to generate sounds of the composition directly. Ideally, to achieve maximum flexibility, an electronic music generation system should include both of these uses of the computer.

chapter 25

Chance Music, Multimedia, and Instrumental Exploration

CHANCE MUSIC

The completely rationalistic, totally controlled method of handling musical materials, which grew out of the serialism of Webern, has been countered since the 1950s by a significant movement to free music from restrictive preciseness through the introduction of the element of chance into its composition and performance. Music based on chance is known as *aleatory* (aleatoric) music. Precedent for the concept of indeterminacy in music is not at all difficult to find. Strictly speaking, all musical performances are to some degree dependent on chance, not only because of the inconsistency of the performers themselves, but also because our relatively limited notational system leaves much to the imagination and creativity of the performer. The improvisational element of aleatoric music finds its historical counterpart in musical performances of baroque music. During this period, a composer often notated only the melody and bass line, figured with numbers to indicate his intent concerning harmonic structures. The keyboard accompaniment and the elaboration of the melodic line were left to the ingenuity of the performers themselves.

Since 1950, indeterminacy has become important as a conscious means of composition in avant-garde circles. It can be introduced into music in two ways: the materials of music may be created by chance methods, such as the tossing of dice, the turn of a card, and the application of the mathematical laws of chance; or the composer may choose to prepare the

346

outline of the work, allowing the performer to fill in the details. In other words, chance may operate at either the compositional level or the performance level. In the latter case, the composer relinquishes part of his responsibility by allowing the performer to collaborate in the creation of the work. Whereas the performer is bypassed altogether in electronic music, in chance music he is glorified. Indeterminacy in music has numerous parallels in the other arts, including the mobiles of Alexander Calder (1898–1976) and the paintings of Jackson Pollock (1912–56).

John Cage (b. 1912)

The use of chance methods at the compositional level was pioneered by John Cage. In the 1950s Cage became increasingly absorbed with Oriental philosophy, particularly that expressed in Zen Buddhism. He adapted this mystical, nonlogical philosophy to music, claiming that the purpose of music was not 'to communicate or entertain but just to be. In creating this "purposeful purposelessness," chance operations played a principal role. Most of the music he has written after this point in his life has been concerned with developing as many devices as possible for achieving unpredictable results. In the *Imaginary Landscape No. 4* (1951) he used twelve radios with two "performers at each radio, one manipulating the dial for the various wave lengths indicated by the composer in

John Cage
BMI Archives.

kilocycles, and the other manipulating the dial for dynamics." Many of his chance procedures are derived from the ancient Chinese book of wisdom *I Ching (Book of Changes)*, which directs actions as the result of six tosses of three coins (originally sticks shaken from a box.) In his *Music of Changes* (1951) for piano, Cage uses *I Ching* to control every aspect of composition, including structure. With structure no longer a part of the compositional means, composition has now become for Cage "an activity characterized by process." He wrote the music for another piano work on various sheets of paper and instructed the performer first to drop the sheets and then play them in the order in which they were picked up. Perhaps his most widely known piece is *4'33"* (*Four Minutes and Thirty-three Seconds;* 1954). The performer (the instrument is not specified) sits in front of a music stand—or piano, as is frequently the case—for four minutes and thirty-three seconds without playing a note of the "score" before him. Instead he is instructed to turn the pages or otherwise mark the end of each of the three movements. Cage's intention, expressed in his book *Silence,* was to make the audience aware of the sounds of life around them, "letting sounds be themselves instead of reflecting my ideas and feelings." Theoretically at least, the same result could be a possibility in his Concert for Piano and Orchestra (1958), in which each of the performers is instructed to play all, any, or none of the notes in his part. "I regard this work as one 'in progress' which I intend never to consider as in a final state, although I find each performance definitive."

Cage's music enrages, amuses, or confounds, depending on the extent of one's devotion to tradition and logic. He has done his best to break down time-honored values and tradition, and in so doing has exerted a strong influence on the young, particularly those in the avant-garde movement in Europe, where he is the most highly regarded among American composers.

Various methods of dealing with the unpredictable were explored by members of the "Cage group," young composers associated with Cage in New York during the 1950s. The most notable among them are Morton Feldman (b. 1926), Christian Wolf (b. 1934), and Earle Brown (b. 1926).

OTHER REPRESENTATIVE COMPOSERS

Pierre Boulez's concept of integrating chance into a composition is to structure many possibilities, giving the performer alternatives rather than complete license. It was he, incidentally, who first used the term *aleatory* (derived from the French *aléa*—chance; Latin *alia*—dice) in reference to chance music. His Third Piano Sonata (1957) contains five movements that may be performed in any order; moreover, each movement consists of a number of structures that can be interchanged, allowing for further variations of sequence. The third movement, for example, contains two "routes," one printed in red and one in green; the performer is given his choice of these, each of which in turn provides various choices for dynamics, duration, and attack. The performer, as a consequence, becomes a collaborator in the final configuration of the work, creating a version that will change with each performer and likely with each performance.

Stockhausen's *Klavierstück XI* (1956) also allows the performer considerable freedom of choice. It consists of nineteen musical fragments that may be played in any order and in any of six different speeds, dynamics, and articulations. The nineteen fragments are printed irregularly on a single large sheet and the performer is instructed to play the first fragment that catches his eye. At the end of each fragment there are tempo, dynamic, and attack instructions, and the performer, looking at random at another fragment, plays it according to the instructions he has just read. Each fragment may be joined to any of the other eighteen, but when one fragment has been played three times, the piece is ended. Stockhausen's other aleatoric works include *Zyklus for One Percussionist* (1959) and *Refrain for Three Players* (1959).

Recently, Lukas Foss became interested in ensemble improvisation and formed an improvising chamber ensemble of five performers: percussion, flute, clarinet, cello, and he himself directing from the piano. He first attempted to use this technique in *Time Cycle* (1960) for soprano and orchestra. His Improvisatory Chamber Ensemble performed improvised interludes between the four songs of the work. In *Echoi* (1961–63), for four soloists (written for the Improvisatory group), there is considerable indeterminacy in performance. Foss uses various signs for unorthodox effects:

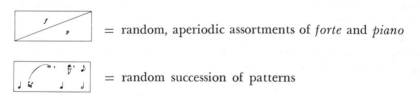

= random, aperiodic assortments of *forte* and *piano*

= random succession of patterns

In *Echoi IV* he inserts a page of "interpolation" in the score, directing that "the music on these pages is interrupted six times by the percussionist hitting an anvil at moments of his choice, at which point the players, without losing a second's time (rather like a jumping phonograph needle), shift to the interpolated page. The interpolations are in turn ended (interrupted) by anvil strokes which command the immediate return (jump back) to the main music. . . ."

MULTIMEDIA

Multimedia is the mid-twentieth-century parallel to the nineteenth-century *Gesamtkunstwerk*. It is a logical development of such composite art forms as the ballet and the musical theatre, and in all probability was also a result of the realization that there is a need for some type of activity during performances of tape recorder music. The concept of multimedia includes works ranging from the occasional buffoonery of John Cage and his followers, with their musical theatre of the absurd, to sincere attempts to form a new creative communication.

In 1952, the composer Cage, pianist David Tudor, artist Robert Rauschenberg, and dancer Merce Cunningham collaborated in a series of multimedia "happenings." They played records, danced, used film, and read lectures from stepladders, all in a random sequence of structured material. By 1960, however, what had started as a serious investigation into the possibilities of collaboration in the arts degenerated into a full-length theatrical performance of the absurd—an outrageous circus of fun and games with little artistic content. As an example, Cage's *Theatre Piece 1960* consisted of a series of incoherent happenings (purposeful purposelessness) in which the performers shot at balloons filled with paint, one shaved himself while a loudspeaker blared out the "March" from *Tannhäuser,* and a contralto sang "Parlez-moi d'amour," all while Cage slowly counted from one to twenty-three! In 1961, Stockhausen presented a piece in Cologne called *Originale,* patterned after the theatrical absurdities of Cage. To the accompaniment of his *Kontakte* for electrical sounds, piano, and percussion, the instrumentalists change clothes (the pianist dons an oriental female costume) and "brew up tea at the piano." The height of something or other was reached in the "happenings" of the Korean Nam June Paik, in which chance operates at both the compositional and performance levels. These works have no end or beginning; everything is determined at the time of performance.

In this country, multimedia has concerned itself largely with exploring the possible relationships between music and color abstractions. Music and projected colors already had been combined effectively by Scriabin in his *Poem of Fire.* This same line of development has been pursued by the composers Morton Subotnick (*Play!,* 1964), Allen Strange (*No Dead Horses on the Moon,* 1969), and Donald Scavarda (*Landscape Journey,* 1964), who have all written works for filmed color projections and either live music or electronic tape. Both arts deal with time, can develop rhythmic concepts, and use color. When we add to this combination choreography and/or spoken text (although not necessarily from a stepladder), a partial indeterminacy is also evident. An example of a carefully structured multimedia work is *Fission,* in which composer Donald Erb collaborated with choreographer Larry Berger and Daniel Hodomarsky, an artist and color engineer.

INSTRUMENTAL EXPLORATION

Contemporary instrumental exploration began with Henry Cowell's experimentation with unusual methods of creating sound on a piano. He directed performers to pluck the strings and use other unorthodox means of sound production. John Cage continued this exploration with piano sounds, principally by introducing various sound-modifying objects into the piano, producing what is called a "prepared piano." Other instrumentalists and composers extended these explorations, seeking new sound resources from all existing instruments. As one composer put it, music is created by performers, not instruments; therefore, all sounds made by a performer on his instrument may be considered legitimate compositional material. Some of the new techniques now demanded include the following:

Stringed Instruments

Striking the back or sides of the instrument with the fingers or bow, playing on the "wrong" side of the bridge, using combinations and extensions of traditional techniques (e.g., harmonic glissandos, fingernail pizzicato, etc.).

Wind Instruments

Use of the mouthpiece alone or of the body of the instrument without the mouthpiece, or of the instrument with a "wrong" mouthpiece, rattling the keys or valves of the instrument without blowing into it; *multiphonics*—two or three notes sounded simultaneously by either humming while playing or using special fingering and blowing techniques; extension of traditional techniques (e.g., glissandos, jazz effects, flutter-tongue, etc.).

Percussion Instruments

Use of instruments of other cultures such as Japanese temple bells or Tibetan prayer stones and finger cymbals, use of unorthodox sound producers (e.g., cowbells, brake drums, airplane motors, etc.), use of many new types of beaters (metal, glass, cloth, etc.), extension of traditional techniques, including striking traditional instruments in the "wrong" places or in an unorthodox manner.

Instrumental exploration has also brought into use many instruments new to the concert idiom (e.g., electric guitar, electric piano, musical saw, etc.) . It has also brought into use electric amplification and modification of existing instruments, giving them a greatly extended dynamic range. Some composers, rather than modifying existing instruments, and not wishing to utilize electric sound sources, have created new instruments capable of playing many different scale constructions. Instruments have been devised that divide the octave into more than the conventional twelve parts and that use tunings other than the traditional ones. For example, Harry Partch (1901–74), seeking the sound qualities made possible through Just Intonation, divided the octave into forty-three parts and devised the instruments for the music he had created.

Many special effects peculiar to a group of composers or a group of works often necessitate special notational systems. Contemporary Polish composers in particular have been inventive in devising new notational schemes. Kazimierz Serocki in *Segments* devotes two pages of explanation to the many new notational symbols he has used. Some of them can be seen in the following example:

Example 207.

Serocki defines the symbols in this example as follows:

↓ = play directly on the strings

▅▅▅ = gradual *ritardando*

↾ = pluck the string with the fingernail

All notes [in the piano score] approximate within the given register

▅▅▅ = strike the keys with the open palm of the hand within the given register

▼ = with plectrum

✱ = non-rhythmicized tremolo

├────┤ = duration of the note

↾ = strike the edge of the instrument

♪ = strike one drumstick with another; the stick that is struck is laid on the membrane

◢◢◢ = gradual *accelerando*

Since 1950, there has been a considerable amount of exploration into the various kinds of sounds that could be produced by the human voice. Schoenberg was the first to use the voice in a nontraditional way (*Sprechstimme*), in *Pierrot Lunaire* (1912). It took over forty years before other composers continued in the path he had begun. Berio, in *Visages* (1960), has experimented with various vocal sounds—cries, laughs, whispers, shrieks, etc. Witold Lutoslawski, in the *Three Poems by Henri Michaux* (1963), requires the choir of twenty individual parts to speak, whisper, moan, and shout, as well as sing, in projecting the drama of the texts. The following example, from *Aventures* (1962) by György Ligeti (b. 1923) illustrates some of the techniques used in contemporary vocal literature. It is scored for three singers and seven instrumentalists. Instead of using words, Ligeti devised an alphabet of 112 sounds, and provided the work with a constant alternation of metric and proportional notation (shown in the example between the first five measures and the sixth measure):

Example 208.

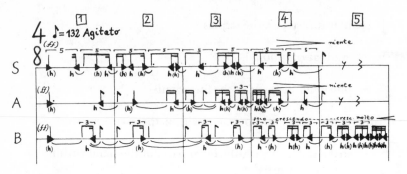

Breathe very intensely, excited, gasping—with the mouth open, and as much air as possible

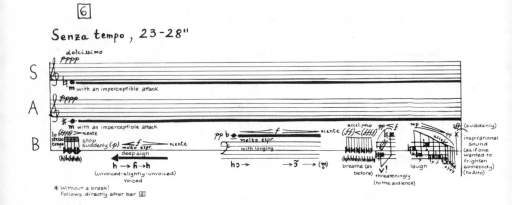

⌐↓↑⌐ denotes breathing (unvoiced but very intensive),

    (▶=inhaling, ◀=exhaling)

(h)   = as in <u>h</u>ang—unmodulated, intensified breath

(ɦ) = voiced (h)

(ɔ) = as in <u>o</u>ral

(ɔ̃) = nasal (ɔ) as in French b<u>on</u>

(m̥) = unvoiced (m) as in French nationali<u>sm</u>e

The creative possibilities for the unconventional use of instruments and the voice are well exemplified in the works of the American, George Crumb (b. 1928). Subtle, vibrant textures, and economy of means, reflecting the influence of Webern, permeate the refined chamber proportion of his world of sound; lyricism and a clear sense of musical direction characterize his expressive reflection of the past. His personalized means of expression centers substantially in the percussion section and in the voice; *Ancient Voices of Children* (1970) as an example, is scored for thirty percussion instruments, mezzo soprano, boy soprano, mandolin, harp, piano, and oboe. Like others of his generation, Crumb is fascinated by the gentle percussion sounds of Asiatic music, which he enhances by chance elements to heighten the improvisatory effect of his works. Vocalists in his compositions explore a wide spectrum of sound possibilities: they are instructed to buz, cry, sigh, fluttertongue, whisper through a speaking tube, and sing into an electrically amplified piano. The highly expressive quality he achieves using these varied instrumental and vocal means, and the resulting accessibility of his music have brought him into particular prominence among composers of his generation.

The poetry of Federico Garcia Lorca, who was killed in 1936 during the Spanish Civil War, has found an important role in Crumb's compositions. *Night Music I* (1963), *Songs, Drones and Refrains of Death* (1968), *Madrigals, Book III* (1969), *Madrigals, Book IV* (1969), *Night of the Four Moons* (1969), and his *Ancient Voices of Children* are prominent among the works in which he uses Lorca's poetry. His considerable ability in writing for "prepared" piano is evidenced in his *Makrokosmos* (Vols. I and II; 1972, 1973). Other significant works include *Echoes of Time and the River* (1967), an orchestral work; and *Music for a Summer Evening* (*Makrokosmos*, Vol. IV; 1974) for two amplified pianos and percussion.

chapter 26

Consolidation

It has become generally accepted by now that all sound is, or can be, proper material for music. Conventional sound sources used in unconventional ways, improvisatory techniques, the sounds and music of other cultures, the sounds of folk music and jazz, and the spatial deployment used in baroque music are all now being incorporated into the mainstream of music, often with remarkably effective results.

The most important demonstration of consolidation among all existing styles and techniques explored since 1950 has occurred, surprisingly enough, in Poland, where since the 1956 uprising the arts have been greatly encouraged and subsidized. The Warsaw Festivals, held every autumn since 1957, have presented an amazingly wide range of works, displaying contemporary techniques and styles from almost every country in the Western world and from Japan. In Poland, as in Germany, creative activity in the arts had largely disappeared during the years between 1930 and the end of the war; then, in 1949, a group of young Polish composers joined forces to form the *Group of '49* dedicated to the cause of new music. Five among them are of particular importance: Grazyna Bacewicz (1913–69), Kazmirz Serocki (b. 1922), Tadeusz Baird (b. 1928), and two who stand well above the others in superior talent and creative imagination—Witold Lutoslawski and Krzystof Penderecki.

356

Witold Lutoslawski (b. 1913)

Lutoslawski received his training in music in his native city at the University of Warsaw. During these formative years, he wrote his Symphonic Variations (1937), his first work to attract attention. World War II created a five-year hiatus in his life at a time when his career might have been developing rapidly. Then in 1945, following the war, he was asked by the Polish Music Publishing Company to compose a cycle of easy pieces based on Polish folk-song and dance themes. This opportunity marked the beginning of a period in his career dominated by the folk idiom. This period culminated in his writing the Concerto for Orchestra (1950–54) in which folk music was "merely the raw material used to build a large musical form of several movements."

Witold Lutoslawski

The Decca Record Company Limited.

The *Funeral Music* (1958) for string orchestra, dedicated to the memory of Béla Bartók, was his first work to achieve international recognition. It is a highly personal serial work whose homogeneity is based on a tone row constructed of semitones and tritones; it is cast in one movement composed of four successive segments: Prologue, Metamorphoses, Apogeum, Epilogue. The Apogeum is based on chords derived from all twelve tones of the octave. This was his first use of a technique that soon became a distinguishing characteristic in his music. In constructing the twelve-tone chords he restricted himself to two or three intervals in order to give the chords a distinctive, recognizable sound. In his own words, "Since 1958 I have been working on twelve-note chords. I am primarily interested in those whose adjoining sounds give a limited number of interval types. . . . Twelve-note chords constructed from one, two, or three types of intervals have for me a distinct, easily recognizable character, while twelve-note chords comprising all types of intervals are colorless—they lack a clearly defined individuality." The resulting sounds bear no relationship to the Viennese atonal school; instead, one can find the influences of Debussy, Stravinsky, Bartók, and Varèse.

Seeking new means of rhythmic expression in his works, Lutoslawski experimented with chance elements in *Jeux Vénitiens* (1961). In this work, the chance element is strictly controlled by the composer as a procedure rather than an end in itself. The title refers to the manner of performance (joyous) and the city of the work's first performance (Venice). Lutoslawski describes his controlled use of aleatory techniques by stating that it consists "in a use of the element of chance which enriches the rhythm and expressionism of the music, without in the least lessening the composer's grip on its final shape." For Lutoslawski, avant-garde techniques have never been an end but merely a means toward the enrichment of his music.

One of his finest and certainly best-known works to date is the *Trois poemes d'Henri Michaux* (1963), commissioned by the Zagreb Festival of Contemporary Music. It is scored for woodwinds, brass, percussion, and a mixed chorus of twenty parts. The expressive and tonal range of the chorus is greatly increased through innovative effects ranging from whispers and moans to glissandos and shrieks. The alternating pattern of aleatoric and controlled passages of this work requires separate conductors for both the chorus and orchestra in performance.

Among his later works, the String Quartet (1964), *Paroles tissées* (*Words Woven Together;* 1965) for voice and chamber orchestra, the Symphony No. 2 (1966–67), the *Livre pour Orchestre* (*Book for Orchestra;* 1968), and the Cello Concerto (1970) are particularly noteworthy. In all of these works, he explores the possibilities of combining strict and free compositional techniques. In the *ad libitum* sections, there is what Lutoslawski in his String Quartet calls *aleatory counterpoint*. In this technique, there is no element of chance in pitch considerations; instead, he confines chance to the independent playing of each instrument and therefore nullifies any harmonic considerations, increases rhythmic complexities, and makes the horizontal, or contrapuntal, flow of sound the music's principal characteristic.

Witold Lutoslawski: *LIVRE POUR ORCHESTRE*

Of the *Livre* Lutoslawski says, "I realized that in my music up to this work, there was one element that had been lacking, an aspect of my musical personality which was not yet represented in my compositions: the irrational." While it may seem paradoxical, the use of the irrational as a structural principle results in a certain formal order in the *Livre pour Orchestre*. The meaning of *Livre* is "book"; consequently, the four sections of the work are called chapters. There are in addition two interludes, one placed after each of the first two chapters; a third interlude, which follows the third chapter, Lutoslawski develops as the final chapter.

First Chapter. The opening movement, played almost entirely by the strings, projects a mysterious, evocative mood. Extensive use is made of glissandos—so much so, in fact, that for the most part, pitch definition is almost nonexistent: only undulating clouds of sound are heard. The instruments begin their glissandos at varying times, moving from *forte* to *piano,* to create a constant flow of shifting sounds:

Example 209.

Example 209. Continued

An *accelerando* leads to a climax by the brass section, and then a very quiet coda presents long-held notes in the strings to which an "irrational" *forte* passage by the piano is added briefly. The chapter then ends as quietly as it began. There are just two small sections in this movement that could be called aleatoric. In the first, the pitches are given but the durations are arbitrarily determined by the performer; in the second, both the indicated pitches and the durations are intended to be merely approximated by the performers.

Following the first chapter, a short interlude is played by three clarinets. According to the composer:

> The three initial movements of this work are rather intense. After each of them a moment of relaxation is required. The short interludes are to serve this purpose. They consist of music of less significance played *ad libitum*. I imagine that the attitude of the conductor when he has given the single beat which begins each interlude should be exactly the same as during a pause between movements. An attitude which should suggest that this is the moment for the audience to relax, change position, cough, etc. After about twenty seconds the conductor raises his baton (a signal that the period of relaxation is at an end), interrupts the *ad libitum* playing and without loss of tension begins the next movement after a pause of only five seconds.

The score indicates the notes and approximate speeds for the interludes, but the exact duration of the beat is left to each of the performers:

Example 210.

Second Chapter. This movement presents a strong contrast to what has gone before. Like the first movement, it is begun by the string section, this time playing pizzicato. Together with the harp, piano, and celesta, who join in, all play different rhythmic figures. There are groups of three, four, five, six, and nine notes to the beat all played simultaneously, resulting in the effect of a continuous texture of plucked strings. When the wind sections join in, the string players alter their texture by striking the strings with their bows. The woodwinds then present a section in which the various instruments are used to create a complex sound tapestry achieved through the combining of many rhythmic figures. The strings then produce waves of sound through successive overlapping *crescendos* punctuated by sharp chords. At the close of the movement, the strings gradually drop out of the ensemble until only the violas remain. As the sound slowly diminishes, an "irrational" burst of sound similar to that played at the end of the first chapter is produced by the keyboard instruments and harp.

The second interlude, played by two clarinets and harp, is very similar to the first.

Third Chapter. Once again the strings begin, but for the first time in the *Livre* they play in clearly defined rhythmic phrases. The movement rushes forward, reaching a climax as the trombones join in, "sliding" from one chord to another. There is a momentary silence, and then the tam-tams play quietly in a hesitant free rhythm. The trombones repeat their outburst twice more, followed successively by another pause, the tam-tams, and then a final trombone sliding passage. Following a final pause, the chapter's opening material is heard briefly, now altered so that the rhythmic impulse dissipates as the chapter closes.

Fourth Chapter. The third "interlude" is scored for piano and harp. Instead of ending with a "five-second pause" as did the previous interludes, this interlude gradually develops into the large final movement. The writing for the movement is largely *ad libitum*—pitches are given but all rhythmic values are no more than approximated. Exquisite sonorities are produced by the *sostenuto* strings and suspended cymbals. As the music gradually builds in volume, the texture thickens and the entire orchestra combines in a rich fabric of sound. The "irrational" intrudes again as a sharp brass chord provokes a rapid outburst from two xylophones and the piano, only to be cut off abruptly by another sharp brass chord. There is a wild flurry of pizzicato notes from the violas and cellos; then repeated brass chords set off various instrumental sections in dramatic bursts of action:

Example 211.

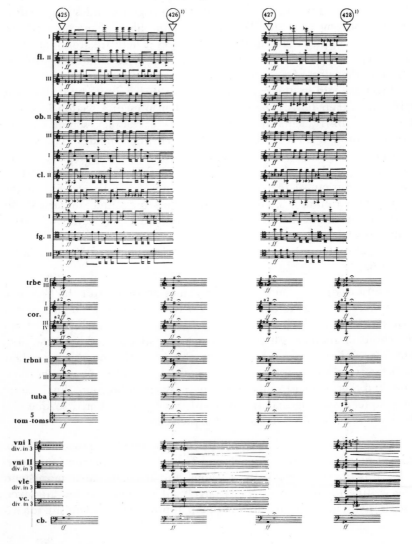

An *accelerando* places the chords closer and closer in mounting tension as the brass are joined by the entire orchestra in a furious burst of sound followed by four seconds of silence. Another crash is followed by five seconds of silence. A final crash is followed by seven seconds of silence. The entire orchestra repeats its outburst with renewed ferocity and then gradually subsides as a steady, very tranquil quarter-note rhythm is heard emerging from the string section.

A postlude resolves all of the tension previously generated as two flutes join in a quiet expressive duet over gently moving strings. The duet is played in a rhythm completely independent of the conductor. The book is finally closed by twelve solo violins playing *pianissimo* chords in their highest registers, and then the sound fades away in a cadence of complete repose.

Krzysztof Penderecki (b. 1933)

As a child, Penderecki witnessed the Nazi massacre of the Jewish population in the small southern town where he was born. This experience had a profound influence on much of his music, which, in many instances, is an expression of his compassion for human suffering. Sudden national prominence was thrust on him when, after his graduation from the Kraków Conservatory in 1958, he anonymously entered three compositions in a Polish composers' competition and won the first three prizes. As the leading representative of the young Polish avant-garde in the sixties, he first attracted international attention with the première of his *Anaklasis* (1960) for percussion and strings. He divided the strings into forty-two parts in this work, moving the separate parts principally in quarter tones and semitones, enhancing the sound through a great variety of articulations and special effects. He was principally concerned with the exploration of new sound qualities and, as a consequence, abandoned the use of specified pitch, intervals, and melodic lines. Intent on constructing new timbres through new means of articulation, he achieved dramatic effects through masterful manipulation of sound sequences and dynamic contrasts. Each of his next three works, all for strings, continued his experimentation with coloristic effects: *Threnody for the Victims of Hiroshima* (1960), for fifty-two string players; *Canon* (1963), for fifty-two players and tape recorder; and *Polymorphia* (1961), for forty-eight players. In these works, Penderecki used a new system of notation in the individ-

Krzysztof Penderecki

BMI Archives.

ual scores for each instrument to indicate the specialized effects he wanted. The score of *Threnody* contains no "normal" notation and the performance contains no "normal" playing. There is no feeling for meter —instead, the duration of the various sound events is indicated in seconds at the bottom of the score. Some of the symbols he invented to convey his musical ideas can be seen in the following example:

Example 212.

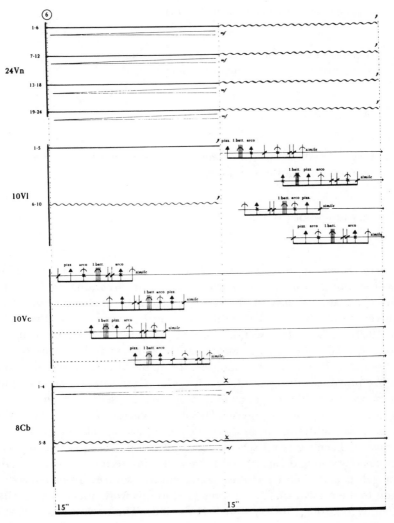

The symbols are defined in the score by Penderecki as follows:

▲   highest note of the instrument (indefinite pitch)

⊤   play between bridge and tailpiece

⧘⧘⧘⧘   arpeggio on 4 strings behind the bridge

ᴌ   percussion effect: strike the upper sounding board
      of the instrument with the nut or finger-tips

〰〰   molto vibrato

〜〜   very slow vibrato with ¼ tone frequency difference
      produced by sliding the finger

𝗓   very rapid not rhythmicized tremolo

His *Passio et Mors Domini Nostri Jesu Christi secundum Lucam*
(*Passion and Death of Our Lord Jesus Christ According to St. Luke;*
1963–65), commissioned by the Cologne Radio for the seven hundredth
anniversary of Münster Cathedral, is one of the most successful works of
the 1960s. It is in two sections, scored for three soloists, three mixed
choirs, speaker, boys' choir, and orchestra. The text includes the Gospel
of St. Luke, Psalm verses, quotations from the *Breviary*, and the composer's previous setting of the *Stabat Mater* for three unaccompanied
choirs. Considerable use is made of a twelve-note series, which includes
the sequence of notes B(B♭)-A-C-H(B♮) in homage to Johann Sebastian
Bach. This traditional musical tribute to Bach is an acknowledgment of
the use of Bach's general scheme for the Passion—the division into two
sections (Passion and Death) and the use of arias, recitatives, parts for the
Evangelist, and choral sections. Many musical sources, from Gregorian
chant to the present time, are represented in this work, including a Polish
religious folk song, "Swiety Boze" (Holy God). The work is a remarkable

confirmation of religious tradition within the language of the new music. The Passion was met with surprise and indignation by many of the avant-garde, who felt that it constituted a betrayal of Penderecki's ideals and a turning toward tradition. Others feel that it is a continuation and logical development of such earlier works as his *David's Psalms, Threnody,* and *Stabat Mater.*

Included among his more recent works are *Dies Irae,* or *Auschwitz Oratorio* (1967); Capriccio for Violin and Orchestra (1967); String Quartet (1968); the opera *Devils of Loudon* (1969); *Utrenja* (1970), for soloists, chorus, and orchestra; and *Cosmogony* (1970), for solo voices and orchestra, commissioned by the United Nations for its twenty-fifth anniversary.

In summary, Penderecki may be described as an eclectic composer whose musical vocabulary includes techniques selected from the past and present to fit into his own intensely expressive style. Actually, the direct emotional and dramatic appeal in his music may be its principal *raison d'être.*

Penderecki: CAPRICCIO FOR VIOLIN AND ORCHESTRA

In seeking new means for expressing his musical needs, Penderecki never lost sight of the need for communication. His Capriccio clearly illustrates this important point; it is structurally logical, technically brilliant, and readily accessible in its expressive content. First performed in 1967 for the Danaueschingen Festival, the Capriccio was premièred in the United States, March 1968, by the Buffalo Philharmonic under the direction of Lukas Foss. It is scored for violin solo and a large orchestra, which, in addition to the usual instrumentation, includes saxophones, electric bass guitar, harmonium, piano, harp, and eighteen assorted percussion instruments.

In requiring unconventional effects from conventional instruments, composers have had to create a new system of symbols to communicate their precise intentions. Penderecki uses a wide variety of new symbols in his Capriccio, particularly in the sections involving indefinite sounds. He indicates $\frac{2}{4}$ meter at the beginning; however, its meaning is conventional only in the fact that the time value for each measure is fairly constant; the number and length of the notes within the measures vary considerably. The work is in a three-part form whose third section is more nearly a variation of the opening section than a repetition. All three sections are approximately the same length.

Capriccio opens with a timpani roll followed by the brass instruments playing in tone clusters dramatized through the overlapping of repeated crescendos by each instrument to a *sf*. The strings then join in, playing in tone clusters "as loudly as possible." A *subito pp* ends the introduction, and the solo violin enters playing a rapid chromatic figuration, *non legato,* beginning with its lowest note and ascending through three octaves. This brief passage constitutes the basic melodic material of the work. The orchestral accompaniment to the violin solo in this extended section is principally in the form of sound effects—very soft tone clusters by the brass and occasional ricochet effects by the strings. A brief cadenza interrupts for a moment, and then the soloist's chromatic passage returns, accompanied this time by the saxophones joined intermittently by other instruments. The first section concludes with the soloist and all the strings sustaining their "highest note" before slowly sliding down in a zigzag glissando while the players hum along (with closed mouth).

The middle section begins following a momentary pause. It contains little of the structured movement of the opening; it is, instead, concerned largely with the interplay of timbres. Long notes are held with and without vibrato; quarter tones are used; and Penderecki further extends his aleatory technique by having the keyboard instruments played in rhythm, but with only relative pitch indications given.

Following a general pause, marked $\underset{\frown}{\text{P.G.}}$, the divisi cellos enter successively, playing in their low register, slowly sliding from one note to another. The soloist then joins them in this bridge to the third part, whose beginning is marked by the soloist quietly playing the chromatic material of the first section. The solo part takes on added complexity as all the inherent virtuoso possibilities of the instrument are exploited. The brass interrupt occasionally with raucous passages in waltz style. Following a more nearly literal repetition of the solo chromatic passage from part one, the soloist again plays a cadenza, and then the work ends with a brief coda.

The following reproduction from the original score is taken from the close of the middle section of Capriccio. The harmonium moves in tone clusters; the pianist is using a jazz brush on the strings of the piano; the twenty-four violins each play a different note and then slide down a fifth in artificial harmonics; and the woodwinds sustain pitches with fluctuations up a quarter tone ($+$) and down a quarter tone ($\downarrow$):

Example 213.

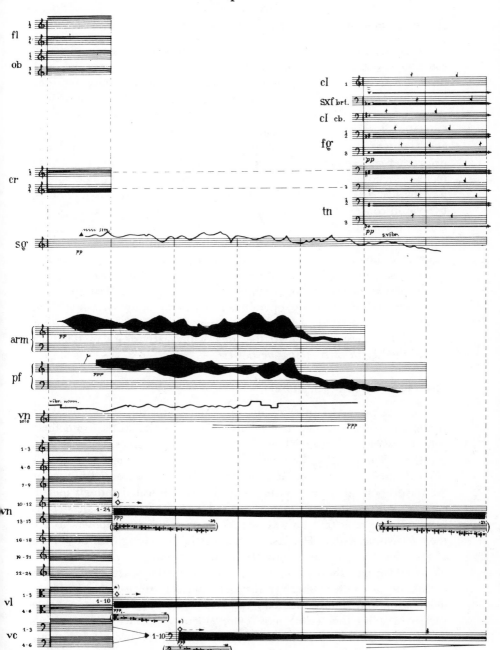

369

Grazyna Bacewicz (1913–69)

Grazyna Bacewicz began her musical career as a concert violinist; soon, however, creative work began to take precedence over her performance activities. During most of her years of shared activity, she composed in a neoclassic style, as is reflected in three violin sonatas, three violin concertos, Concerto for String Orchestra, and the Third String Quartet. These works are characterized particularly by their objectivity and frequent use of sonata-form. Her music written after 1949 and before her retirement from the concert stage in 1954 is marked by an increased emotionalism and reflects a preoccupation with the new sounds used by her compatriots. Works of this period include four symphonies, two violin concertos, two string quartets, a ballet, and two piano sonatas. During her final period, she achieved a synthesis between the avant-garde and tradition. In her own words, "I have not crossed so far, and now never will, the line that separates us from the 'absurd'. . . . In my music, a great deal happens, it is aggressive, and at the same time, lyrical.". Works of this period include the prize-winning Music for Strings, Trumpets and Percussion (1958); a radio opera, *Adventures of King Arthur* (1959); *Pensieri notturni* (1961), Second Cello Concerto (1963), and Concerto for Viola and Orchestra (1967). At the time of her early death in 1969, she was at the height of her creative powers.

Kasimierz Serocki (b. 1922)

Serocki destroyed most of his early music, feeling that it was too crude, not truly representative of his style and personality. From these youthful works he preserved just his first two symphonies, two cantatas, and some piano works. Two separate paths have characterized Serocki's musical career. On the one hand he writes fairly conventional music for the theatre and films, and on the other he has dedicated himself to self-expression through experimentation and technical inventiveness. It is interesting to note that he was one of the first Polish composers to use the twelve-tone system. His first efforts in serialist writing include a Suite of Preludes (1952), Piano Sonata (1955), and two song cycles, *Heart of the Night* (1956) and the *Eyes of the Air* (1957). In the *Musica concertante* (1958), he attempted total serialization and has since explored space modulation and chance methods. His latest works present a remarkable variety of styles and techniques: *Niobe* (1966), a poem for two reciting voices, choir, and orchestra; *Forte e piano* (1967), for two pianos, choir, and orchestra; *Continuum* (1966) for percussion; *Swinging Music* (1970); and *Fantasia elegaica* (1972) for organ and orchestra.

370

Tadeusz Baird (b. 1928)

The postromantic monumentalism in such works as Baird's First Symphony (1950), the *Colas Breugnon Suite* (1951), Concerto for Orchestra (1953), and Lyric Suite (1953), for soprano and orchestra, gives early evidence of the highly emotional character so closely associated with his mature style. Baird was not attracted to the techniques of the avant-garde; instead, he availed himself of resources from the past as disparate as archaic modal language and dodecaphonic techniques. The personal style that he evolved in the fifties can be considered an outgrowth of the Viennese twelve-tone school. While strictly dodecaphonic, it is also characterized by its subjective, intensely lyric quality. Representative works of this period include the String Quartet (1957), *Four Essays* (1958), *Homily*, for reciting voice, choir, and orchestra, and *Four Dialogues* (1964), for oboe and chamber orchestra. The music critic Karl Woerner, writing for the *Musical Quarterly*, calls Baird "Poland's most significant musical lyricist since Szymanowski" and goes on to say:

> Here a modern composer is writing modern beautiful music, without a dubious or inferior aspect being in the least associated with the word 'beautiful'. . . . It is an expressive type of music, which now and then pushes on into the heights of the ecstatic—Alban Berg reborn and rejuvenated in the Slavic world.

In 1968 he was awarded the Koussevitsky Award "for outstanding contributions to the music of our times." His latest works, which further intensify his highly individual style, include *Sinfonia Breve* (1958), Third Symphony (1969), *Goethe's Letters* (1970), and *Psychodrama* (1972).

Some of the many other young Polish composers whose music is being heard with increasing frequency are Henryk Górecki (b. 1933), Boguslav Schäffer (b. 1929), Wlodzimierz Kotonski (b. 1925), and Augustyn Bloch (b. 1929). One important factor in the emergence of Poland as a major contributor to the mainstream of music is the proliferation of musical organizations in that country. There are now over nineteen orchestras, nine opera companies, and numerous chamber ensembles actively performing in Poland, all subsidized and supervised by state and municipal governments.

Postscript

An overview of twentieth-century music affirms the fact that during the first three-quarters of the century there have been two periods of major fundamental music change separated by a period of consolidation. The first period of fundamental change occurred shortly after the turn of the century and continued for approximately twenty years, until just after World War I. During these years of exploration, long-held precepts of functional tonality were significantly challenged and then abandoned. A parallel exploration of the possibilities of Asian, African, and East European resources yielded further new directions in Western music. Looking back on these decades, however, we can now see that what appeared to many at first sight to be revolution may more accurately be described as a period of rapid change within the continuum of an evolutionary process. Eventually, the pace of change slowed, and the process of consolidation of new practices with those of the past began. This period is most closely associated with the neoclassic movement and its retrospective look particularly at the baroque and classic periods. Within this period of synthesis, other trends, including neoromanticism, nationalism, progressivism, and experimentation also played significant roles.

Then, during the years following World War II, a new period of intense activity began. New rejections, new explorations, and new freedoms unfettered by the past, were sought. The avant-garde composers in particular systematically abandoned nearly every traditional aspect of musical expression—melody, harmony, rhythm, form—and adopted a wholly new vocabulary of their own. Explorations of this period have included serialization of new musical parameters, indeterminacy and the abandonment of closed forms, use of noise, new media and multimedia, new applications of conventional media, and the innovative use of electronically generated sounds. In the view of many, the only link this music has with the past is polyphony. Unlike composers of the earlier part of the century, avant-garde musicians have declared revolution their avowed intent. Individuals have displayed an almost insatiable thirst for uniqueness in their quest for self-expression, making common denominators difficult to find within the pluralistic nature of their creativity.

How long will this period of intense rapid change continue? There is considerable evidence, discussed in the last chapter, to indicate that although the avant-garde is actively continuing its explorations, the intensity of the process has diminished considerably, and that for a rapidly increasing number of composers, the process of consolidation is already well under way. The evolutionary directions that this synthesis with the mainstream will take, together with the new possibilities implicit in the ever-continuing process of experimentation, give every promise of exciting developments in the music of the future.

Selected Bibliography

GENERAL

Austin, William W., *Music in the Twentieth Century*. New York: W.W. Norton & Company, Inc., 1966.

Brody, Elaine, *Music in Opera*. Englewood Cliffs, N.J.: Prentice-Hall, Inc., 1970.

Collaer, Paul, *A History of Modern Music*. New York: Grosset and Dunlap, Inc., 1961.

Cooper, Martin, ed., *New Oxford History of Music*. Vol. 10, "The Modern Age." New York: Oxford University Press, 1974.

Copland, Aaron, *Our New Music*. New York: McGraw-Hill Book Company, 1941.

Davies, Laurence, *Paths to Modern Music*. New York: Charles Scribner's Sons, 1971.

Demuth, Norman, *Musical Trends in the Twentieth-Century*. London: Rockliff, 1952.

Deri, Otto, *Exploring Twentieth-Century Music*. New York: Holt, Rinehart and Winston, Inc., 1968.

EWEN, DAVID, *The Complete Book of Twentieth-Century Music.* Rev. ed. Englewood Cliffs, N.J.: Prentice-Hall, Inc., 1959.

————, *Composers of Tomorrow's Music.* New York: Dodd, Mead & Company, 1971.

————, ed., *The New Book of Modern Composers.* 3rd ed. New York: Alfred A. Knopf, Inc., 1961.

GOSS, MADELEINE, *Modern Music Makers.* New York: E.P. Dutton & Co., Inc., 1952.

GROUT, DONALD J., *A Short History of Opera.* 2nd ed. New York: Columbia University Press, 1965.

HANSEN, PETER S., *An Introduction to Twentieth-Century Music.* 3rd ed. Boston: Allyn & Bacon, Inc., 1971.

HODEIR, ANDRÉ, *Since Debussy: A View of Contemporary Music.* Translated by N. Burch. New York: Grove Press, Inc., 1961.

HOWARD, JOHN TASKER, *Our Contemporary Composers.* New York: Thomas Y. Crowell Company, 1941.

MACHLIS, JOSEPH, *Introduction to Contemporary Music.* 2nd ed. New York: W.W. Norton & Company, Inc., 1979.

MELLORS, WILFRED, *Romanticism and the Twentieth Century.* Fairlawn, N.J.: Essential Books, 1957.

MEYER, LEONARD B., *Music, the Arts, and Ideas; Patterns and Predictions in Twentieth-Century Culture.* Chicago: University of Chicago Press, 1969.

MITCHELL, DONALD, *The Language of Modern Music.* New York: St. Martin's Press, Inc., 1970.

MORGENSTERN, SAM, ed., *Composers on Music.* New York: Pantheon Books, Inc., 1956.

MYERS, ROLLO, *Music in the Modern World.* London: Arnold, 1948.

PAULY, REINHARD G., *Music and the Theater.* Englewood Cliffs, N.J.: Prentice-Hall, Inc., 1970.

PEYSER, JOAN, *The New Music.* New York: Dell Publishing Co., Inc., 1971.

PLEASANTS, HENRY, *The Agony of Modern Music.* New York: Simon and Schuster, Inc., 1955.

Rossi, Nick, and Robert Choate, eds., *Music in Our Time*. Boston: Crescendo Publishing Company, 1969.

Salazar, Adolfo, *Music in Our Time*. New York: W.W. Norton & Company, Inc., 1946.

Salzman, Eric, *Twentieth-Century Music: An Introduction*. 2nd ed. Englewood Cliffs, N.J.: Prentice-Hall, Inc., 1974.

Schwartz, Elliott, and Barney Childs, eds., *Contemporary Composers on Contemporary Music*. New York: Holt, Rinehart and Winston, Inc., 1967.

Sessions, Roger, *The Musical Experience of Composer, Performer, Listener*. Princeton, N.J.: Princeton University Press, 1950.

Slonimsky, Nicolas, *Music Since 1900*. 4th ed. New York: Coleman-Ross, 1971.

Stuckenschmidt, H. H., *Twentieth-Century Music*. Translated by Richard Dereson. New York: McGraw-Hill Book Company, 1969.

Thomson, Virgil, *The Musical Scene*. New York: Alfred A. Knopf, Inc., 1945.

Vinton, John, ed., *Dictionary of Contemporary Music*. New York: E.P. Dutton & Co., Inc., 1974.

Whittall, Arnold, *Music Since the First World War*. London: J.M. Dent & Sons, Ltd., 1977.

Yates, Peter, *Twentieth Century Music*. New York: Pantheon Books, Inc., 1967.

PART I

Chapter 2

Abraham, Gerald, ed., *The Music of Sibelius*. New York: W.W. Norton & Company, Inc., 1947.

Cardus, Neville, *Gustav Mahler*. New York: St. Martin's Press, Inc., 1965.

Carner, Mosco, *Puccini: A Critical Biography*. 2nd ed. New York: Holmes and Meier, 1977.

Del Mar, Norman, *Richard Strauss: A Critical Commentary on his Life and Works*. 3 vols. London: Rockliff, 1962, 1969, 1972.

EKMAN, KARL, *Jean Sibelius.* Translated by Edward Birse. New York: Alfred A. Knopf, Inc., 1938.

GRAY, CECIL, *Sibelius.* London: Oxford University Press, 1931.

HULL, A. EAGLEFIELD, *A Great Musical Tone Poet: Scriabin.* London: K. Paul, Trench, Trubner & Co. Ltd., 1918.

JOHNSON, HAROLD, *Jean Sibelius.* New York: Alfred A. Knopf, Inc., 1959.

KRAUSE, ERNST, *Richard Strauss.* Boston: Crescendo Publishing Co., 1969.

LA GRANGE, HENRY-LOUIS DE, *Mahler.* Vol. 1. London: Victor Gollanz, Ltd., 1974.

MAHLER, ALMA, *Gustav Mahler.* New York: The Viking Press, 1946.

MAREK, GEORGE, *Richard Strauss: The Life of a Non-Hero.* New York: Simon and Schuster, Inc., 1967.

MITCHELL, DONALD, *Gustav Mahler: The Early Years.* London: Rockliff, 1958.

————, *Gustav Mahler: The Wunderhorn Years.* London: Rockliff, 1976.

NEWMAN, ERNEST, *Richard Strauss.* London: John Lane, 1908.

RINGBOM, NILS-ERIC, *Jean Sibelius.* Translated by G.I.C. de Courcy. Norman: University of Oklahoma Press, 1954.

STEFAN, PAUL, *Gustav Mahler, a Study of His Personality and Work.* Translated by T. E. Clark. New York: G. Schirmer, Inc., 1913.

SUCKLING, NORMAN, *Fauré.* London: J.M. Dent & Sons, Ltd., 1946.

SWAN, ALFRED, *Scriabin.* London: John Lane, The Bodley Head, Ltd., 1923.

WALTER, BRUNO, *Gustav Mahler.* New York: Alfred A. Knopf, Inc., 1958.

Chapter 3

DEMUTH, NORMAN, *Ravel.* London: J.M. Dent & Sons, Ltd., 1947.

LOCKSPEISER, EDWARD, *Debussy.* 4th ed. New York: McGraw-Hill Book Company, 1972.

MANUEL, ROLAND, *Maurice Ravel.* Translated by Cynthia Jolly. London: Dobson, 1947.

MYERS, ROLLO, *Debussy.* New York: A.A. Wyn, Inc., 1949.

——, *Ravel.* London: Gerald Duckworth & Co., Ltd., 1960.

ORENSTEIN, ARBIE, *Ravel, Man and Musician.* New York: Columbia University Press, 1975.

PALMER, CHRISTOPHER, *Impressionism in Music.* New York: Charles Scribner's Sons, 1973.

SCHMITZ, ELIE ROBERT, *The Piano Works of Claude Debussy.* New York: Duell, Sloan & Pearce-Meredith Press, 1950.

SEROFF, VICTOR, *Debussy, Musician of France.* New York: G.P. Putnam's Sons, 1956.

——, *Maurice Ravel.* New York: Holt, Rinehart and Winston, Inc., 1953.

THOMPSON, OSCAR, *Debussy: Man and Artist.* New York: Dodd, Mead & Co., 1937.

VALLAS, LÉON, *Claude Debussy: His Life and Works.* Translated by Maire and Grace O'Brien. New York: Dover Publications, Inc., 1973.

——, *The Theories of Claude Debussy.* New York: Oxford University Press, 1937.

WENK, ARTHUR B., *Claude Debussy and the Poets.* Berkeley: University of California Press, 1976.

PART II

Chapter 4

BACKUS, JOHN, *The Acoustical Foundations of Music.* New York: W.W. Norton & Company, Inc., 1969.

BORETZ, BENJAMIN, and EDWARD T. CONE, eds., *Perspectives on Contemporary Music Theory.* New York: W.W. Norton & Company, Inc., 1972.

COWELL, HENRY, *New Musical Resources.* New York: Something Else Press, 1969.

DALLIN, LEON, *Techniques of Twentieth Century Composition.* 3rd ed. Dubuque, Iowa: William C. Brown Company, Publishers, 1974.

FORTE, ALLEN, *Contemporary Tone-Structures.* New York: Columbia University Press, 1955.

HINDEMITH, PAUL, *The Craft of Musical Composition.* Translated by Arthur Mendel. New York: Associated Music Publishers, 1945.

MARQUIS, G. WELTON, *Twentieth-Century Music Idioms.* Englewood Cliffs, N.J.: Prentice-Hall, Inc., 1964.

PERLE, GEORGE, *Serial Composition and Atonality.* 4th rev. ed. Berkeley: University of California Press, 1977.

PERSICHETTI, VINCENT, *Twentieth-Century Harmony.* New York: W.W. Norton & Company, Inc., 1961.

RETI, RUDOLPH, *Tonality, Atonality, Pantonality.* New York: The Macmillan Company, 1958.

RUFER, JOSEF, *Composition with Twelve Notes Related to One Another.* London: Rockliff, 1954.

SAMSON, JIM, *Music in Transition; a Study of Tonal Expansion and Atonality 1900–1920.* New York: W.W. Norton & Company, Inc., 1977.

SEARLE, HUMPHREY, *Twentieth-Century Counterpoint.* London: Williams & Norgate, Ltd., 1956.

SPINNER, LEOPOLD, *A Short Introduction to the Technique of Twelve-Tone Composition.* London: Boosey and Hawkes, 1960.

ULEHLA, LUDMILLA, *Contemporary Harmony.* New York: The Free Press, 1966.

Chapter 5

ARMITAGE, MERLE, ed., *Schoenberg.* New York: G. Schirmer, Inc., 1937.

BORETZ, BENJAMIN, and EDWARD T. CONE, eds., *Perspectives on Schoenberg and Stravinsky.* Princeton, N.J.: Princeton University Press, 1968.

LEIBOWITZ, RENÉ, *Schoenberg and His School.* New York: Da Capo Press, 1975.

NEWLIN, DIKA, *Bruckner, Mahler, Schoenberg.* Rev. ed. New York: W.W. Norton & Company, 1978.

PAYNE, ANTHONY, *Schoenberg.* New York: Oxford University Press, 1968.

RUFER, JOSEF, *The Works of Arnold Schoenberg.* Translated by Dika Newlin. London: Faber & Faber, Ltd., 1963.

STUCKENSCHMIDT, HANS H., *Arnold Schoenberg*. New York: Grove Press, Inc., 1960.

WELLESZ, EGON, *Arnold Schoenberg*. Translated by W. H. Kerridge. New York: E.P. Dutton & Co., Inc., 1925.

Chapter 6

BERG, ALBAN, "A Word about Wozzeck," *Modern Music* 5 (1927):22–24.

CARNER, MOSCO, *Alban Berg*. London: Gerald Duckworth & Company, Ltd., 1975.

DEMAR, IRVINE, ed., *Anton Webern: Perspectives*. Seattle: University of Washington Press, 1966.

KOLNEDER, WALTER, *Anton Webern: An Introduction to His Works*. Berkeley: University of California Press, 1968.

REDLICH, HANS F., *Alban Berg: the Man and His Music*. New York: Abelard-Schuman, 1957.

REICH, WILLI, *The Life and Works of Alban Berg*. Translated by C. Cardew. London: Calder, 1965.

REIHE, DIE, No. 2, *Anton Webern*. Bryn Mawr, Pa.: Theodore Presser, Inc., 1957.

WILDGANS, FRIEDRICH, *Anton Webern*. London: Calder & Boyars, 1965.

Chapter 7

ARMITAGE, MERLE, ed., *Igor Stravinsky*. New York: G. Schirmer, Inc., 1936.

BORETZ, BENJAMIN, and EDWARD T. CONE, eds., *Perspectives on Schoenberg and Stravinsky*. Rev. ed. New York: W.W. Norton & Company, 1972.

LANG, PAUL HENRY, ed., *Stravinsky: A New Appraisal of His Work*. New York: W.W. Norton & Company, Inc., 1963.

STRAVINSKY, IGOR, *Poetics of Music*. Cambridge, Mass.: Harvard University Press, 1970.

STRAVINSKY, IGOR, and ROBERT CRAFT, *Conversations with Igor Stravinsky*. New York: Doubleday & Company, Inc., 1959.

———, *Themes and Episodes*. New York: Alfred A. Knopf, Inc., 1966.

STROBEL, HEINRICH, *Stravinsky: Classic Humanist.* Translated by Hans Rosenwald. New York: Merlin Press, 1955.

TANSMAN, ALEXANDRE, *Igor Stravinsky; the Man and His Music.* Translated by Therese and Charles Bleefield. New York: G.P. Putnam's Sons, 1949.

VLAD, ROMAN, *Stravinsky.* 2nd ed. Translated by Frederick and Ann Fuller. New York: Oxford University Press, 1967.

WHITE, ERIC WALTER, *Stravinsky: A Critical Survey.* New York: Philosophical Library, 1948.

————, *Stravinsky, the Composer and His Works.* Berkeley: University of California Press, 1966.

Chapter 8

FASSETT, AGATHA, *The Naked Face of Genius.* Cambridge, Mass.: The Riverside Press, 1958.

HARASZTI, EMIL, *Béla Bartók, His Life and Works.* Paris: Lyrebird Press, 1938.

HELM, EVERETT, *Bartók.* London: Faber and Faber, Ltd., 1971.

LENDVAI, ERNÖ, *Béla Bartók, An Analysis of His Music.* London: Kahn & Averill, 1971.

LESNAI, LAJOS, *Bartók.* Translated by Percy M. Young. London: J.M. Dent & Sons, Ltd., 1973.

MOREUX, SERGE, *Béla Bartók.* Translated by G. S. Fraser and Erik de Mauny. New York: Vienna House, 1974.

STEVENS, HALSEY, *The Life and Music of Béla Bartók.* Rev. ed. New York: Oxford University Press, 1967.

Chapter 9

HINDEMITH, PAUL, *A Composer's World.* Garden City, N.Y.: Doubleday and Company, Inc., 1961.

KEMP, IAN, *Hindemith.* London: Oxford University Press, 1970.

REICH, WILLI, "Paul Hindemith." *Musical Quarterly* 17 (1931):486–496.

SKELTON, GEOFFREY, *Paul Hindemith*. London: Victor Gallancz Ltd., 1975.

STROBEL, HEINRICH, *Paul Hindemith*. 3rd ed. Mainz: B. Schott's Söhne, 1948.

Chapter 10

ABRAHAM, GERALD, *Eight Soviet Composers*. London: Oxford University Press, 1943.

BAKST, JAMES, *A History of Russian-Soviet Music*. New York: Dodd, Mead & Co., 1966.

HANSON, LAWRENCE, and ELISABETH HANSON, *Prokofieff, the Prodigal Son*. London: Cassell, 1964.

KAY, NORMAN, *Shostakovich*. London: Oxford University Press, 1971.

MARTYNOV, IVAN, *Dmitri Shostakovich: The Man and His Works*. New York: Philosophical Library, 1947.

NESTYEV, ISRAEL V., *Prokofieff*. Translated by Florence Jonas. Stanford, Calif.: Stanford University Press, 1960.

————, *Sergei Prokofiev, His Musical Life*. Translated by Rose Prokofieva. New York: Alfred A. Knopf, Inc., 1946.

PROKOFIEV, SERGE, *Autobiography, Articles and Reminiscences*. Moscow: Foreign Languages Publishing House, 1941, 1946.

SEROFF, VICTOR, *Dmitri Shostakovich*. New York: Alfred A. Knopf, Inc., 1943.

Chapter 11

DAY, JAMES, *Vaughan Williams*. New York: Farrar, Straus and Giroux, 1961.

DICKENSON, ALAN E., *Vaughan Williams*. London: Faber & Faber, Ltd., 1963.

HOWARD, P., *The Operas of Benjamin Britten*. London: Barrie & Rockliff, 1969.

HOWES, FRANK S., *The Music of Ralph Vaughan Williams*. New York: Oxford University Press, 1954.

MITCHELL, DONALD, and HANS KELLER, eds., *Benjamin Britten*. New York: Philosophical Library, 1953.

WHITE, ERIC WALTER, *Benjamin Britten: a Sketch of His Life and Works*. Rev. and enl. ed. London: Boosey & Hawkes, 1954.

YOUNG, PERCY, *Vaughan Williams*. London: Dennis Dobson, 1953.

PART III

Chapter 12

COOPER, MARTIN, *French Music*. New York: Oxford University Press, 1951.

DEMUTH, NORMAN, *Albert Roussel*. London: United Music Ltd., 1947.

HELL, HENRI, *Francis Poulenc*. New York: Grove Press, Inc., 1959.

MILHAUD, DARIUS, *Notes without Music*. New York: Alfred A. Knopf, Inc., 1953.

MYERS, ROLLO, *Erik Satie*. New York: Dover, 1968.

ROSTAND, CLAUDE, *French Music Today*. Translated by H. Marx. New York: Merlin Press, 1958.

TEMPLIER, PIERRE-DANIEL, *Erik Satie*. Translated by Elena L. and David S. French. Cambridge, Mass.: M.I.T. Press, 1969.

Chapter 13

ABRAHAM, GERALD, *Eight Soviet Composers*. London: Oxford University Press, 1943.

BAKST, JAMES, *A History of Russian-Soviet Music*. New York: Dodd, Mead & Co., 1966.

CHASE, GILBERT, *The Music of Spain*. New York: Dover Publications, Inc., 1959.

EÖSZE, LÁSZLÖ, *Zoltán Kodály, His Life and Work*. London: Collet, 1962.

FRANK, ALAN, *Modern British Composers*. London: Dennis Dobson, 1953.

GARDAVSKY, CENEK, *Contemporary Czechoslovak Composers*. Prague: Panton, 1966.

HARTOG, HOWARD, ed., *European Music of the Twentieth Century*. New York: Frederick A. Praeger, Inc., Publishers, 1957.

HOLLANDER, HANS, *Leoš Janáček: His Life and Work.* Translated by Paul Hamburger. New York: St. Martin's Press, Inc., 1963.

HOWES, FRANK, *The Music of William Walton.* 2nd ed. London: Oxford University Press, 1973.

LANG, PAUL HENRY, and NATHAN BRODER, eds., *Contemporary Music in Europe: A Comprehensive Survey.* New York: W.W. Norton & Company, Inc., 1967.

OLKHOVSKY, ANDREY, *Music under the Soviets.* New York: Frederick A. Praeger, Inc., Publishers, 1955.

PAHISSA, JAIME, *Manuel de Falla: His Life and Works.* London: Museum Press, 1954.

REESER, EDUARD, ed., *Music in Holland: A Review of Contemporary Music in the Netherlands.* Amsterdam: J.M. Meulenhoff, 1959.

SEARLE, HUMPHREY, and ROBERT LAYTON, *Britain, Scandinavia and the Netherlands.* Twentieth Century Composers, vol. 5. New York: Harper & Row, Publishers, 1973.

TIPPETT, SIR MICHAEL, *Moving into Aquarius.* St. Albans: Paladin Books, 1974.

VLAD, ROMAN, *Luigi Dallapiccola.* Translated by Cynthia Jolly. Milan: Suvini Zerboni, 1957.

YOUNG, PERCY M., *Zoltán Kodály: A Hungarian Musician.* London: Ernest Benn Limited, 1964.

PART IV

BERETZ, BENJAMIN, and EDWARD T. CONE, eds., *Perspectives on American Composers.* New York: W.W. Norton & Company, Inc., 1971.

CHASE, GILBERT, *America's Music from the Pilgrims to the Present.* New York: McGraw-Hill Book Company, 1966.

COWELL, HENRY, *American Composers on American Music.* New York: Frederick Unger, 1962.

HITCHCOCK, H. WILEY, *Music in the United States.* 2nd ed. Englewood Cliffs, N.J.: Prentice-Hall, Inc., 1974.

HOWARD, JOHN TASKER, *Our American Music.* New York: Thomas Y. Crowell Company, 1954.

————, *Our Contemporary Composers.* New York: Thomas Y. Crowell Company, 1941.

LANG, PAUL HENRY, ed., *One Hundred Years of Music in America*. New York: G. Schirmer, Inc., 1961.

MELLERS, WILFRED, *Music in a New-Found Land*. 2nd ed. New York: Hillstone, 1975.

REIS, CLAIRE, *Composers in America*. New York: The Macmillan Company, 1947.

Chapter 14

BOATWRIGHT, HOWARD, ed., *Essays before a Sonata, The Majority, and Other Writings by Charles Ives*. New York: W.W. Norton & Company, Inc., 1962.

COWELL, HENRY, and SIDNEY COWELL, *Charles Ives*. New York: Oxford University Press, 1955.

WOOLRIDGE, DAVID, *From the Steeples and Mountains, A Study of Charles Ives*. New York: Alfred A. Knopf, Inc., 1974.

Chapter 15

CHOU WEN-CHUNG, "Varèse: A Sketch of the Man and His Music," *Musical Quarterly* 52 (1966):151–170.

COWELL, HENRY, "The Music of Edgard Varèse." *Modern Music*, Jan.–Feb. 1928, pp. 9–19.

EDWARDS, ALLEN, *Flawed Words and Stubborn Sounds: A Conversation with Elliott Carter*. New York: W. W. Norton & Company, Inc., 1971.

GOLDMAN, RICHARD FRANKO, "The Music of Elliott Carter." *Musical Quarterly* 43 (1957):151–170.

OUELLETTE, FERNAND, *Edgard Varèse*. New York: Orion, 1968.

Chapter 16

BERGER, ARTHUR, *Aaron Copland*. New York: Oxford University Press, 1953.

COPLAND, AARON, *Music and Imagination*. New York: Mentor, 1959.

SMITH, JULIA, *Aaron Copland*. New York: E.P. Dutton & Co., Inc., 1955.

Chapter 17

CARTER, ELLIOTT, "Walter Piston." *Musical Quarterly* 32 (1946):354–375.

SCHEIBER, FLORA, and VINCENT PERSICHETTI, *William Schuman*. New York: G. Schirmer, Inc., 1954.

Chapter 18

BRODER, NATHAN, *Samuel Barber*. New York: G. Schirmer, Inc., 1954.

HORAN, ROBERT, "Samuel Barber." *Modern Music,* March–April 1943, pp. 161–169.

Chapter 19

ARVEY, VERNA, *William Grant Still*. New York: J. Fischer and Bro., 1939.

HAAS, ROBERT BARTLETT, ed., *William Grant Still*. Los Angeles: Black Sparrow Press, 1975.

HOOVER, KATHLEEN, and JOHN CAGE, *Virgil Thomson: His Life and Music*. New York: T. Yoseloff, 1959.

THOMSON, VIRGIL, *Virgil Thomson*. New York: Alfred A. Knopf, Inc., 1966.

PART V

Chapter 20

HARRISON, LOU, *About Carl Ruggles*. New York: Alicat Bookshop, 1946.

SCHUBART, MARK A., "Roger Sessions: Portrait of an American Composer." *Musical Quarterly* 32 (1946):196–213.

Chapter 22

CHASE, GILBERT, *A Guide to the Music of Latin America*. Washington, D.C.: Library of Congress, Music Division, 1943.

———, "Alberto Ginastera: Argentine Composer." *Musical Quarterly* 43 (1957):439–460.

CHAVEZ, CARLOS, *Musical Thought*. Cambridge, Mass.: Harvard University Press, 1961.

LIST, GEORGE, and JUAN ORREGO, eds., *Music in the Americas*. Bloomington: Indiana University Press, 1967.

SLONIMSKY, NICOLAS, *Music of Latin America*. New York: Thomas Y. Crowell Company, 1945.

STEVENSON, ROBERT, *Music in Mexico*. New York: Thomas Y. Crowell Company, 1952.

PART VI

BECKWITH, JOHN, and UDO KASEMETS, eds., *The Modern Composer and His World*. Toronto: University of Toronto Press, 1961.

CAGE, JOHN, *Silence*. Middletown, Conn.: Wesleyan University Press, 1961.

COPE, DAVID H., *New Directions in Music*. Dubuque, Iowa: William C. Brown Company, Publishers, 1976.

————, *New Music Composition*. New York: Schirmer Books, 1977.

————, *New Music Notation*. Dubuque, Iowa: Kendall/Hunt, 1976.

COTT, JONATHAN, *Stockhausen*. New York: Simon and Schuster, Inc., 1973.

HARVEY, JONATHAN, *The Music of Stockhausen*. Berkeley: University of California Press, 1975.

KARKOSCHKA, ERHARD, *Notation in New Music*. Translated by Ruth Koenig. New York: Frederick A. Praeger, Inc., Publishers, 1972.

KOSTELANETZ, RICHARD, *John Cage*. New York: Frederick A. Praeger, Inc., Publishers, 1970.

MACONIE, ROBIN, *The Works of Karlheinz Stockhausen*. London: Oxford University Press, 1976.

PARTCH, HARRY, *Genesis of a New Music*. 2nd rev. ed. New York: Da Capo, 1974.

WÖRNER, KARL H., *Stockhausen*. Translated by Bill Hopkins. Berkeley: University of California Press, 1973.

Chapter 24

APPLETON, JON, and RONALD PERERA, eds., *The Development and Practice of Electronic Music*. Englewood Cliffs, N.J.: Prentice-Hall, Inc., 1974.

CROWHURST, NORMAN H., *Electronic Musical Instruments.* Indianapolis: Howard W. Sams & Co., 1962.

HILLER LEJARON A., and LEONARD M. ISAACSON, *Experimental Music.* New York: McGraw-Hill Book Company, 1959.

HOWE JR., HUBERT S., *Electronic Music Synthesis.* New York: W.W. Norton & Company, Inc., 1975.

MATHEWS, MAX, *The Technology of Computer Music.* Cambridge, Mass.: The M.I.T. Press, 1969.

SCHWARTZ, ELLIOTT, *Electronic Music: A Listener's Guide.* New York: Frederick A. Praeger, Inc., Publishers, 1973.

STRANGE, ALLEN, *Electronic Music.* Dubuque, Iowa: William C. Brown Company, Publishers, 1972.

Chapter 25

BARTALOZZI, BRUNO, *New Sounds for Woodwind.* London: Oxford University Press, 1967.

BRINDLE, REGINALD SMITH, *Contemporary Percussion.* London: Oxford University Press, 1970.

BUNGER, RICHARD, *The Well-Prepared Piano.* Colorado Springs: The Colorado Music Press, 1973.

KIRBY, MICHAEL, *Happenings.* New York: E.P. Dutton & Co., Inc., 1965.

Chapter 26

ERHARDT, LUDWIK, *Music in Poland.* Warsaw: Interpress Publishers, 1975.

JAROCINSKY, STEFAN, ed., *Polish Music.* Warsaw: Polish Scientific Publisher, 1965.

Index